George and Darril Fosty's

SPLENDID IS THE SUN

The 5,000 Year History of Hockey

with contributions by
John Jelley

Stryker-Indigo Publishing Company, Inc. / New York

Cover Design by Steve Klinkel www.vonkinlk.com

Printed in Canada

For

Stryker-Indigo Publishing Company, Inc.,
37 Rolling Lane, Levittown, New York 11756

ISBN 0-9651168-1-6

First Edition

This book is dedicated to our families.
You have supported us all these years asking nothing in return.
We love each one of you dearly.

There is nothing new under the sun but there are lots of old things we don't know.

Ambrose Bierce (1842-1914)

*Give me the splendid silent sun with all
of his beams full-dazzling.*

Walt Whitman (1819-1892)

What is your substance,
Whereof are you made,
That millions of strange shadows on you tend?

William Shakespeare (1564-1616)

HISTORICAL TIMELINE

3000 BC 1275 BC	Gilgamesh and Pikku-Mikku c.2750-c.2500 BC	Earliest bone skates found in Budapest, Hungary c.2800-c.2000 BC	Egyptian hockey image Beni-Hasan c.1975-c.1640 BC	Manapuri ancient scripture Puyus written c.1900 BC – polo and hockey being played by the Gods.	Battle of Kadesh c.1285 BC and emergence of Phoenician Empire
1275 BC 750 BC	First account of Hurley in Battle of Moytura c.1272 BC	Mahram Bilqis build c.1200 BC	Utica founded c.1100 BC followed by Carthage in c.800 BC	Homer's, Iliad Funeral Games c.800 BC	First Olympic Games played c.776 BC

7

750 BC 300 BC	*"Hit the ball to the field of Apis"* inscribed on Egyptian tomb, c.600-500 BC	About 50 sets Olympic type games being held throughout Mediterran ean c.500 BC	Aristotle c.384-322 BC	Artaxerxes III's conquest of Egypt c.342 BC.	*Mahabhar ata* written c.300 BC
300 BC 1 AD	Hannibal begins to cross Alps c.218 BC	King Lowry Loingseach c.200 BC	Cuchulain and the Red Branch Warriors c.100 BC	Diodorus Siculus, *Biblioteca Historica* c.90-21 BC	Londinium founded c.50 BC
1 AD 750 AD	King Ezana Christianizes Aksumite Empire c.325-350 AD	Emperor Theodosius ended Greek Olympics in name of Christianity c.393 AD	Fields and ball courts appear in Mexico c.400 AD	St. Patrick arrived in Ireland c.432 AD	Destructio n of the Donar Oak c.726 AD

750 AD 1000 AD	Copan, Honduras, elephant headdress dated to at least c.750 AD	Mayan game changes c.800 AD	First evidence of Lacrosse c.800 AD	Danes sacked Canterbury Cathedral c.851 AD rebuilt c. 950 AD	Leif Ericson c.970-1020 AD
1000 AD 1365 AD	Thorfinn Karlsefni Sagas c.1003-1008 AD	Wupatki culture c.1075-1225 AD	*Het Kolven, Jeu de Mail* played on ice c.1200-1300 AD	Kensington Runestone c. 1362 AD	King Edward III bans the play of shinny c.1365 AD
1365 AD 1575 AD	Last reference to a Norse settlement in North America c.1374 AD	Tyler's Rebellion c.1381 AD	John Cabot Expedition c.1497 AD	*Brueghel's Winter Landscape and Skaters and Hunters in the Snow* c.1565	"Sea Beggers" and the evidence of widesprea d use of iron skates c.1572 AD

1575 AD – 1820 AD	First account of Mi'kmaqs playing hockey in 1749	Thomas Chandler Haliburton "Hurley on ice" at King's College School in Windsor 1802-1810	*Boys' Own Book* records British ice hockey rules in 1810	Sir John Franklin account of playing hockey in Kingston, Ont. 1813	Hockey being played in Bury Fen 1813
1820 AD – 1855 AD	Cambridgeshire parish-league formed 1827	Sir John Franklin account of soldiers playing ice hockey in Northwest Territories, 1825	1837 Staffordshire China sugar bowl commemorating hockey being played on the ice in Britain.	Blackheath Hockey Club formed in 1840	Hockey by Paine's Bridge March 3, 1855, predating Royal Canadian Rifles in Kingston, Ont. 1855

10

Kolven Player, Holland, c.1720 AD. The Fritz Locher Collection.

Table of Contents

Foreword

    The history of hockey is the story of human cultural interaction and geographic migration. It is a game that spread worldwide from its original home in ancient Mesopotamia, along the banks of the Tigris and Euphrates Rivers, moving over the centuries across much of the ancient and modern world. Evidence of ancient hockey's migration exists. However, like many early and historic roads the path is, at times, difficult to map. Yet, in the case of hockey, the signposts are many. In the end, these signposts allow the researcher to link the past to the present. Once linked, these signposts serve as a chronicle of history revealing new insights on current societies and the human past.

    It has long been argued the game of hockey is the earliest of man's sports. This argument is based on the knowledge that man has always been a competitive creature and has used 'sport' as a method of creating stronger, faster and more cunning members of his society. In their book, *War Without Weapons*, Philip Goodhart and Christopher Chataway remind us that as man progressed, he learned to walk upright and to swing a club. Fashioned from animal bone or a tree limb, the club became a tool for survival. But the club required skill, hand and eye coordination and the ability to think. As man mastered his weapon, this self-taught coordination became a form of competition. Swinging an object downwards to hit stones, primitive man created a game played among opposing individuals and tribes. Combining a hunter's skill with physical strength this primitive pastime would eventually evolve into a more complex form of play. In time, this play would become the first recognized form of ancient hockey.

    As human society developed, primitive hockey became closely associated with the practices of religion. Though we do not know the origins of religion one can surmise that religious beliefs existed for tens of thousands of years predating the written word and that these beliefs coincided with the development of ancient hockey. At one point ancient hockey and religion merged with the end result being that these two unique elements of ancient society would became part and parcel of one. Ancient hockey would become a celebration of religion. It would become the sport of legends. It would become a game of man and his gods.

    Five thousand years have past, and though much has changed, much remains the same. The sport of hockey is today a game played on ice. Its spiritual home is the country of Canada. At first glance, to the untrained observer, Canadian-style hockey is a misunderstood, seemingly violent sport dominated by boys and men. In truth,

Canadian hockey is far more complex than first appearance. In Canada, it is a record of a nation's achievement. It is the past, the present, and for many Canadians, the future. It is the soul of a people. A game which is the culmination of legends, myths, and history. A game of gods, heroes, warriors and demons; a complex tradition of heroism, teamwork, skill, strategy, and self-sacrifice. In their book, *The Death of Hockey*, Bruce Kidd and John Macfarlane sum up the reality of the Canadian hockey experience in a way that few have ever expressed. They write:

> *Hockey captures the essence of the Canadian experience in the New World. In a land so inescapably and inhospitably cold, hockey is the dance of life, an affirmation that despite the deathly chill of winter we are alive.*

Often the most obvious, is that which is unseen. In modern annals there exists the great myth that Canadians invented hockey. In fact, the converse is true; *hockey invented Canadians.*

Over six years of research and writing went into the creation of this book in an effort to identify all sources pertaining to hockey and its history. Some of the research took weeks to locate, study and disseminate. More often, however, the efforts took months or years. In the end, over six thousand books and articles specific to the sport were identified worldwide. In addition, hundreds of additional sources pertaining to religion, military history, politics, cultural anthropology, archaeology, and ancient history were also reviewed or identified in order to aid in the research. Attempts to obtain as many of these sources, and translations, as possible were initiated. Particular efforts were made to gather primary accounts in order to confirm actual statements and/or historic facts. Often, when original source materials were obtained, differences between the original sources and the secondary sources came to light. Such discrepancies are an indication of how poorly researched many books on hockey history truly are. In the end, of the six-thousand sources reviewed or identified over one-thousand were utilized. Yet even with this number some books stood out above-all-others. If we were to compile a list of 'the best' books on hockey we would cite, among the many, the following: 1) Scott Young's *War On Ice: Canada In International Hockey.* The writing and research was superb and the book difficult to put down. 2) Doug Beardsley's *Country On Ice* is perhaps the most eloquent and intelligent book ever written on hockey. 3) Bruce Kidd and John Macfarlane's *The Death Of Hockey* forced us to reach into our souls and ask ourselves what it meant to be Canadian. 4) Ken Dryden's two books *The Game* and

Home Game took us into the lives of professional and amateur Canadian hockey players allowing us to reflect on the lives of athletes while reminding us of the simplicity of the game and the sacrifice made by individuals at all levels.

Splendid is the Sun: The 5,000 Year History of Hockey is not your typical sports history. It is a book which attempts to identify the historic development of the game of hockey and its cultural migration as well as its profound impact on human history. Based on the assumption that hockey originated in one place, and moved outwards over time to other regions of the world, the book attempts to show hockey's migration as it moved across the centuries impacting and reshaping cultures that shared in its play. In the end, the book creates a timeline for the sport. By accomplishing this task, the reader is able to understand, to a much greater degree than ever before, the complexities of hockey's history. In addition, by creating a timeline and linkage between the game, showing its development and the explaining the cultures who played the sport, one can credit those groups and individuals who helped transform the game.

We will never know who invented hockey. We will never understand the full story of the game's past. But we can at least, given the limited information we possess today, learn to appreciate the impact this sport has had on cultures, societies, and history. Hockey is not just a game. *Hockey is the first game.* Its development has impacted man and human history in ways no other sport has. It is Doug Beardsley who reminds us of the legend of the ancient Wichita Indians of North Texas and Arkansas who claim the game of hockey was born from inside the body of man. According to the Wichita:

> *When the first soul came down from the heavens it entered man in search of a place to exist. Looking behind the left rib cage, it found a ball. Behind the right rib, the soul discovered a stick. As there was no room for the spirit to dwell within man, the objects were removed and given to the body to be carried in the outside world - a sign to all that he who carried the ball and stick, were at one with the soul. Immediately man began to hit the ball with the stick. Later, more souls came down from the heavens and inhabited the bodies of other men. They too learned to hit the ball. In time, the men divided themselves into tribes and began to compete with each other. Thus the first games of hockey were played.*

In its truest form, the history of hockey is a chronicle of all which has gone before and much, which remains unseen. It is the story of a game derived and played by ancient man as a symbol of eternal life and man's celebration of religion. It is the legacy of the Sun God in all its splendor.

George and Darril Fosty
July 21, 2003

The First Period

Chapter One

The Cult of the Sun God

The religious concept of *"the Bird and the Serpent"* has been around since the dawn of man. So widespread is this phenomenon that roots of this ancient religious practice can be found in the early records of European and African civilizations as well as throughout the native tribes of North and South America. The Bird has the power of flight and with it, to be all-seeing. It moves skyward soaring towards heaven where it dwells with the gods. The Serpent is a symbol of all earth-bound creatures. It is a symbol of every living thing that must walk the planet. What differentiates the serpent, or snake, from most other creatures is its ability to shed its skin. This shedding of skin allows the creature to regenerate anew, and to be reborn, making it a symbol of eternal life. In *The Bible*, the *Book of Genesis,* the Serpent in the Garden of Eden is portrayed as both evil as well as a deceiver of man. For though it was once dwelled in the branches of the *Tree of Life,* and was considered the most beautiful of all living creatures, God punished it for its actions, removing its splendor and forcing the animal to crawl on its belly as a sign that it was the lowest form of all animals.

At first glance, the story of the Serpent in the Garden seems to be an innocent tale. In reality, the story is actually a written account of the final days of man's first great religion. The Serpent and the Tree of Life were the cornerstones of pre-biblical belief. They were the symbols of a Pagan religion that worshipped the Sun and the Sun God, the religion of the ancient Sumerians of Mesopotamia. Referred to in ancient cultures by different names, the Sumerians had named their great god *Utu.* Later the Egyptians would call him *Ra, Amun, Ptah, Khnum* or *Aten.* To the Hittites and Hurrians he was *Kumarbi.* The Assyrian-Babylonians called him *Shamash*, but to all he was the King of all Gods, the God of Justice, the Creator of Life.

Each culture used the same symbolism of the Bird and the Serpent to represent God. The Egyptians portrayed Ra with a sun disc above his head carrying an *ankh* or *Crux Ansata* in one hand and a scepter or staff in the other. The sun disc was the symbol of God the Creator. The ankh, an ancient cross with a circular top, symbolized fertility and the eternal Tree of Life. The scepter was a symbol of the snake. Held in the left-hand, the staff symbolized the snake's power of eternal life and rebirth. Held in the right-hand the staff symbolized the snake's power to strike out and administer justice. In Egyptian religion the staff possessed a forked bottom designed to trap the head of those to be judged and an upper hook designed to move and redirect them to their fate. Ra was symbolized by the image of a man with the head of a falcon. Being half bird he possessed the ability to see over all lands making him all-seeing.

It is in the accounts of the Sun God religion that we find the first records of a hockey-like game being played. Referred to by the Sumerians as *Pukku-Mikku*, the game was designed to honor the rebirth of man and creation. The first archaeological evidence of the story and the game date to c.2750 BC to c.2500 BC and is found on twelve clay tablets. Known as the *Akkadian Legend of Creation*, or the *Epic of Gilgamesh*, the tablets recount the tale of the great warrior-king and athlete Gilgamesh who resided in the Sumerian city of Uruk, located in present day Southern Iraq. It is on the twelfth tablet, the tale of *Gilgamesh and the Huluppu Tree*, which the first mention of Pukku-Mikku, being played on a flat dirt surface using a curved stick and a circular hollow wooden ring, occurs.

To the ancient Sumerians, the Pukku, the ring, represented the Sun God and the heavens wrapped within the coils of the Serpent. The Mikku, the stick, was representative of the Tree of Life, the tree that had brought forth the family of man. A tree that, following the Great Flood, had been rescued from the waters and planted on the richly soiled bank of the Euphrates River - the river which we today proclaim in our wisdom as the birthplace of ancient civilization. In addition, the Mikku also represented the Serpent, due to its shape as well as the serpent's symbolic representation of all earth-bound creatures and life. The *Epic of Gilgamesh* parallels the biblical *Book of Genesis* and today we know this as the story of *Noah and the Great Flood*.

By the Egyptian Middle Kingdom period (c.1975 BC to c.1640 BC), Pukku-Mikku had spread west to North Africa and the region of the Nile River Valley. At Beni-Hasan, the site of thirty-nine Middle Kingdom tombs near Minia, the first Egyptian image of two hockey players, armed with curved sticks and a circular ring, can be found painted on the tomb of Prince Kheti. The two ancient athletes stand opposite each other in a timeless testament to human rivalry and sport. Neither is prepared to yield; both are oblivious to the passage of time.

It would be the Egyptians who would eventually transform the game utilizing a small ball in replacement for the hollowed ring. The first written evidence of this modified change appears in an Egyptian religious text inscribed on the walls of a tomb from the 6th century BC. It reads: *"Hit the ball to the field of Apis."* Apis was the bull-god deity also known as *Orisis-Apis*, the physical manifestation of the Sun God Ra on earth, and the same bull-god deity, *Enkidu*, found in the *Epic of Gilgamesh*. Festivals were held to honor the bull-god in celebration of the sun's path, or ecliptic, into the Taurus constellation. This celebration marked the spring equinox, the start of the flooding of the Nile, and the planting of the spring crops.

For the Egyptian and the Hittite Empires the areas around present day Lebanon were each other's furthest frontier. With empires being the weakest at their edges, it would be here, where the two great ancient kingdom's lands met, that a new ancient power would emerge. Ramses II's failure to recapture the Hittite held city of Kadesh, located in present-day southwestern Syria, in c.1285 BC, marked the beginnings of declining Egyptian control of the Mediterranean region around Southwest Asia Minor. With a diminishing Egyptian influence, combined with the subsequent decline of the Hittite Empire (controllers of the lands of present day Turkey, Iraq, Iran, and Syria), a turbulent power vacuum was created in the Mediterranean enabling the Canaanite peoples of Lebanon, Israel, Palestine, and Syria to emerge independently from the shadows of these two great empires. It would be the Canaanite people of the port cities of Sidon (Zidon) and Tyre (Tyrus), on the coast of Lebanon, who established what would later become the Phoenician Empire. It is of note to understand that the term Canaanite refers to a series of tribes with similar culture and language, of which included the Phoenicians, and also includes Sumerian, Assyrian, Babylonian, Scythian, Ethiopian, and Hittite along with other cultural groups of the region.

The Canaanite-Phoenicians would travel the length of the Mediterranean spreading their culture, later founding the colonial cities of Utica c.1100 BC and Carthage c.800 BC in what is now Tunisia. These navigators and traders from Sidon-Tyre would eventually turn Utica-Carthage into the Phoenician Empire's economic center making the Phoenicians (also referred to as Carthaginians) chief rival to the Greeks and later the Romans for the control of the Mediterranean. In their quest for resources and trade, the Phoenicians would travel throughout the port cities of Italy, Greece, and Spain passing through the Straits of Gibraltar and journeying up the Western European coastline as far as ancient Ireland. In addition, they traveled south of the Straits of Gibraltar hugging the West Africa coastline down as far as current day Angola.

Masters of economic trade and sea travel, theirs was a world based on the import and export of raw materials and finished products; import skills that could only be realized through the careful study and exploitation of multicultural traits, beliefs, and practices. Due to their advanced trade network, and secret knowledge of the Atlantic Ocean north of the Straits of Gibraltar, it is reasonable to assume the Phoenicians were one of the great ambassadors of ancient hockey. In all likelihood, early Phoenicians, or Canaanite peoples, would be the first to introduce the concept of the stick and ball game to the ancient tribes of Ireland and Britain, sometime between c.1800 BC to c.1300 BC. Here it took on a violent form and was recorded in *The Irish Annals* under the name *hurley*.

The history of ancient Ireland is one of slow but constant migration of Indo-Europeans from Eastern Europe and Central Asia. One of these groups was the *Tuatha de Danann*, a mixed-race European-Canaanites tribe with cultural ties to the people of Phoenicia. It has even been suggested the Tuatha de Danann are descendants of the *Tribe of Dan* (*Tuatha* meaning tribe and *Danann* being Dan) linking this ancient Irish tribe to the Danites and the city Dan, in Syria. In Biblical terms, the Dans were one of the *Ten Lost Tribes of Israel*, there symbol, or crest, being the image of the Serpent. The city of Dan, today Tel-Dan (Tell el-Qadi in Arabic), is about thirty miles inland from the port of Tyre and was an important point connecting Tyre and Damascus along the Silk Road. Their frequent contacts with the people of Tyre, in which they had a common heritage, had allied the ancient Danites with Tyre-Phoenicians.

In *The Irish Annals*, a body of work mixing Irish history with legend and mythology, records the first account of hurley in association with the Tuatha de Danann. The annals record that in c.1272 BC, the strongest and most skilled warriors of the Tuatha de Danann defeated their rivals, the *Firbolgs*, in a match to the death at *The First Battle of Moytura*. There were twenty-seven men on each side and when the game was over, the casualties were afforded a funeral of honor and were buried together under a huge stack of rocks known as a cairn, an ancient equivalent of our modern day monuments and burial headstones. At the *Second Battle of Moytura*, the Tuatha de Danann leader Nuada would be killed by the Formorians, another of the original inhabitants of Ireland. The Celtic Sun God *Lugh*, one of the Danann warriors, would emerge as a hero having killed the Formorian warrior Balor, by shooting a stone into the giant's eye. Later becoming Danann leader and Irish High King, Lugh would be honored in the ancient games of *Lughnasadh* (the Irish equivalent to the Olympic Games), an event still celebrated to this day.

The Battles of Moytura are an important turning point in the history of ancient hockey. For though the First Battle of Moytura appears a simple sporting legend, it is in fact not a sporting contest at all but rather an account of a religious war. Moytura was a Pagan match between Sun God believers, Tuatha de Danann, and non-believers, Firbolgs, for the control of Ireland's religious beliefs.

Although the Dananns were the victors, what the Moytura

22

account fails to mention is that the tribe assimilated with the Firbolgs and, in doing so, the native Irish Firbolgs would adopt the Dananns religion and culture. Years later, these descendants would author the *Brehon Laws* and serve as the overall masters of pre-Christian religious ceremonies throughout Ireland, as well as other parts of the British Isles. In the *Brehon Laws*, such was the violence and danger associated with ancient hurley that it was declared a form of Irish military service. The laws asserted if a man was killed or injured by a hurley, either his surviving family or himself were eligible for life-long financial assistance. This could be considered the earliest example of a military disability or widow's pension. Also stipulated in the laws, all sons of kings and chieftains were to be supplied with hurley sticks during the traditional period of fosterage with another noble family. Today, we now know these descendants as the Druids. Their religion, the worship of the Serpent and Sun God, is symbolized by the great stone monoliths that exist throughout ancient Ireland, Wales, and England - the best known being Stonehenge.

It is at Stonehenge where one sees the archeological link between the ancient tribes of the British Isles and the Canaanite-Phoenicians. Stonehenge is a Sun God religious shrine. It also serves as an ancient astrological calendar. Its purpose was to serve as a sacred place of worship allowing the high priests the ability to determine the seasonal equinox of both spring and winter. Across the top of the monolith are large stones that would have originally been linked to represent a Serpent. Believing that the universe was an egg wrapped in the coil of a snake, the shrine represents the clearest evidence we have of today of the spread of the Sun God religion from its original home in ancient Iraq across much of Western Europe.

While the Canaanite religious game of ancient hockey was being introduced to the British Isles, the Egyptians, during the New Kingdom period (c.1539 BC to c.1075 BC), were in control of Lower Nubia (Northern Sudan). This region would later become part of the Aksumite Empire, an empire that stretched from the Red Sea inland across northern Ethiopia to the Nile River encompassing much of modern day Yemen. Since the 10th century BC Ethiopia has existed as an identifiable state and was a chief African supplier of gold dust, ivory, leather hides, and aromatics to the ancient Egyptians, Greeks, and later the Romans. This area was a major trading power and cultural force from c.1000 BC to c.700 AD with Axum, home to the legendary Queen of Sheba, serving as its capital.

Here the people of Ethiopia began to play *Ganna*, a game similar to that of modern day hockey. Named after the Ethiopian word for Christmas, Ganna is played by the country's youth each January 7 in celebration of the birth of Christ. January 7 being in accordance to the traditional, old Julian calendar, day of Christmas. According to Ethiopian legend, after receiving word of the birth of Christ, shepherds tending to their sheep used their crooks as sticks and began celebrating by playing a ball game. In truth, Ethiopians have been playing this ancient stick and ball game long before the birth of Jesus, learning the game through cultural contacts with the people of the Mediterranean, specifically the ancient Egyptians.

In 2000 AD, the University of Calgary professor, Dr. Bill Glanzman, and a team of international researchers revealed they had found the 3,000-year-old temple of Mahram Bilqis buried beneath the sands of Rub al-Khali desert in Yemen. This sanctuary was a sacred site for pilgrims throughout the region from c.1200 BC to c.550 AD, and believed to have been used throughout the reign of the Queen of Sheba. Glanzman wrote to the Canadian Press news agency:

> *Although they were off the beaten path as far as European history is concerned, they were just as cosmopolitan and culturally important in that they served as a crossroads to a variety of cultures: Egyptian, Sudanic, Arabic, Middle Eastern, and Indian. Perhaps an indication of this cosmopolitan character can be found in the fact that the major Aksumite cities had Jewish, Nubian, Christian and even Buddhist minorities.*

Glanzman's observations show that this region was an epicenter of ancient culture where knowledge would be sought and exchanged. The Temple of Mahram Bilqis would have been a place where this ancient stick and ball game could be shared and spread to other cultures.

King Ezana ruled Aksumite at its cultural peak from c.325 AD to c.350 AD. About c.333 AD, he converted to Christianity and declared Aksumite the first Christian state in the history of the world. It was at this time that many Ethiopian cultural legends were created. Throughout the ages these legends became very vital and uplifting and have endured to the present day, a testimony to the living expressions and lasting values of Christian-Ethiopian culture. Unfortunately, what Christianity failed to explain, Christianity simply appropriated. In the case of Ganna, the ancient Sumerian religious game was *Christianized* and made to appear to be of Christmas origin rather than of a more ancient religious source.

The winter solstice, the shortest day of sunlight, was the time when ancient religious worshippers celebrated the birth of the Sun God - the Creator. With King Ezana's conversion to Christianity in the 4th century AD, Aksumite essentially converted Ganna from a Pagan game, celebrating the Sun God, to a Christian game, celebrating Jesus Christ. It is ironic that today, the Sumerian religious game of Pukku-Mikku, and the tale of the Tree of Life, still exists and is recreated in simplistic form each Christmas in Ethiopia.

In addition to spreading westward, and later down the Nile River Valley, the ancient Sumerian game of Pukku-Mikku had also spread eastward via the ancient trade routes of western Asia. Evidence of this is found in Manipur, by North Eastern India, were the games of *Khong Kangjei, hockey on foot,* and its evolved form of *Sagol Kanjei, polo,* are played. The Manipuri people trace the origins of their games back to the ancient scripture *Puyas,* written c.1900 BC, and a mythological age when the game of hockey was played by the gods.

It is here, among the Manipuri, the Meitei, and the ancient horse-riding peoples of current-day Iran, that the horse became revered as a divine creature. In the ancient religious scripture, *The Story of the Mahabharata,* written c.300 BC to c.300 AD, the Sun God *Surya* is described as riding in a horse drawn chariot carrying the sun across the sky. The people of Manipur believe *The Mahabharata,* and its description of the *Jewel City (Mani = Jewel* and *Pur = City* or place), is evidence that they are the lost ancient Aryan civilization of India.

Manipuri hockey is a seven-a-side game in which each player plays with a cane stick, shaped very much like a present day hockey stick. The game starts when a small ball, made from the root of a white bamboo plant, is lobbed into play at center field. A player is permitted to carry the ball with his stick and kick the ball with his feet while the ball is in play. However, a goal can only be scored when the stick strikes the ball over the goal line. Generally, children play this game until they are of age to play the game on horseback. As in Ethiopia, the Manipuri play Khong Kangjei and Sagol Kanjei as part of their Christmas celebration. It is these ancient horse-riding peoples who adapted the game of hockey-on-foot to horseback, becoming the game of polo, and where today religion remains a key factor in both games continued play.

It is this binding of religion and games that links hockey to its past. It is apparent that by c.600 BC a version of hockey had become common among the ancient Greeks. It appears that the Greeks went so far as to incorporate the sport into their Isthmian and Olympic Games. The first record of the Olympic Games, dedicated to the supreme god *Zeus,* appears in c.776 BC. In Waldo E. Sweet's book *Sport and Recreation in Ancient Greece,* he writes *"the games of 776 BC were not the innovations of a new ceremony but rather the reorganization of older games."* Sweet describes some of the early history of the Olympics:

25

[Greece] was not a political entity. It was a group of independent city-states that shared many attributes . . . They had a belief in a common origin and in a tradition of migrations from the North. They had common religion and a colorful mythology. They inhabited not only the area called Greece today but also most of the islands of the Aegean, Egypt, Cyrene on the coast of Africa, the lower half of Italy, Sicily, and the coast of the Black Sea. They all stressed athletics and their cities sent their best athletes to Olympia and other religious festivals.

In 500 BC . . . there were about 50 sets of games held at regular intervals. Six centuries later, in 93 AD, the number of games had increased to over 300. Among these many sets of games, 4 were preeminent: Olympic Games, Pythian Games, Isthmian Games, and Nemean Games. The sites for all 4 were religious shrines.

The Greek philosopher, Homer writes in the *Iliad, Book 23*, that the first games were held to honor Patroclus' funeral. In Greek legend Patroclus was a slain hero who fought against the Trojans at Troy. Homer's "Funeral Games" in other words, are rooted in the religious ideal of eternal life. The late University of Cincinnati professor, P. V. Myer wrote:

The celebrated games of the Greeks had their origin in the belief of the Aryan ancestors that the souls of the dead were gratified by such spectacles as delighted them during their earthly life. During the Heroic Age these festivals were simple sacrifices or games performed at the tomb, or about the pyre of the dead [pyre: a combustible heap for burning a dead body as a funeral rite]. *Gradually these grew into religious festivals observed by an entire city or community, and were celebrated near the oracle or shrine of the god in whose honor they were instituted; the idea now being that the gods were present at the festival, and took delight in the various contests and exercises.*

Though the popular belief remains that no team sports were being played by the Greeks in their Isthmian or Olympic Games, many scholars indeed believe evidence of the playing of unknown ball games, by teams of men, does exist. The ancient Olympic Games would last about 1000 years before disappearing. It would be the Roman Emperor Theodosius who would order all Pagan sites destroyed in the name of Christianity, effectively ending the Greek Olympics in c.393 AD.

The evidence of the widespread use of primitive skates by early man has given rise to the theory of ancient winter sports. The first skates were fashioned from the shank bones of oxen, reindeer, horses, or sheep. From ancient archaeological sites near Budapest, Hungary, remains of bone skates dating to the Early Bronze Age c.2800 BC to c.2000 BC have been found implying the practice of ice-skating in ancient times was widespread in Eastern Europe. It has even been suggested that ancient hockey may have been played on the frozen winter ponds of ancient Hungary and Macedonia, effectively making the mysterious lake dwelling Illyrian tribes the first known practitioners of a recognizable form of ice hockey as early as c.500 BC. In addition, bone skates have also been uncovered among the Roman ruins of early Londinium dating back to c.50 BC. This discovery may indicate that during times of severe winters primitive ice hockey may very well have also been played along the banks of the River Thames by early Romans.

This theory of a possible Roman link to ice hockey seems practical given the Roman love of team sports and competition, as the Romans were major innovators in the development of stick and ball games. For it was the Romans who invented the *cambuca* or *chole* stick, a three and a half foot shaft with a curved blade. Borrowing from the Egyptians, the Romans also adapted the use of a lightweight ball, incorporating horse hair, feathers and linen into the lining of the leather, allowing the ball to be hit harder, to roll faster, and to be hurled skywards rather than merely passed along the ground. They called this new form of play *Pila Paganica* - a complex reference to the games of cambuca and chole being played on the ground using sticks and small goal posts.

Chapter Two

Mariners of the Sun

The earliest known European references of a hockey-like game being played in the New World are found in 16th century Spanish accounts of the Araucanos Indians of South America. At first, the Spanish referred to this tribe as the "Aucas" meaning the people of the Eastern regions. This was a reference to their original place of habitation, present day Eastern Argentina. Later, as the tribe moved inland towards Chile, in response to Spanish and Portuguese aggression, they were renamed the Araucanos for the Arauco region of Southern Chile where they subsequently resided. So fierce were the Araucanos that they hold the distinction of being the only South American tribe to effectively defeat the Incas at the height of the Inca Empire. In addition, they were the only South American tribe never conquered by the Spaniards and their allies.

Proof of the linkage between the pre-Columbian Araucanos and the ancient peoples of the Mediterranean can be found in the Araucanos legend of the Great Flood, as well as the religious significance placed in a hockey-like game of which they played. According to Araucanos legend, there once existed a great serpent that dwelled on the bottom of the sea. His name was *Cai Cai*. Cai Cai ruled all the waters. He wanted to rule the earth so he caused the rains to fall flooding all the lands. Warned of the impending flood, *Ten Ten*, the serpent of the mountains, told the Araucanos to seek refuge in the mountains. Unfortunately, many of the Araucanos were unable to reach high ground and died. After the water receded the surviving members of the tribe returned to the lands and created a new world. In memory of the great flood and their rebirth they celebrated by playing a game using a stick and a ball.

The Araucanos called their stick and ball game *Chueca* or *the twisted one*, a game that took its name from the curvature of the player's stick, which was used to hit a small leather ball. In addition to being a ritual celebration incorporating prayers, dances, and feasting, the Araucanos believed the sport was a great source of physical conditioning and warfare training. This early form of hockey was played between two teams over a flat field roughly three hundred-foot long by thirty-foot wide. At each end there was a designated line, which served as a goal marker. Played mainly for enjoyment, the Araucanos also used the game to settle differences between rival tribes in order to avoid conflict, although the game itself would sometimes directly lead to warfare. In his study of the Araucanos, Father Diego de Rosales recorded the violence that could result from Chueca in his manuscript, *Historia General del Reino de Chile*, written between c.1652 AD and c.1673 AD. He wrote:

> *The most ordinary game is the Chueca . . . They hit a ball with some twisted sticks curved in one end . . . which have a natural curve at one end and is used as a mallet. They form two gangs to fight against each other to carry the ball, placed in the middle of a hole, to their own team until they take it out from the line, marked on both side . . . They get a point when the ball goes through the line on their side. The game is over after six or four lines, and they can play a whole afternoon . . . After the game, they sit down to drink chicha and get completely drunk. Sometimes during these meetings, they come to agreements for uprising, because they call for other Indians from the whole Earth, and at night, they talk and agree on rebellions. Thus governors sometimes forbid this game and these meetings for the damages experienced. In order to be comfortable while running, they play the game naked, wearing only a loincloth to cover their indecency. Women sometimes play this game, but they wear some cloth, and they all attend to the field to see them play and run.*

A question which has never been answered by historians or experts of South American Indian cultures is: "How did such a geographically isolated tribe possess a stick and ball game almost identical in rules, format, dress, and concepts to that of the ancient Mediterranean and Near Eastern cultures?" The most obvious conclusion is the most controversial - the implied notion that at some point in the pre-Columbian past, the Araucanos were in contact with ancient old world peoples. Such a conclusion goes to the heart of popular history and modern beliefs. However implausible as this theory may seem, proof in fact does exists showing a direct link. Aristotle (c.384 BC to c.322 BC), in his *Minor Works*, credits the Phoenician-Carthaginians with the discovery of a large island west of the Pillars of Hercules (the pillars being two mountains on each side of the Straits of Gibraltar where the Mediterranean meets the Atlantic Ocean). Aristotle states:

> *In the sea outside the Pillars of Hercules they say that an island was found by the Carthaginians, a wilderness having*

wood of all kinds and navigable rivers, remarkable for various kinds of fruits, and many day' sailing away. When the Carthaginians, who were masters of the western ocean observed that many traders and other men, attracted by the fertility of the soil and the pleasant climate, frequented it because of its richness, and some resided there, they feared that knowledge of this land would reach other nations, and that a great concourse to it of men from various lands of the earth would follow. Therefore, lest the Carthaginian Empire itself should suffer injury, and the dominion of the sea be wrestled from their hands, the Senate of Carthage issued a decree that no one, under penalty of death, should thereafter sail thither, and they massacred all who resided there.

Later, in c.50 BC, the Sicilian historian Diodorus Siculus wrote, in his book *Biblioteca Historica*, of the Carthaginians and their accidental discovery of South America:

Over against Africa lies a very great island in the vast Ocean, many days' sail from Libya westward. The soil there is very fruitful, a great deal whereof is mountainous, but much likewise a plain, which is the most sweet and pleasant part, for it is watered with several navigable rivers . . . The mountainous part of the country is clothed with very large woods, and all manner of fruit trees and springs of fresh water . . . There you may have game enough in hunting all sorts of wild beasts . . . This island seems rather to be the residence of some of the gods, than of men.

Diodorus goes on to describe in detail how the Phoenician-Carthaginians had established a number of trading centers and colonies throughout the known world and had discovered the region of South America by chance, when one of their West African merchant vessels had reached the Eastern South American shoreline after being blown off course during a fierce storm. The late Columbia University historian, Frederick J. Pohl in his 1961 book, *Atlantic Crossings before Columbus*, argues the Phoenician-Carthaginians were the first people to discover the Americas stating there is historical record of their circumnavigation of Africa. Pohl's argues based on detailed historical study and observations of what Diodorus wrote:

"Over against Africa" (not west of Gibraltar or west of Cadiz) strongly supports the idea of an Atlantic crossing; for

if the Phoenicians crossed the ocean it must have been westward from Africa, as it was only there that the prevailing winds and currents would have made a westward crossing possible. Readers of course demanded that every voyage have a storm.

What is important to note from the Diodorus description is the detail and knowledge he displays in terms of South American geography. He describes a continent surrounded by water. He describes the southeastern rivers and the estuaries and the direction they flowed. More amazingly, he describes the entrance to the Parana River, the region of the Rio de la Plata near Buenos Aires, and the lands of Great Plains and Andean Mountains, near the junction of the Pilcomayo and Paraguay rivers areas - the traditional home to the Araucanos Indians.

Captain Alan Villiers, in his book *Men, Ships and The Sea*, explains that the Phoenicians were the inventor's of the ship's keel. They were also the first peoples to create streamlined ships, which utilized complex sails and rigging. At the height of their empire, ships capable of transporting 100 tons of cargo moved regularly along the coastlines often traveling in excess of 100 miles a day. So advanced were these vessels that not until the 17th century would comparable ships sail the world's oceans. During the time of Hannibal, Phoenician-Carthaginian ships transported an army of elephants across the Mediterranean to aid in the war against the Romans. Hannibal would use these mammals to cross the Alps Mountains; a feat that to this day is considered one of the great logistical marvels of the ancient world.

If one argues the point of contact between the old and new worlds, based on the historic records of Aristotle and Diodorus, were the lands inhabited by the Araucanos (making the Araucanos the first people of the New World to play the game) then as the game took root in South America it would have spread northwards into the regions of Central and North America. In effect being a South-North migration. Given what we know of the ancient trade routes among the tribes of the Americas, and archaeological dating of native artifacts and settlements, such a theory seems plausible. This theory is also consistent with the fact that the South American tribes were among the most developed of all the New World groups. Discovered on the cliffs of the Bay of Paracas in Peru is a 600-foot carved Tree of Life. This ancient symbol of early Near Eastern religion and ancient hockey stands like a cairn in the face of critics who contend that South America was void of old world contact prior to the arrival of the Spanish. In addition, at Copan, Honduras, archaeologists have found a stone carving of an

31

elephant headdress dated to at least c.750 AD, though likely much later, evidence yet again, of a Mediterranean connection.

Over the last two centuries, archaeological discoveries in both Central and South America have continued to produce evidence of New and Old World links. At Chichen Itza, a Mayan city located on the Yucatan Peninsula, archaeologists have documented the images of lotus blossoms carved on the walls of an encircled sports field. The images of lotus blossoms raise much interest in archaeological circles for the fact that no such flower is native to that region. Instead, the lotus blossom is both a native plant as well as a religious symbol of eternal life and a common image found on the walls of ancient buildings and tombs of the Mediterranean. Again at Beni Hasan we find images of the lotus on the tomb wall of Prince Kheti.

In Mayan religion the earth is symbolized in the form of a ball court. It is an arena where man confronts the powers of life, death, and rebirth. It is on these ball courts that the Mayan's played a game called *Chaah* as part of an elaborate religious ceremony reenacting the story of creation. According to the Mayans, the heroes of the story were descendants of a feathered serpent named *Kukulcan*. Around c.800 AD the Mayan game witnessed a transformation from its earlier form. The stick and ball play declined in popularity and was replaced by a violent soccer-like game using a larger ball. Stone circles or hoops, attached to the sides of the stone playing field walls, were also added.

In total, over 600 ball courts have been unearthed in Mexico alone, evidence of the game's widespread play and religious significance. Not counting the ancient game of hockey, there are over 230 cultural similarities between the peoples of Central and South America and the peoples of the ancient Mediterranean. Among the similarities one finds are the Tree of Life, the creation story, Bird-and-Serpent legends, and the worship of the Sun God.

Chapter Three

Serpents of the Sky

Prior to the arrival of the Europeans a network of Indian trade routes existed along the western coasts of the North American Pacific Northwest and Mexico. Archaeological evidence of their extensiveness can be found on Gabriola Island, in British Columbia, Canada. It is here one finds some of the most extensive examples of ancient petroglyphs in the world. Of particular interest are images of mythical birds, serpents, and the sun. In addition two images of an anteater have been found. Anteaters are not native to Canada; instead they are Central American in origin. How these images came to exist on an isolated coastal island in Western Canada can only be explained when placed in context with the ancient trade routes. Partly due to naivety, as well as a lack of understanding of the past, archaeologists have all but ignored these images claiming instead that they represent mythical forms. This inability to recognize the obvious is an indication of exactly how little modern man understands the cultures and history of the native peoples who once inhabited this region.

The Indians of British Columbia and the Pacific Northwest traded extensively with other tribes, including those of the American Southwest and Northern Mexico. Far from isolated, theirs was a world of economic and cultural interaction over great distances, the likes of which were not replicated again in North America until after the completion of the first Continental Railroad. Far from primitive, they were in fact some of the most complex societies to predate modern man.

Additional evidence of a link between the Indians of the Pacific Northwest and those of American Southwest exists. Beaver-teeth dice and beaver-teeth inline staves used in Pueblo Indian games have been found. The beaver teeth have been traced to the Columbia River region, well north of the traditional hunting grounds of the Pueblo. It is along this trade route that the ancient cult of the Sun God and the religious sport of ancient hockey spread, as it made its way north from the Mexican interior to the northern fringes of the Canadian West Coast.

In the book *Ancient American Indians,* Paul R. Cheesman describes the Wupatki Ruins near Flagstaff, Arizona, as a place where ancient Indian tribes came together and shared their culture and knowledge. Its rich fertile land served as a natural meeting place for native farmers from the tribes of the Anasazi, the Hohokam, the Mogollon, the Patayan and the Sinagua. Cheesman contends that a melting pot of native culture existed in this one area for over 150 years prior to its abandonment around c.1225 AD. He adds: *"The ball court found at Wupatki bears a dramatic resemblance to the famous ancient ball courts found in Mexico and South America."*

Wupatki appears to have been a key site for tracing and dating the spread of ancient hockey throughout North America. The tribes that came together here around c.1075 AD were agrarian societies, less violent than their Mayan counterparts. These tribes were practitioners of a form of the stick and ball game. The fact they did not adopt the Mayan hoop game indicates that these tribes possessed knowledge of ancient hockey prior to the changes precipitated by the Mayas in c.800 AD. Here too one finds the legends and worship of the Sun God, the Serpent as well as tales of a once great flood.

Moving west from Arizona, the trade routes crossed into California spreading the game to the Pima-Papago, the Hopi, the Yuma, and over to the California coast, home of the Sycuan tribes. Again the Sun God cult and the game of hockey took hold. Once more the story of the flood appears among tribal legends. Northward along the coastal regions of California, the Sun God religion and the practice of hockey continued to spread. In the present day Contra Costa country region near San Francisco, this religious and sports phenomena found root among the tribes of the Miwoks, the Yokuts, the Pomos and the Ohlone. It is also at this point where significant developmental changes to both the religion and the practice of ancient hockey occur, as the sport takes on two different styles of play. In the first instance it continues to be a traditional ball and stick game. However, a second version, utilizing blocks of wood tied together with sinew - creating an aerial method of play, also emerges. With this change an object could now be tossed skyward, symbolic of a flying serpent, from player to player to be caught on the curved end of the stick, as participants moved quickly up the field. This new twist on the ancient game of hockey would spread and be adopted by other tribes of the region, particularly the Pomos.

Other changes also took place. Though the Sun God myth continued to be symbolized by a mythical bird, more and more the image becomes one of a bird-like creature known as a Thunderbird. As was the case with the ancient Egyptians, this bird-god would be viewed as an all-wise and all-seeing entity. One to be worshipped and feared by man on account of it being the ruler of the heavens as well as the purveyor of justice.

Later, as the game would continue its northern journey, the Hupa, the Yurok, and the Wintun Indians would adopt its play. By now the game was reaching a zenith in terms of development and impact on the native cultures of the Pacific Northwest. Loosely allied with each other, the Indian tribes along the West Coast would converge annually along the Columbia River for the seasonal salmon runs. Tribes as far north as Alaska, as far south as California, and as far east as North Dakota, would journey to the point where the river narrowed to only a couple hundred feet coming together in one spot to trade, to exchange stories, and to share knowledge. Today we know this area as "The Long Narrows" or the "Dalles." Due to the confined channel, this area was possibly the best place in North America to catch fish. In David Wynecoop's book, *Children of the Sun: A History of the Spokane Indians,* he writes:

> . . . the 15-mile stretch of rapids where canoe travel in both directions had to stop. Here lived . . . the Wishram, and every year they held a huge market or fair. The Yakimas held one out on the plains, where 6,000 Indians might camp in a circle six miles around. The people from the wet country met those from the dry country and exchanged goods from as far east as North Dakota and as far north as Alaska.

In Emory Strong's book, *Stone Age on the Columbia River,* he states an *"Indian with his crude instruments could have taken about 100 fish a day, averaging 20 pounds each."* He adds:

> [For] the interior and coastal groups . . . between California and Canada, the Long Narrows became the great trade mart of the West, and the permanent residents were the middlemen in the traffic. The western Indians traded dried clams, dentalium shell, baskets, wappato, and wooden implements for furs, feather, robes, dried fish, and slaves; all might be sold again further up or down the river. More natives came to the Long Narrows to enjoy the festivities and the gambling than to fish, for the best fishing places were limited and individually owned, and fish could be caught at many other places on the river.

Canadian fur trader and pioneer, Alexander Ross, who traveled on the Astor Expedition of 1811 (the second greatest American overland crossing after Lewis and Clark) wrote in *Adventures of the First Settlers on the Oregon or Columbia River, 1810-1813*:

> The main camp of the Indians is situated at the head of the Narrows and may contain, during the salmon season, 3,000

souls, or more; but the constant inhabitants of the place do not exceed 100 persons, and are called Wyampams [Wishram]. The rest are all foreigners from different tribes throughout the country, who resort hither not for the purpose of catching salmon, but chiefly for gambling and speculation, not in fish, but in other articles.

According to Indian accounts, the different tribes would meet along the long flats next to the Narrows at a point called Colowesh Bottom, named after an Indian Chief, to compete in athletics and games. It was at Colowesh Bottom where groups representing numerous western and mid-west tribes learned the game and its legends. As David Wynecoop describes, the various tribes would come together and play a form of ancient hockey, similar to that of today's Scottish shinny, *"on a mile-long stretch of beach using a wooden ball and long, curved sticks of vine maple."*

The tribes of the Columbia were closely aligned with an Interior Salish tribe known later as the Thompson Indians of British Columbia. Great innovators, they would be among the first to transform the curved stick by tying netting of mesh between the lower part of the stick's shaft and the curved blade. This innovation would allow them to elevate the traditional ball and eliminate the blocks of wood-tied together with sinew. By doing this, the two versions of the Pacific Northwest game could be merged. James Teit writes in his 1898 book, *The Traditions of the Thompson Indians of British Columbia:*

These sticks were about three feet long, and had a very crooked head, so that the players could catch the ball with them, and throw it from them towards the goal of the enemy. Many men ran with the ball held in the crook of the stick until stopped by an opponent, when they threw the ball towards the intended goal. Others preferred, if they had the chance, to lift the ball with the toe, and before it fell strike or catch it with their stick. When bending the end of the stick to the desired crook, bark string was used, connecting the latter to the straight part of the stick. Some Indians played with the strings still attached, thinking to get a better hold of the ball, but this was considered unfair. In some games all the players used crooks with nets similar to those of lacrosse sticks. Often a guard-stick was used to protect the ball from the players of the opposite party.

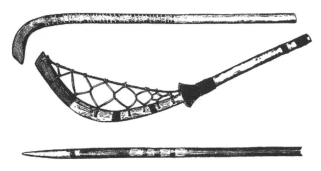

Illustration of stick types Teit had observed and recorded in *The Traditions of the Thompson Indians of British Columbia.* Top: Original style shinny stick. Middle: Adapted shinny stick for lacrosse type game. Bottom: Guard-stick for protecting ball during play.

What James Teit had witnessed was not a game similar to lacrosse but rather a game which was the forerunner to lacrosse. Teit's observations are important in terms of both the presentation of a timeline as well as a visual record. For his accounts allows us to glimpse briefly at a lost link in the development of ancient hockey. In addition, Teit shows us the cultural complexity of the native tribes and how they were able to borrow the customs and skills of others in order to serve their own basic requirements and lifestyle needs. Referring again to the Thompsons he wrote:

> *When analyzing the culture of the Thompson Indians, we find much evidence of a strong influence of eastern culture by way of the Nicola Valley. The style of dress, the use of feather ornaments, the cradle of the Nicola band are decidedly due to contact with the east. The Nicola band have always been in close contact with the Okanagan; and eastern products, such as pipes and painted buffalo-hides, and eastern fashions and customs, such as styles of dress and the method of building round tents instead of square lodges, have been introduced in this manner. Even the first vague traces of Christianity seem to have found their way to the tribe along this route.*
>
> > *In many respects these resemblances between their culture and eastern culture are common to them and to other tribes of the western plateaus. The sinew-lined bow, the occurrence of the tubular pipe, the peculiar woven rabbit-*

37

skin blanket, the high development of the coyote myths, and the loose social organization, combined with the lack of elaborate religious ceremonials, characterize them as resembling still more closely the culture of the western highlands . . .

Ornaments made of dentalia and abelone shell must be considered as evidence of trade rather than copies of ornaments worn on the coast. The hand-hammer, harpoon, and fish-knife may also be counted as copies of implements used by the Coast tribes.

One of the elements of their culture that is most difficult to explain is the occurrence of the beautiful basketry made of cedar-bark, and of woven fabrics made of mountain-goat wool, among the Lower Thompsons. Coiled basketry of this type is found in many places along the Pacific coast . . . coiled basketry of the Arctic Athapascans, which belongs to this type, may be related to the coiled basketry of the Apache and Navajo . . . This same type of basketry is found not only among the Athapascan tribe of the Mackenzie Basin . . . but also among the Chilcotin of British Columbia. It occurs all along the Coast Range and the Cascade Range in British Columbia and Washington, and attains its greatest beauty in California.

Teit was not aware of the annual migration of the native tribes to the region of The Long Narrows. He did not understand the significance that the salmon run played on the cultural interaction of the tribes. If he had known he would have been able to answer the mystery of why the Indians all displayed similar styles of basketry. He would have also understood why similarities existed between the Thompson Indian stick game and that of East Coast lacrosse. Contrary to beliefs, lacrosse was not an East Coast invention. Its origins were found along the Columbia River where the salmon migrated and where the cultures of native America came to exchange knowledge and to play.

There has always been a popular notion that the game today called lacrosse originated in Eastern North America among the native tribes of the Great Lakes. It has been assumed that lacrosse's migration had been both a north-south journey down the Mississippi River to the Gulf of Mexico as well as westward migration across the Great American Plains. Such logic seemed correct given the natural development of European colonial history in the New World. The Europeans had come from the east and had moved west. As a result, most histories pertaining to the tribes and peoples of North America have attempted to explain history and developments with east-west logic. We know that like a compass, human history and development often moves in more than one direction. In the case of early hockey the route has been a south-north migration from the farthest corners of South America to the Columbia River, and then an eastward journey to the Great Lakes, moving much in the same direction and shape as a hockey stick. Only when one thinks in terms of a south-north migration do the archaeological dates and timelines of history, like pieces of a puzzle, fall into place.

Historians do not give a date for the first evidence of lacrosse being played in the Great Lakes regions. The popular assumption has always been that the sport first appeared around the 13th-15th centuries (coincidentally the same time as the first European contact with the New World). This assumption seems implausible given the northern migration of hockey and the fact that ruins of fields and ball courts appear in Mexico as early as c.400 AD. Regardless of when hockey first appeared along the Great Lakes region, the fact that the religious significance of the game remained consistent throughout cannot be ignored. This factor is both a credit to the oral tradition of storytelling of the ancient Indians as well as an indication of just how little the legends had changed over the centuries. The Iroquois tribes played lacrosse when celebrating their mid-winter festival, *Hodigohsosga*. Hodigohsosga, was a festival honoring their supreme deity, *Shagodyowehgowah,* or *Great Protector*, which, according to the Seneca Indians, is the author of creation.

The first European references to lacrosse is recorded in the 1636 AD accounts of the Jesuit missionary Jean de Brebeuf in *The Jesuit Relations and Allied Documents, Travels and Explorations of the Jesuit Missionaries in New France 1610 - 1791 Vol. X, Huron.* Describing a game played by the Huron and other Algonquin tribes of the St. Lawrence, using a ball and a stick reminiscent of a bishop's crosier or *la crosse*, Brebeuf, who himself was later savagely killed by the Iroquois, wrote:

> *There is a poor sick man, fevered of body and almost dying, and a miserable Sorcerer will order for him, as a cooling remedy, a game of crosse. Or the sick man himself, sometimes, will have dreamed that he must die unless the whole country shall play crosse for his health; and, no matter how little may be his credit, you will see them in a beautiful field, Village contending against Village, as to who will play crosse the better, and betting against one another Beaver robes and Porcelain collars, so as to excite greater*

interest...

Sometimes, also, one of these jugglers will say that the whole Country is sick, and he asks a game of crosse to heal it; no more needs to be said, it is published immediately everywhere; and all the Captains of each Village give orders that all the young men do their duty in this respect, otherwise some great misfortune would befall the whole Country.

In the Book *The Jesuit Relations and Allied Documents: Travels and Explorations of the Jesuit Missionaries in New France, 1610-1791: The Original French, Latin, and Italian texts, with English Translations and Notes*, it is written:

. . . they had tired themselves to death playing crosse in all the villages around here, because this sorcerer had affirmed that the weather depended only upon a game of crosse . . .

These accounts, though somewhat puzzling to the Jesuits, as they were unfamiliar with native folklore, reflect the widespread belief among many of the regional tribes that the game held magical powers, as it was associated with eternal life. It seems rather straightforward to assume that individuals near death, or tribes suffering from a calamity, would turn to the game as a way of bringing forth good luck and healing. A tribal *Shaman* (Medicine Man) would declare the whole country as sick, and that a game of lacrosse was needed for its recovery. This belief and practice would be in keeping with the game's original purpose dating back centuries to the time of the Sumerians. The game was also invoked as a preparation and ceremony for war, as the eternal life concept associated with its play would seemingly strengthen the believers and, in theory, make them impervious to death. In other words, allowing them to be reborn.

Alexander Henry gives one of the earliest accounts of lacrosse in his book, *Travels and Adventures in Canada and the Indian Territories between the Years 1760 and 1776.* He writes:

A favorite game amongst the Ojibwe is described as The Hurdle [Lacrosse]. When about to play, the men of all ages would strip themselves almost naked, but dress their hair in great style, put ornaments on their arms and belts around their waist, and paint their faces and bodies in the most elaborate style. Each man was provided with a hurdle, an instrument made of a small circle, in which a loose piece of network is fixed, forming a cavity big enough to receive a leather ball about the size of a man's fist. Everything being prepared, a level plain about half a mile long was chosen, with proper barriers or goals at each end. Having previously formed into two equal parts, they are assembled in the very middle of the field, and the game began by throwing up the ball perpendicular in the air, when instantly both parties, painted in different colors, held their rackets elevated in the air to catch the ball. Whoever was so fortunate to catch it in his net ran with it to the barrier with all his might, supported by his party, while the opponents were pursuing and endeavoring to knock the ball out of the net. He who succeeded in doing so ran in the same manner to the opposite barrier, and was of course pursued his turn.

If in danger of being overtaken he might throw it with his hurdle to an associate who happened to be nearer to the barrier. They had a peculiar knack of throwing it a great distance, so that the best runners did not always have the advantage; and by a peculiar way of working their hands and arms while running, the ball never dropped out of their hurdle.

The best of three heats wins the game, and besides the honour acquired on such occasions, a considerable prize is adjudged to the victors. The vanquished, however, generally challenge their adversaries to renew the game the next day, which is seldom refused. The game thus becomes more important, as the honor of the whole village is at stake, and it is carried on with every impetuosity. Every object which might impede them is knocked down and trodden under foot without mercy; and before the game is decided, it is a common thing to see members sprawling on the ground with wounded legs and broken heads - yet this never creates disputes or ill-will after the game is decided.

It is Alexander Henry, who, aside from presenting the reader with the most detailed account of lacrosse prior to the 1800's, is also the source for one of the most amazing episodes in lacrosse history.

Fort Michilimackinac, originally built in 1715 AD by the French on the south shore of the Straits of Mackinac which links Lake Michigan to Lake Huron, was a strategically located, fortified trading post used by the French to link their trade system. After their loss in the French-Indian Wars, the French relinquished control of the outpost to the British in 1761 AD. The Ottawa and Chippewa tribes from the

41

area found British control to be grave compared to that of the French, and under the coordination and control of Chief Pontiac, they planned a rebellion to take over the fort.

The Chippewas sent word to Captain Etheruyton, who was in charge of the fort, that the Ottawa and Chippewa tribes would hold a lacrosse game to honor King George III's birthday celebration for June 4, 1763. The English, unaware of a newly formed alliance between the two Indian tribes, were cautious but never suspected that the Indian intent was to capture the fort from the British. Many men came outside the fort standing along the sidelines placing wagers on which side would achieve victory, leaving the fort gate open. Upon an agreed signal the Indian warriors, aided by native women who had hidden their men's tomahawks under their clothing, attacked their unsuspecting British spectators. Before the British could respond, over 400 Indians had penetrated the fort's wall. When the battle ended, 71 British soldiers and civilians were dead. Only three British who were the fort's commanders survived - Captain Etheruyton, L. T. Leslie, and Alexander Henry. Etheruyton and Leslie were later ransomed off and Henry escaped, eventually settling in New York City where he later penned his autobiographical account.

Perhaps the most ominous lacrosse story is about the former Erie Indians who lived around the southern shores of Lake Erie, stretching from present day Buffalo, New York, to Sandusky, Ohio. According to an 1845 edition of the *Buffalo Commercial Newspaper*, Seneca Chief Blacksnake recounted the slaughter and subsequent demise of the Erie Indians. The incident occurred when the Erie, a traditional enemy of the Seneca, had challenged the Seneca to a ball game similar to lacrosse. As the Chief explained:

> *Traditionally the Erie were stronger, wiser and more prosperous than their neighboring tribes. They built wooden dwellings, planted gardens and grew fields of grain. When the soil was spent, they moved to new sites.*

In their match against the Seneca, it would be the Seneca who would walk away victorious. The Erie, upset in defeat, proposed several other athletic challenges which included a foot race and wrestling bouts, which they subsequently also lost. They were so humiliated by their defeats that they later formed a war party intent on destroying the opposing Five Nations tribes in which the Seneca were a part of (the League of Five Nations included the Seneca, Mohawk, Oneida, Cayuga, and Onondaga tribes and later expanded to six nations with the inclusion of the Tuscarora). Blacksnake continued:

Erie warriors fought bravely, but had no firearms. The combined alliance forces, wielding muskets and using their canoes as ladders to scale the wall of the Erie stronghold, finally killed most of the defenders. Following the conflict, the Erie lost their identity. Eventually, the few who remained were absorbed by other tribes. Nearly all of the Erie braves were killed.

The game would continue to spread from the St. Lawrence and the Great Lakes, into the Mississippi River heartland to the tribes of the Natchez, the Choctaw, the Creeks and eventually, all the way south to the Seminoles of Florida. It is estimated that a total of forty-eight separate North American tribes played this adaptation of the ancient form of hockey, a game we still refer to today as *lacrosse.*

Chapter Four

The Viking Sagas

One of the strangest yet most interesting links to the ancient game of hockey pertains to the legends and history of the Norse. We know from archaeological evidence that the Vikings, as they were called, arrived on the shores of Eastern Canada as early as c.1000 AD and that numerous forays to the region followed. Norse accounts of their voyages are numerous. Many of these writings contain references to the natives of Eastern Canada. Some historians have argued that Norse settlements may have existed as far inland as Lake Michigan. In terms of ancient hockey, evidence to support the belief of Viking forays to the Great Lakes does exist, however, often it has been refuted by skeptics more inclined to criticize new theories rather than assume traditional historic thought may be incorrect.

One obvious linkage, never fully explored, is the similarities between the oral histories of the Great Lakes Indians and the Norse Sagas. On at least one occasion, Jesuit missionaries reported that they had been told by the natives that lacrosse, in addition to holding religious importance, was associated with the remembrance of an event in which one of their own warriors bloodied a human giant while engaging the stranger along the shoreline. The stranger received a serious head wound at the hands of the warrior - proof that the individual was mortal and not a visiting supreme being or a god. Jesuit missionary Jean de Brebeuf accounts of this Huron legend tied to the game of lacrosse:

> *During these songs and dances, some take occasion to knock down, as if in sport, their enemies. Their most usual cries are hen, hen, or héééé, or else wiiiiiii. They ascribe the origin of all these mysteries to a certain Giant of more than human size, whom one of their tribe wounded in the forehead when they dwelt on the shore of the sea.*

This insignificant account or legend seems to hold little importance until it is reviewed in the context of Norse history.

In the *Thorfinn Karlsefni Sagas (c.1003 AD to c.1008 AD)*, Karlsefni is credited with seeing more of the North American continent than any other Viking. *The Hauk's Book* details Karlsefni's voyage southward along the coast where it is said that he and his men sailed far to a river that flowed down from the land into a lake and thence into the sea. Could this be referring to the Great Lakes region? It was here they built shelters and where they would encounter a hostile tribe of natives. The saga describes one early spring morning when Karsefni's party saw a great many skin canoes filled with Indians:

> . . . *looking like coals flung out beyond the bay, and staves being swung about on every boat . . . Nothing was seen of them for three weeks, but at the end of that time, such a great number of the boats of the savages appeared that they looked like a floating stream, and their staves were all revolving in a direction opposite to the course of the sun, and they were all whooping with great outcries. Then Karlsefni's men took red shields and held them up to view. The savages leaped from their boats, and they met and fought. There was a heavy shower of missiles, for the savages had war slings. Karlsefni observed that the savages had on the end of a pole a great ball-shaped object almost the size of a sheep's belly, and nearly black in color, and this they flung from the pole up on the land above Karlsefni's men, and it made such a terrifying noise where it struck the ground that great fear seized Karlsefni and all with him, so that they thought only of flight and of making their escape up along the river bank. It seemed to them that the savages were driving at them from all sides, and they did not make a stand until they came to some jutting rocks where they resisted fiercely. In front of her she* (Freydis) *found a dead man, Thorbrand Snorrason, whose skull had been split by a flat stone . . .*

It would be this battle that would cause Karlsefni and his men to leave and return home.

It was the Norwegian historian Ebbe Hertzberg in his 1904 article entitled *Old Ball Games of the Norsemen ('Nordboernes Gamle Boldspil'),* who first pointed to the similarities between the ancient Norse stick and ball game of *knattleikr* and Indian Lacrosse. Hertzberg argued both games were in fact the same and that the games were evidence of early Norse contact with the Americas. Hertzberg's arguments concluded that the game of knattleikr was given from the Vikings to the tribes of the Americas. Hertzberg would have perhaps been more correct if he had concluded the opposite; that knattleikr was a game adopted by the Vikings from their contact with the Indians. Regardless, Hertzberg's arguments of similarities have continued to stand the test of time and to conclusively link the two games. Hertzberg identified at least ten similarities between knattleikr and lacrosse:

1) Both games are played on both dry land and ice;
2) Both Games are played with well defined boundaries;
3) Both games are played by two opposing teams;
4) Both games require a referee;
5) Each player is matched against an opposing player of equal skill or strength;
6) Both games require players to carry the ball across the opponent's boundary line or to throw the ball through the goal of the opposition;
7) Both games are noted for their sanctioning of extreme violence;
8) Both games are seen as a test of male strength and warrior masculinity;
9) Opposing players, once paired off, were required to maintain close proximity to each other; and
10) Both games utilize a wooden ball and a shinny-like stick with meshed ball holder.

Though many of these similarities appear trivial, and can be dismissed individually as coincidental, the overwhelming number of similarities is too many to be deemed a coincidence. If one accepted the Hertzberg argument, then the next question that must be answered is: "When did the Norsemen-Indian contact occur?" Archaeological evidence suggests the game of lacrosse dates back to at least c.800 AD. Coincidentally, this is well before the first Norse expeditions to America occurred. During the period between c.874 AD to c.930 AD numerous Norse settlements were successfully established in Iceland and Greenland. At the height of Norse expansion and sea power, around c.1100 AD, Norse census records record a population of 50,000 individuals in Iceland alone. These individuals were ruled over by 400 different chieftains who individually oversaw their own clan communities and warriors, each of whom competed for glory, wealth, and land holdings. Competition among the chieftains and their clans was intense and often led to violence as groups struggled to maintain control of their own lands and economic power bases. In order to alleviate this cultural strain, expeditions of resettlement by landless clan members were often initiated. In fact, given the tremendous demands such a large population would have had on the Icelandic communities and fertile farmlands, resettlement was in all likelihood promoted.

The Norse sagas record numerous expeditions to the uncharted lands in and around the North Atlantic. Until last century, many scholars have assumed that the few expeditions mentioned in the sagas were limited in numbers. However, more recently, some researchers have suggested that in fact the sagas were an amalgamation of "many" voyages and not just a limited few. This theory would account for the often-contradictory descriptions of the lands that the Norse explorers discovered and would explain the difficulties researchers have faced in terms of identifying the lands described.

If one assumes Norse exploratory and resettlement expeditions were commonplace among the chieftain-led clans, then it is safe to assume that these settlement attempts were more numerous than currently believed. Such a theory would also imply that the Norse settlements, which have been suggested to have existed in America in at least 3-5 locations, were larger in number than previously thought. Though evidence of Norse settlements has been slow in coming, in recent years, as the 1961 discovery of the Viking settlement of L'Anse Aux du Meadows site in Newfoundland shows, Norse settlements in America did exist. Given what we know today of the existence of Norse settlements along the Eastern Canadian shores, the comparison of knattleikr, and lacrosse seems all but fitting.

The closest resemblances of lacrosse to knattleikr can be found in the games played by the Indians of the interior Great Lakes of Canada. The tribes who played this sport were known to have trade links and contact with other groups that included the Mi'kmaqs of the Eastern shores and the Inuit of Labrador and Baffin Island. Is it possible that Norse explorers, aided by Inuit and Mi'kmaq scouts, sailed inland via the St. Lawrence to the Great Lakes and/or down the Hudson Bay where they came into contact with the Eastern tribes? Many scholars would disclaim such a theory, however; compelling evidence suggests that in fact both possibilities may indeed have occurred.

In 1888, Dr. Franz Boas, in his book *The Central Eskimo* recounted an Inuit legend from Baffin Island. He wrote:

> *In olden times the Inuit were not the only inhabitants of the country in which they live at the present time. Another tribe similar to them shared their hunting-ground. But they were on good terms, both tribes living in harmony in the villages. The Tornit were much taller than the Inuit and had very long legs and arms. Almost all of them were blear-eyed (blue-eyed). They were extremely strong and could lift large boulders, which were by far too heavy for the Inuit. But even the Inuit of that time were much stronger than those of*

47

to-day, and some large stones were shown on the plain of Miliaqdjuin, in Cumberland Sound, with which the ancient Inuit used to play, throwing them great distances. Even the strongest men of the present generation are scarcely able to lift them, much less swing them or throw them any distance.

The Tornit lived on walrus, seals, and deer, just as the Eskimos do nowadays, but their methods of hunting were different . . . There method of hunting deer was remarkable. In a deer pass, where the game could not escape, they erected a pile of cairns across the valley and connected them by ropes. Some of the hunters hid behind the cairns, while others drove the deer towards them. As the animals were unable to pass the rope they fled along it, looking for an exit, and while attempting to pass a cairn were lanced by the waiting hunter, who seized the body by the hind legs and drew it behind the line . . . The old stone houses of the Tornit can be seen everywhere. Generally they did not build snow houses, but lived the whole winter in stone buildings, the roofs of which were frequently supported by whale ribs . . . Though both tribes lived on very good terms, the Inuit did not like to play at ball with the Tornit, as they were too strong and used large balls with which they hurt their playfellows severely.

What makes this passage remarkable is the detail of the descriptions of both the Tornit as well as their hunting practices and sports. Stone-tossing was common among the Norse. It is a sport played in parts of Scotland, a former Norse settlement, and other areas of the North Atlantic. In addition, the style of hunting was similar to the herding and hunting methods of the early Europeans. Lastly, the description of the people and their ball play seems to describe Norse physical features and the game of knattleikr.

If indeed the Tornit were Norsemen, then what could have happened to them? Where did these blue-eyed Indians go? Again, the answer may surprise us. We know from the historic Roman Catholic clerical accounts of the 1600's that the last reference to a Norse settlement was recorded in c.1374 AD. After that date, all record of Viking colonization on Greenland appears to have been abandoned. Some suggest that these Norse colonists sailed east and southeast toward the shores of Iceland and Ireland. However, evidence does not support this theory. Others, less willing to discount the arguments of continued westward movement, believe the lost Greenland settlers went west into the heartland of the Canadian Arctic lands eventually becoming assimilated with the dominant Eskimo tribes. In his book, *The Voyages of the Norsemen to America*, William Hovgaard writes:

> *Thus the final disappearance of the Norsemen was due in part, to their absorption by the more numerous Eskimo population. This theory is most important, since it opens up fresh possibilities and a new field of research as to the ultimate fate of the Norse colony in Greenland. It might be objected that if such a fusion had actually taken place, we would have heard more about it; but this does not follow. The comparative silence of the reports on this point may be due to the fact that intercourse with the heathen was strictly prohibited by the Church. Such intercourse was regarded with the greatest abhorrence by all good Christians, and every effort must have been made to prevent reports of it from reaching the outside world, especially the ecclesiastical authorities in Norway and Rome. Judging from the Eskimo traditions, the Norsemen did actually associate with the Eskimos and even took pains to learn their language. Little by little, since the Church no longer infused new religious life in the colony by sending out priests, the Norsemen relinquished the Christian faith and merged completely with the Eskimo population. In spite of all efforts to conceal the fact, reports of it reached Iceland, as is seen from the annals of Bishop Gisle Oddson, written in Iceland before 1637. At the year 1342 we read: "The inhabitants of Greenland voluntarily forsook the true faith and the Christian religion, after having abandoned all good morals and true virtues, and were converted to the peoples of America."*

In 1656 AD, reports of tall, blond haired Eskimos were recorded by Dutch explorers who had ventured as far north as Baffin Island. As late as 1910 on Victoria Island, an area located midway between Baffin Island and Alaska, European explorers again recorded the existence of Eskimos with European features. The Victoria Eskimos were said to have had white skin and blue eyes and some were even said to have had curly hair.

We do not know the total population of the Norse Greenland colonies; we can assume their population was comparable to that of Iceland. The Norse Greenland colonies were in existence for more than 400 years. During this period, the entire Greenland coastline had been sailed and explored. Most of the Norse settlements had been established on the western side of the island with the largest

49

concentration of communities being near the Davis Strait, a body of water separating Greenland from Baffin Island. At its shortest point, the Davis Strait separates Baffin Island from Greenland by only 165 miles. In terms of Norse sailing abilities, this distance could be easily covered in just two days of normal sailing.

Given the type of ship utilized by the Norsemen, and their excellent navigational skills, the idea that they reached Baffin Island is not so much a question of when but rather a question of how often? During 400 years of existence, and being less than 300 miles from Baffin Island, the Greenland settlements seem to have been the likely starting point of Norse exploration westward into the Hudson Bay and south towards the Great Lakes. From c.985 AD to c.1014 AD, a thirty-year period, we know of at least ten Norse expeditions of discovery being initiated in the North Atlantic. Six of these expeditions reportedly sailed to or were key in the discovery of Leif Ericson's Vinland, a territory speculated to be either Newfoundland, the Eastern United States in the area of present day Chesapeake Bay, or farther inland towards the Great Lakes. Such major undertakings, on average once every three years, indicate just how widespread Norse travels and explorations were. To assume, over a 400-year period of settlement in Greenland, the Norse did not continue their westward journeys is not only a narrow interpretation of history, but one which also ignores the navigational skills possessed by the Norse during these times.

An argument for Vikings reaching the Great Lakes, besides the similarities between Jean de Brebeuf recorded account of the Huron legend and its similarities to the Karlsefni Norse Saga and the similarities between knattleikr and lacrosse, is the controversial Kensington Runestone. Found in 1898 by farmer Olaf Ohman near Alexandria, Minnesota, the stone reads:

> *8 Goths and 22 Norwegians on opthagels journey from Vinland over the West. We had camp by 2 skerries one days journey north from this stone. We were and fished on day. After we came home found 10 men red with blood and dead Ave Maria Save from evil.*
>
> *Have 10 of our party by the sea to look after our ships 14 days journey from this island Year 1362.*

According to the The Runestone Museum in Alexandria, modern research evidence supports the artifact's authenticity. Recent work by linguist Richard Nielsen, an expert in Middle Age Swedish language, shows that the engraving is of 14th century origin. According to

Nielsen, the inscribed word *"opthagels,"* indicates a journey of *"acquisition"* not one of discovery meaning it was a trip based on commerce and exchange. This indeed lends credence to support the argument that cultural interaction between the tribes of the Great Lakes and the Norse occurred. This would also explain how the Norse came to play knattleikr. Geologist Scott Wolter, who has studied the Kensington Stone's mineralogical and geological weathering, claims the stone is authentic based on the degree of mica weathering found on the stone. In an interview with Wolter, he argues:

> *Based on comparison of weathering characteristics of the chip samples obtained from slate tombstones, the biotite mica that was exposed at the time of the original inscription on the KRS [Kensington Runestone] took longer than 200 years to completely weather away. Having said this, the only other evidence there is to put the KRS at some point in past, is the date inscribed on the stone - 1362.*

The religious priest and historian Adam of Bremen, after sailing the lands of the North Atlantic and documenting the kingdoms of the Norsemen, wrote in his book *On the Propagation of the Christian Religion in the North of Europe* in c.1073 AD:

> *. . . there is still another region, which has been visited by many, lying in that Ocean which is called Vinland, because vines grow there spontaneously, producing very good wine; corn likewise springs up there without being sown. . . This we know not by fabulous conjecture, but from positive statements of the Danes.*

Bremen, like many other scholars of his generation, was well aware of the Norse journeys westward, and the lands of their discovery. Skeptics claim that there is no evidence of Norse settlements outside of Greenland, Iceland, and Newfoundland. However, these same skeptics cannot explain the similarities between Norse and Indian legends as well as the similarities between lacrosse and knattleikr?

Chapter Five

The First Canadians

Though the ancient Mi'kmaq Indians of Nova Scotia were known to trade well inland along the shores of the St. Lawrence River, the ancient hockey stick and ball game to which they play is in fact closer in design and rules to European hockey than the native game of lacrosse or Norse game of knattleikr. The Nova Scotia Mi'kmaqs, part of the Algonquin tribes, and not traditional sun worshippers, played a form of ancient hockey that mirrored Scottish shinny. It was British soldiers, at the time of the founding of Halifax, Nova Scotia in c.1749 AD, reported that the Mi'kmaqs played primitive shinny. How the Mi'kmaqs, the true originators of *"modern Canadian hockey on ice"* came to play such a game is one of the great mysteries of history. The most likely explanation for this mystery may be found in two controversial legends referred to as the Mi'kmaq legend of *Glooscap* and the Scottish legend of the *Voyage of Sinclair.*

In the late 1800's, when British and Canadian sports writers were busy trying to discover the origins of Canadian hockey, they were forced to acknowledge the fact that the Mi'kmaqs had been playing a shinny-like game for as long as anyone could remember. Because no one in the establishment sports communities wished to credit non-whites with the early development and origins of Canadian hockey, the Mi'kmaq game was politely dismissed with the conclusion that even though the Indian game was similar to that of shinny, these similarities were purely coincidental.

At the time, no one examined the history of the Mi'kmaqs, their legends, or the legends of the Scots. If such an examination had been attempted, more questions than answers concerning the Mi'kmaq game and its origins would have been raised. Of all the early native tribes likely to have contact with Northern Europeans, the most likely would have been the Mi'kmaqs, as they would have been the first tribe that Europeans traveling the North Atlantic Ocean currents would have encountered, either through exploration or shipwreck. In addition, due to their friendly nature and knowledge of the region, they would most likely have served as guides for anyone wanting to explore the inland regions west of the eastern seaboard or anyone interested in benefiting from the establishment of a trading network between themselves and other tribes.

Though accounts are sketchy, early written reports of Europeans journeying to Canada, following the John Cabot Expedition of c.1497 AD, indicate on more than one occasion when Europeans encountered the Mi'kmaqs they were able to communicate with them, as the natives were said to possess limited knowledge of a number of European languages including Basque. At least one account claims the Mi'kmaqs could speak half a dozen or more languages, including a primitive form of Gaelic.

According to the Mi'kmaqs, a great white god named Glooscap had once lived among them and taught them various skills including fishing with a net. The legend describes how he built an island on which he placed large trees. Once he had completed his work, he floated away on the winds and over the waters. In recent years historians examining the legend have concluded the reference to an island and trees is likely a description of the building of a boat with masts. This spectacle would have been unknown to the early Mi'kmaqs and one that would be explained by them utilizing the only forms of description they would have understood. Even more intriguing is the Scottish argument that Glooscap was of Scottish descent. Known in the Scottish annals as Henry Sinclair, Prince of Orkney, Sinclair is said to have led an expedition from the Orkney Islands westward to an unknown land in c.1398 AD, ninety-four years before Columbus.

Sinclair was born near present day Rosslyn Castle, outside of Edinburgh, in c.1345 AD and was of Norman ancestry. This means that he was of Viking origin. His father, a knight, had died battling the Lithuanians in c.1358 AD when young Henry was 13. Prior to this, Henry's grandfather had died in Spain battling the Saracens. By the time Henry had turned 21 he was himself a Knight Templar, a member of a mysterious band of warriors that to this day conjures up romantic images. At age 24, King Hakon V of Norway declared him the Earl of Orkney.

The recorded evidence of his voyage to the New World is found in the c.1558 AD *Zeno Narrative*, a series of maps and old letters by Antonio Zeno, a former admiral of the Orkney ruler and a reputed participant of the voyage. In 1961, the historian Frederick J. Pohl, in his book *Atlantic Crossings Before Columbus,* convincingly argued that Glooscap was indeed Earl Henry Sinclair. As described in the *Zeno Narrative,* Sinclair decided to embark on a westward journey after being intrigued by Antonio Zeno's tale of a fisherman who had been blown westward 26 years earlier to an incredible and very fertile land called Estotiland. The account states that in c.1398 AD an expedition of 13 ships, manned by Knight Templars and armed with the latest in cannonry, sailed west in hopes of discovering the territory and to lay

53

claim to the region in the name of the Norwegian monarchy. The Zeno documents go on to describe the journey recounting the first lands encountered as home to hostile natives forcing the ships to move south until they reached a new landfall and a safe harbor. Pohl argues that this land was in fact Nova Scotia and the harbor in question was the area known as Chedabucto Bay on the Eastern Shore of Nova Scotia.

According to Zeno, while the ship sailed through the region, Sinclair's party saw smoke from a distant hill and Sinclair subsequently ordered 100 of his men to leave their boats and move forward in the direction of the smoke, with the intent of identifying the source. After eight days the soldiers returned and brought word that the smoke was a natural occurrence from a great fire in the bottom of a hill. It was from here that a pitch-like substance ran like a spring into the sea. The soldiers also reported the presence of a large number of primitive natives living in nearby caves.

If this account is accurate, then the most likely location of the burning pitch and caves appears to be the region in and around present day Stellarton, Nova Scotia, an area rich in asphalt deposits and home to Mi'kmaq Indians whose forefathers were said to have lived in caves. Pohl states:

> *Open deposits of viscous pitch are rare. In the New World, the two best known, one in Trinidad and the other in Venezuela, were over 2000 miles south of Newfoundland . . . There were oil seepages in Eastern Canada . . . but none of these, except the one at Stellerton, was associated with an open burning coal seam, and was near a river and a harbor. . . As for the burning coal seam at the bottom of the hill at Stellarton, the so-called Foord seam there has been on fire repeatedly; for its bituminous coal is exceptionally rich in oil and gas. It was on fire three times between 1828 and 1830, a fire that began in 1832 burned for more than a year until the East River was turned into it to extinguish it. After 1860 it was on fire several times, and again there was a fire in it, which burned continuously from 1870 to 1901.*

Glooscap, the legendary cultural hero of the Mi'kmaqs, is in a number of tales and had always been believed by scholars to be European - but always assumed to be after Columbus. Pohl found no less than 17 places where the Mi'kmaq legend was identical with that of Prince Henry Sinclair, as some of Pohl's comparisons show:

> *The visiting hero was a 'prince'. He was a 'king', who had*

often sailed the seas. His home was in a 'large town' on an island, and he came with many men and soldiers. He came across the ocean via Newfoundland and first met the Mi'kmaqs at Pictou. His principal weapon was 'a sword of sharpness'. He had three daughters. His character was unusual, and was precisely that which biographical study of Sinclair reveals. He explored Nova Scotia extensively. He slept for six months in the wigwam of a giant named winter. He remained in the country only from the sailing season to the next sailing season.

Beatrice M. Hay in the December 30, 1927 edition of *Canadian National Railways Magazine* said of the Mi'kmaqs:

Their missionaries believe that they had learned something of Christianity before the arrival of the first French priest, and that they acquired this knowledge from Norsemen who are known to have visited the shores of North America long before.

Hay continued, stating in historian N. E. Dionne's 1891 biography of Samuel de Champlain that the 17th century French explorer discovered the remains of a moss-covered decayed cross along an inlet north of Cape Forchu, Nova Scotia. Other historian have recorded that the Mi'kmaqs were extremely devoted to the cross equating the object with their earlier legends.

Although the Mi'kmaq legends of the Glooscap and the *Zeno Narrative* account of the expedition of Sir Henry Sinclair correspond, the question still remains: "Is there archaeological evidence to support the accounts?" It is the Scottish account that describes how the Sinclair expedition spent their winter teaching the natives various Scottish games and dance. The Mi'kmaqs would later claim to have knowledge of shinny for hundreds of years. Given that shinny was a popular pastime of the Scots, this strongly implies that shinny was one of the games introduced to the Mi'kmaqs at the time of the Henry Sinclair expedition to Nova Scotia. Furthermore, in 1883, a burial stone marker was discovered near present day Westford, Massachusetts, depicting a 14th century knight with a sword and shield. An oval-shaped "boat stone," measuring about two feet in diameter was found in the 1940's by a farmer who had kept it in his barn for approximately twenty years before deeding it to the J. V. Fletcher Library, in Westford. On the stone is a carved image of a 14th century ship, an arrow, and the numbers 184, presumably carved at the same time as the Westford Knight burial stone marker.

Zeno's fairly accurate map made in the 1390's show both sides of Greenland. This map, with its clockwise shift of Greenland and Newfoundland, shows compass bearings and latitudes where there were progressively larger magnetic declinations the farther north one went. (Magnetic declinations are caused from a compass pointing to the magnetic north and not the geographic North Pole.) It would not be until c.1534 AD, 140 years later, following the journey of Jacques Cartier to the coasts of Canada, that a more accurate map of the region was made.

Maybe the most intriguing discovery to date in Nova Scotia is that of a cannon found at Louisburg Harbor, Cape Breton, Nova Scotia, in 1849. The cannon dates back to the late 1300's and is identical in design to those used by the Venetian Navy during this period. Since the Zeno was related to Carlo Zeno, an admiral in the Venetian Navy and a man who had achieved naval victories utilizing primitive cannons on his ships, such a find adds yet more evidence to a Sinclair link to Nova Scotia and subsequent Mi'kmaq contact.

Ten kilometers outside of Edinburgh, Scotland, stands the Rosslyn Chapel. The Chapel was built in c.1446 AD by Sir William Sinclair, third and last Prince of Orkney. The building was specifically constructed to house Knight Templar artifacts. Inside the chapel are a number of detailed carvings depicting religious, historical and botanical images. Included in the carved botanical depictions are over a dozen different leaves and plants. Among these are Cacti and Indian corn. Though such depictions may appear innocent, one wonders how such plants could have been known by the Orkney builders forty-six years prior to Columbus' expedition to the New World? Upon his return to Scotland Sinclair was murdered by the English. In the end, we may never know the complete story of Sinclair and the Glooscap. What we do know is, in addition to the previous mentioned archaeological discoveries, as early as 1749 AD the Mi'kmaqs were playing a form of primitive shinny on the frozen ice of the Dartmouth lakes making them the first recognized Canadians to have played hockey on ice.

The Second Period

Chapter Six

The Red Branch Warriors

In c.200 BC *The Irish Annals* recorded the childhood exploits of King Lowry Loingseach. Lowry, said to be mute, only uttered his first words after being hit with a stick during a hurley match. It is not known what he said but it is believed to be unrepeatable. During this period, the game of hurley was so important in Ireland that it even featured prominently in the folklore of the rural peoples. It was believed that the leprechauns played the game under moonlit skies on the surface of lakes, with some even playing their matches under water.

Around c.100 BC the Ulster warrior Cuchulain, leader of *The Red Branch Warriors* and son of the Celtic Sun God Lugh, gained youthful fame on account of his hurling abilities. In one legendary incident, he single-handedly defeated one hundred and fifty warriors in a hurling match on the Field at Armagh. Angered by their defeat the men attacked Cuchulain, but he fought back killing fifty men with his bare hands before the others fled the field. Considered the greatest warrior of ancient Ulster, Cuchulain was known for his uncontrollable temper and physical deformities, such as having seven fingers on each hand and seven toes on each foot. He was said to go insane with uncontrollable rage and, during times of insanity, was reported as having seven pupils in each eye. On one occasion he had reportedly carried the ball on the blade of his hurley stick a distance of nine miles, in a repetitive motion of throwing the ball into the air and catching it on his blade, before it could drop to the ground.

Cuchulain was the nephew of King Conchobar. At the age of seventeen, Cuchulain singularly defeated warrior Queen of Connacht and her forces of Maeve when they tried and failed in an attempt to capture Ulster. Tales of all kinds are told about him. At the age of twenty-seven, Cuchulain finally met his match when he was killed in an ambush. His attackers are said to have severed his head using the great warrior's own hurley stick.

Hurley continued to be popular in Ireland but according to the Irish texts, *The Dun Cow* c.1100 AD and *The Book of Leinster* c.1160 AD, it was not until the 3rd century AD that the Irish had their next great hurley warrior. Fionn MacCumhail, popularly known as Finn MacCool, was the mythical leader of the fighting band *Fianna Eireann*. Said to be a descendant of the god Nuada, former king of the Tuatha De Danaan, MacCumhail's most notable hurley accomplishment occurred when he defeated fifty men by scoring the decisive goal in a match at Tara. His reward for his deed was a kiss from King Cormac MacArt's daughter - the woman he was to subsequently marry.

Even in the religious records of ancient Ireland one finds mention of hurley. Such is the example and story of the visit of Saint Colmcille to Tara. In the 5th century, Tara was reputed to have been a powerful and sacred place of gods and an entrance to the other world. During his time there, a Connacht prince used a hurley to kill a young boy. Although Saint Colmcille attempted to intervene, the prince was summarily executed on the spot, for such was the anger of those who had witnessed this savage act.

It was at this time that St. Patrick arrived in Ireland (c.432 AD) on a mission to convert the island tribes to Christianity. Although only partly successful, Patrick did however succeed in laying the foundations of the Christian faith allowing for future Christian clerics to continue his efforts. By the 6th century, primitive Christianity and Druidism co-existed throughout Ireland and other regions of the British Isles. During this period an amalgamation of the Sun God and Christian religions occurred across Ireland, Britain, and Western Europe. This merging of religions would in turn lead to the creation of modern Christianity. Among the Druid or Sun God worshipping symbols borrowed by the Christians was the Ankh or ancient Cross. In addition, the scepter or staff carried by Druid high priests, long symbolic of the religion of the snake, was adopted by high ranking Christian clergy becoming the Bishops Staff or Crosier. The amber beads on a necklace, referred to by the ancients as Hesiod's Tears and carried by Druid believers as a symbol of early creation and rebirth, became the Christian Rosary. Marriages performed by the Church continued to allow for the bride and the groom to exchange rings - symbols of the serpent coiled around the heavens as well as a symbol of wealth. Even the symbol of God, long recorded by the Druids and other ancients in the form of three straight rods, became the cornerstone of the triangular symbolism behind the Christian concept of the Father, the Son, and the Holy Ghost - an ironic and deliberate attempt to equate the trio as a Tree of Life.

Of course not all Sun God beliefs were adopted by the Christians. The idea of worshipping the Sun God and paying homage to the Serpent were both concepts rejected outright as falsehoods. And, even though the Tree of Life was utilized to the benefit of Christian symbolism, the idea of a tree as a religious symbol to worship was also rejected. A case in point, the c.726 AD destruction of the Donar Oak, long believed to be a sacred tree of life by St. Boniface near German village of Fritzlar, Hesse, was a way for the Church to send a message to all non-Christian believers of the power of Christianity over the Sun

God religion. The myth of St. Patrick ridding Ireland of snakes was not so much a miracle of man over nature as it was Christianity over Druidism. The rejection of Druid temples as places of worship was also promoted as these temples were designed as symbols of the ring of the snake and the stages of the ancient zodiac. To add to the Church's argument that Christianity was the rightful religion, many of the desecrations of the Sun God symbols of worship and shrines occurred during the time of calamities in order to enhance a belief among the disbelievers of *"God's punishment for praying to a false god."* The fact that Christianity witnessed its greatest regional conversions in Sun God areas during the time of the Plague, when half the population of Western Europe was decimated, is a coincidence that cannot be overemphasized.

Yet, regardless of the Christian attempts to reinterpret religion, and the devastating depopulation of Europe by the Plague, some Druid and Sun God customs thrived. The concept of the cutting of a pine tree (a symbolic Tree of Life) and displaying it in one's home each December 21st in honor of the winter solstice continued eventually becoming a *Christ's Tree,* today's modern Christmas tree. Colored eggs, long symbols of the ancient Sun God religion and symbolic of a world reborn after the Great Flood, became Easter Eggs. In fact, it can be argued, that many of these changes were designed to mainstream Christianity as it competed for the religious, social, and economic control over the Western European masses. Even though all religious symbolisms associated with hockey were also rejected, the game continued to be played in many forms throughout Western Europe.

In c.851 AD the Danes sacked Canterbury Cathedral on one of their many raids into England. In c.950 AD the church was rebuilt. Among the new stained glass windows were six images depicting the timeline of man. Included in this grouping, was the image of a boy holding a curved hurley stick and ball. It is known as the *Puerilitia*, or Childhood, and is reflective proof of the impact of the sport among the European peasant classes.

By c.1100 AD, the game had become a common sight throughout the British Isles. In Ireland it was still called hurley. In Wales, it was known as *Bandy* but in Scotland, having become the favorite pastime of the High King Alexander I, also called "Alexander the Fierce", the game was known as *Shindy* or *Shinty* (now known as *Shinny*). A name derived from the cry, *"Shin t' ye"* (shin to you) that was shouted when players collided or hit one another with their sticks.

Shinty has similar origins and connections to hurley. In Scottish Gaelic the game is known as *Camanachd*, whereas the Irish version was called *Camanacht* (the winter version of hurley). The similarities continue with the prominence of national heroes in the game. Where the Irish proclaim and exult such mighty warriors and players of the game as Cuchulain, the Scots have sagas that boast the heroic deeds and Shinty prowess of their own hero, Conal Gulban. However, unlike in Ireland, the Highland chieftains never resorted to using Shinty as a replacement, or a precursor, to warfare. Shinty was patronized purely for the love of the game.

The English social historian William Fitzstephen, in his c.1175 AD work *Description of the Most Noble City of London,* gave the first written mention of the sport being played in winter when he proclaimed:

> *Let us come to the Sports and Exercise . . . for the scholars of every school have their ball and bastion in their hands . . . When the great fenne or moore . . . is frozen, many young men play upon the yce, . . . some tye bones to their feete, and under their heels and shoving themselves by little picked staffe, doe slide as swiftly as a birde flieth in the air or an arrow out of a cross-bow. Sometimes two runne together with poles, and hitting one the other eyther one or both doe fall not without hurt. Some break their armes, some their legs, but youth desirous of glorie, in this sort excerciseth itselfe against the time of war.*

The sport had become so popular in England by c.1365 AD that King Edward III, fearing its impact on military discipline, banned its play. He cited the excuse that it took time away from the practice of archery.

Earlier in c.1348 AD, England had been ravaged by the Black Death resulting in the death of half the population. In terms of economics and politics the ramifications would be tremendous. Though the peasantry of England had been subject to a "tributary" or "head tax" made payable to the English Nobility, the c.1215 AD Magna Carta has ensured that the exploitation of the peasantry was, in relation to other regions, limited. The Black Death changed this. With fewer peasants to pay tribute greater pressure fell on those remaining to produce and pay out more. Taxes were increased and enforcement efforts strengthened. With the judicial system devastated by the large loss of legal experts, regional interpretation of laws became the norm. Few cases moved through the judiciary and those that did often took years to adjudicate. Peasant rights were not of priority.

In c.1381 AD, tensions came to a head with the outbreak of *Wat Tyler's Rebellion.* Tyler, a roofer and farmer in County Kent, had been out in his field working on the day a local tax commissioner arrived at his home to collect the annual head tax. A dispute erupted between Tyler's wife and the man concerning the age of Tyler's daughter. The tax collector claimed the girl was fifteen and was thus eligible for taxation. The mother claimed otherwise. In an effort to prove the girl's age the man forced the young girl to disrobe in order to examine the girl's breasts and genitalia. He then proceeded to rape the young child. Hearing the screams of his wife and daughter, Tyler ran in from the field and killed the attacker by smashing in the man's skull with a hammer. As word of Tyler's actions spread, local farmers rallied to Tyler's side. Determined to resist any attempt at taxation, or prosecution by authorities, the peasantry organized themselves into a makeshift fighting force. Tyler and two priests from neighboring Essex County, John Ball and Jack Straw, were elected military leaders. The mob of disgruntled poor farmers and villagers assembling in force at Black-Heath, Kent, and set out west towards the inland city of London.

The events that would transpire would go down in history as the *"hurling time,"* a reference to the fact that among the assortment of weapons carried by the peasants were hurley sticks. It would be the first time in history that hockey sticks would be used on a large scale as a weapon of warfare. By the time Tyler and his followers had reached London they numbered over 100,000. Along the way the group seized Canterbury Cathedral, killed the Archbishop of Canterbury, burned dozens of homes of noblemen, and destroyed the Savoy Palace. In addition, they raided the notorious prisons of Fleet and Newgate freeing all the prisoners. Not satisfied with these successes they attacked and captured the Tower of London and sent a demand for an immediate audience with the 14-year old boy-king Richard II. Following a quickly arranged meeting with the King, in which Richard II agreed in principle to all of the demands presented including the immediate abolishment of serfdom, Tyler and his followers retreated back to the Tower of London where they set about preparing additional demands for presentation. The next day the two groups met at Smithfield, where Tyler, Ball, and Straw presented the King with new conditions. During the meeting, and on the orders of King Richard II, the Mayor of London attacked Tyler stabbing him in the throat and stomach. Tyler died a short time later. Ball and Straw were also killed. In the case of Jack Straw, his head was cut off and placed on the end of a horsemen's lancet and was subsequently paraded through London before being hung by a rope from London Bridge. In the weeks that would follow, King Richard II would order the execution of 1500 peasant leaders. All reforms promised would also be revoked.

In c.1385 AD the Cathedral of Gloucester was completed. Among the images placed in the cathedral's stain glass windows was a depiction of a man swinging a hurley stick at a ball. Again the symbolism is unique given the date of its creation and the fact that two of the three main leaders of the Wat Tyler Rebellion were priests. Taken into context with the events of c.1381 AD, the stain glass image serves not only as a subtle reminder and tribute to the "hurling time" but also as a form of social and political commentary.

In c.1388 AD, as the repression of the peasant classes continued in England, Richard II ordered the burning of all hurley sticks throughout the country. Those caught in possession of such items faced severe punishment and fines. Those found guilty of allowing the game to be played on their lands faced fines of twenty pounds and three years imprisonment. The move, believed by some to be an effort to limit the sport's popularity, was instead an effort to eliminate as many potential weapons in the hands of the peasantry as possible and avoid another peasant revolt. It was only after the invention of firearms that this punitive law would be revoked.

At the age of 32, and following his marriage three years earlier to the seven year old Isabella of Valois, the daughter of Charles VI of France, Richard II was murdered becoming the first victim of the War of the Roses in c.1399 AD.

Today, at the Copenhagen Museum one can find a large silver flagon used for holding wine or other liquors. The flagon is believed to be of French origin and has been dated to the late 14th century. The image on the flagon is quite revealing. It shows a headless man swinging a hurley stick. It is highly probable that this ceremonial flagon was part of the silverware at the wedding of King Richard II and Isabella of Valois as it appears to symbolize the death of Jack Straw. Of course we will never know if this is in fact the case. In his work *Richard II*, William Shakespeare sums up the life of the boy-king with the words: *"Heaven hath a hand in these events."* More appropriate words have seldom been spoken.

The Wat Tyler Rebellion is not the only reference to ancient hockey being played in England during the thirteen hundreds. The English writer Thomas Rymer, in his c.1740 AD work *Foedera Conventiones, Litterae Et Cujuscunque Generis Acta Publica Inter Reges Angliae Et Alios Quosuis Imperatores, Reges, Pontifices, Principes Vel Communitates Ab Ingressu Gulielmi I In Angliam A.D 1066. Ad Nostra Usque Tempora. Volume 4*, records a game played by the peasantry in c.1363 AD utilizing a *"crooked stick or curved club or playing mallet with which a small wooden ball is propelled forward."*

By the 13th century, a form of early hockey, using wooden golf-like sticks and a ball, called *Het Kolven*, was being played on the frozen ponds and rivers of Holland. At the same time, the game called *Hurley on Ice* or the French equivalent *Jeu de Mail* was being played on the ponds and rivers of Luxembourg, Belgium, and France. During this period, however, the Dutch would develop skating to a higher form with the invention of iron-blade wooden skates. By the 1500's, these skates were increasing in use, as more and more of the Dutch peasantry turned away from locally made ox bone skates to manufactured iron blades. It would be the iron blades that would allow the Dutch to skate faster and to cover more distances. Ironically, this achievement would not only serve as an aid to travel and leisure during winter, but also would help the Dutch wage war.

In c.1572 AD, a group of Dutch pirates known as the *Sea Beggars* would become victims of Dutch technology when they would be attacked by local peasants on skates, after the pirates had their ships frozen in the ice. Before they took to sea these Dutch pirates were originally known as the *Wild Beggars*. Starting in the early 1550's, they had gained a reputation for robbing and plundering Catholic churches and monasteries on land, often cutting off the noses and ears of priests and monks who were unfortunate enough to cross their path. By the late 1560's, during the start of the 80-Year War (c.1568 AD to c.1648 AD), these murderers and thieves were given ships and organized into sea raiding parties by William of Orange for the purpose of preying on the Spanish Navy. Unruly and treacherous, these pirates were non-discriminating finding great success in disrupting Spanish shipping lanes while also attacking vessels of almost any nation including those of local fishermen from peasant villages and towns along the Dutch shoreline.

In February of c.1572 AD three pirate ships under the control of Captains Willem Blois van Treslong, Jelte Eelsma, and Pieter Simonsz Meyns became stuck in the ice off the small island of Wieringen, a predominant Catholic area near the village of Oosterland. With no imminent escape in sight, the pirates began to walk across the ice pillaging the local villages. After almost a month of raids, the poor victimized locals organized a large group of farmers and threatened to attack the ships if the pirates continued their plundering.

Trapped on the ice and vulnerable to attack, Blois van Treslong, a veteran military naval officer, tried to negotiate a settlement with the locals. In his arrogance his colleague Meyns refused, daring the farmers to attack. In the night a group of Wieringen farmers, armed with clubs, skated quickly and silently out towards the boats. Unseen or heard, they attacked the ships successfully boarding the vessels and beating to death seventeen pirates, including Captain Meyns. The farmers forced Treslong to swear to not exact revenge for this act, and in doing so the captain offered his sword to the people as a token of his friendship. Treslong, still trapped by the ice and no longer wishing to remain vulnerable to further attack, asked the farmers if they could aid him and his surviving crew in freeing the stricken ships from the ice. Using skates and ropes the local peasantry helped the ships break free and reach open sea. Treslongs sword still hangs today in the Catholic Church of Oosterland in Wieringen, Holland, and is a testament to the event and to the widespread use of skates by the peasant masses during this period.

Though visual evidence of early hockey exists in scattered form throughout much of the European medieval and renaissance periods, it is not until the mid-1500's that a large body of visual imagery emerges, thanks in part to the efforts of the Dutch painter Peter Brueghel. Brueghel was hockey's first true sports artist and documentarian. He painted the ancient games and the lower classes that played them. Though fewer than two hundred of his works survive today, of those that do, at least twenty depict participation in sports. No fewer than ten display images of *Het Kolven* on ice. Brueghel has, for the most part, been the subject of scorn or simply ignored by the art world because the subjects he painted reflected the story of the poor and the games of the common people. As a result, most sports historians are unaware of his contribution to the history of hockey. He saw hockey and recorded it for posterity. His art is a virtual timeline on hockey history linking the ancient game to the contemporary claims of modern hockey origins. His are the eyes of the past, his canvass the ultimate record of ancient hockey roots. His work is proof, through artistry and the visual historic record that the so-called modern game had existed for centuries.

Among the more famous paintings and images of Kolven include Pieter Brueghel's c.1565 AD paintings *Winter Landscape* and *Skaters and Hunters in the Snow.* In addition, other artists such as Frans Huys' *Ice Skating in Front of St. George's Gate, Antwerp* c.1558 AD, Elias van de Veldes' *Amusement on the Frozen Moat,* c.1618 AD; David Vinckeboons' *Annual Market,* and Hendrick Avercamp's *A Scene on the Ice,* c.1625 AD further provides visuals depicting primitive ice hockey.

65

Chapter Seven

Rules Britannica

By the 1820's Welsh bandy was becoming a favorite all-seasons game in the small isolated villages and towns throughout Wales. Writing in the English periodical *Sporting Magazine* in 1830, under the title *The Kalendar of Amusements*, Heliwir Morganwg states:

> *There appears to be a peculiar proneness in the disposition of the Welsh towards all sorts of sports and diversion . . . the most popular of all the vale of Glamorgan is the important game of Bandy.*

It is clear that the main piece of equipment needed for Welsh bandy was similar in type and shape to that used later for hockey. The Welsh word of band*y* is the name associated with the standard curved stick used to play the game. The stick was preferably made of ash and bent at the bottom, although it was not unknown for players of the Glamorgan coal mines to substitute a pick or a shovel handle so that they could play. The ball was ideally made from yew, box, or even crabapple, although a ball of rags or even tins was used if necessary. The game's flexibility meant it could be played anywhere, on street or field, depending on the location and number of the players. However, in its heartland, bandy was played on the seashore of the Glamorgan Coast. The beach near Margam and Kenfig hosted many exciting games featuring the *Margam Bando Boys* who were one of the most famous of the 19th century teams. A well-known Welsh ballad recorded the Margam boys poking fun at the English neighbors:

> *Let cricket players blame*
> *And seen to slight our game*
> *Their bat and wicket never lick it,*
> *This ancient manly game.*

The Museum of Welsh Life in St. Fagans has two examples of early *bando* sticks. Senior Museum Curatorial Assistant Dylan Jones dates one of the sticks to 1845, used by Thomas Thomas, of the *Glamorgan Margam Bando Boys*. He describes the elm bando sticks as having a clubbed end, curved by steaming, and a shaved face for striking ball.

The early 19th century saw the advent of the modern era in sports. The beginning of this period is marked by the growing need to formalize the rules for games that had been played informally for centuries. This was particularly driven by Britain's elite private schools which started to set formal rules and began to publish them in an effort to regulate national and international standards of play. The first published set of early ice hockey rules along with recommendations on how to play the game appeared in the *Boys' Own Book*, written in 1810, published in 1813. The rules state:

> *In choosing a hockey, the young player should be careful not to over-weight himself; all the real work of the game is done by pure 'wrist work'; the hockey, therefore, must not be of a greater weight than he can easily manage . . . With a good player the hockey is scarcely ever lifted above the shoulder, the ball being driven along by a succession of taps, and is guided in and out between the opposing ranks of hockeys by the mere action of the wrist.*

> *The game may be played by ten to a dozen on a side with advantage if the space be not too confined; but a game with only six or eight on a side gives more room for individual skill, and is therefore preferable. Under all circumstances a 'crowded' game is to be avoided . . . In the confined space of a few yards, it cannot but be that some blows must be inflicted upon the heads and faces of those engaged.*

> *Hockey is an amusement for all seasons - in the summer on the turf, in the winter on the ice. Sides are chosen by the two best players, selected alternately . . . In the North of England the game is called "Shinney," from the custom of players striking the shins if the bung, or ball, gets between the legs; but we protest against this practice as tending to create angry feeling. With a party of good skaters this game affords fine sport; but of course can only be played on a sheet of ice of great extent. The following are the rule:*

> 1. *The ball must be struck with the stick, and not kicked with the foot or touched by hand.*

> 2. *The ball must be struck fairly through the goal before the side can claim the game.*

> 3. *The goals must be marked by lines at either end; and in the centre a line must be drawn across to determine the side*

which has possession of the ball.

4. *If the ball bounds against the person of a player, he must allow it to fall to the ground before he strikes at it.*

5. *Any player striking another with stick or hand, kicking or otherwise unfair playing the ball, is out of the game.*

6. *A captain on each side is to be chosen to regulate the game, and it is the duty of any player, when directed by the captain, to fetch the ball when struck a distance.*

These six rules will be sufficient.

The winter of 1813 would also bring the so-called the first "official" reference to *bandy on ice* being played in the English marshlands of Cambridgeshire, northeast of London, in and around the village of Bury Fen. An example of this can also be found again in the *Boys' Own Book*:

After they had walked for some time in a path, which skirted a wood, they came to an open place, where some well-looking boys were at play. Each of them had a sort of hooked stick, with which they were beating a ball. Thomas stood for some time looking at them, and then asked his father what game they were playing at.

Mr. White. It is called hockey. Those boys seem to play well; but I cannot say it is amusement of which I am very fond.

Thomas. Why not sir? It seems a very pretty game...

Mr. White. I cannot help thinking it a rather dangerous one; though I believe it is in reality, not more than many others. It was a favourite amusement among us when I was a boy at school . . . You have heard me speak of James Robson, a boy of whom I was particularly fond? . . . he lost his eye playing at hockey . . . A boy . . . missed his aim, and gave him so severe a blow as to occasion the loss of his eye . . . he had nearly lost the sight of the other eye in consequence of the violent inflammation which the pain occasioned . . .

Thomas. Pray, sir, will you tell me some of the rules of it, for I do not very well understand the game from only seeing it played?

Mr. White . . . do not you see a piece of stick with both ends stuck in the ground? That is called a goal, and there is another which answers to it at some distance, the other side of the boys . . . Well when the goals are erected the players divide into two parties, to each of whom belongs the care of one of them. The game consists in endeavouring to drive the ball (called a hockey) . . . through the goal of your antagonist. Both parties meet in the middle space between the goals, and the ball is then tossed up . . . In this the art of the game consists, for it requires a good deal of skill to send it through so small a space at such a distance. I have known the game to last for more than two hours if the parties have been well matched.

Thomas. Ah! Look, it is over, is it not? The tall boy has driven the hockey through the sticks - the goal I think you call it.

Mr. White. Yes, it is usually so called; and the sticks are known by the name of hockey-sticks.

Thomas. I think hockey seems a pretty game. I wonder whether I could play at it.

Mr. White. Not without a good deal of practice, I dare say; but it is not a game, which is now in very general use. The eagerness with which boys are too apt to play at it has been the occasion of many accidents, and it is, I believe, forbidden in many schools.

It is clear from these early rules and accounts that, although the teams may have been referred to as bandy clubs, indeed the game they were playing was early *ice hockey*. By the beginning of the 19th century the term *hockey* was now being used to describe the standardization of rules and equipment used in organized *bandy on ice* in England. By 1827, the villages in the county of Cambridgeshire had become a hotbed for early hockey as teams from the regional villages of Bury Fen, Sutton, Willingham, Cottenham, Swavesey, Nepal, Chatteris, Somersham, St. Ives, and Bedford competed in parish-sponsored matches. This could be considered the first recorded ice hockey league in history as teams competed in annual matches, staged on the frozen rivers and canals, in a quest for victory and the promise of kegs of ale and legs of mutton for the winners.

In 1837, a severe winter hit England freezing the River Thames allowing for hockey to be played on the ice near Richmond. A permanent reminder of the unusual winter was captured on an image emblazoned on a Staffordshire China sugar bowl. The bowl is significant due to the fact that it features the images of two hockey players skating on an idyllic pond. It is the oldest image of hockey being played on ice in England.

The game's popularity led to the establishment of the earliest known upper-class ice hockey club in England, the Blackheath Hockey Club, in 1840. However, the lack of suitable ice then, as today, ensured that ice hockey would not become a truly major sport in Britain. It would not be until another eighteen years later, in 1855, that the Thames River would again freeze over. This time artists recorded the images of local Londoners playing hockey near Paine's Bridge with the images appearing in the March 3, 1855, *Illustrated London News.* This event is significant for it marked the first incident in hockey's history when an actual calendar date together with location was given where hockey was played. It also predates traditional Canadian claims that modern hockey was first played on Christmas Day in 1855 at Kingston, Ontario, by soldiers of the Royal Canadian Rifles.

By the 1860's hockey had become so popular in England that it had once again become the focus of public rebuke. An editorial, which appeared in 1862 in *The Times of London,* read:

> *Hockey . . . ought to be sternly forbidden, as it is not only annoying, but dangerous. In its right place, hockey is a noble game and deserving of every encouragement; but on ice it is in its wrong place and should be prohibited. Any weak spot on the ice is sure to give way if the ball should happen to pass near it or over it; for the concourse of fifty or a hundred persons all converging on the same point is a test which no ice, save the strongest, is able to bear. When a mass of human beings precipitates itself recklessly in any direction, accidents are certain to follow*
> *. . . The game is by no means what it ought to be, as it is impossible to enforce the rules in such a miscellaneous assembly . . . It is more than annoying to have the graceful evolutions of a charming quadrille broken up by the interruptions of a disorderly mob, armed with sticks and*

charging through the circle of skaters and spectators to the imminent danger of all. I should be truly glad to see the police interfere whenever hockey is commenced.

Yet regardless of the views expressed, hockey was by now an increasing popular form of recreation in England. With its growing popularity it was logical that a formal definition for the game would eventually be constructed. In the 1867 edition of *Cassell's Popular Educator* in England one reads:

Hockey consists of driving a ball from one point to another by means of a hooked stick . . . No precise rule is laid down as to the form this stick should take. It is simply a weapon with a bent knob or hook at the end, large or small, thick or thin, according to the option of the player . . . Now for the game itself, which in its principle bears a great resemblance to football and contains at least the germ of the Canadian 'La Crosse.'

By the late 1860's, hockey on ice was being played in over a dozen countries on the European continent. At the same time Canadian hockey, as it was also now called, was regionally well established in parts of the British Isles, the Eastern United States, Canada and the British colony of Newfoundland. In Britain, normally mild winters meant that there was little natural ice, which in turn guaranteed there would be few natural skaters. Artificial ice was the only practical solution in Britain. Ice plants were incredibly expensive and as a result very few rinks had been built, with the few that were built, being elite private clubs patronized by Britain's Victorian and Edwardian gentry. The first artificial ice rinks in Britain were built in 1876, in London, at Charing Cross and Chelsea. A third rink was opened, and closed within a year, at Rusholme in Manchester, due to what was reported as the *"inelastic characteristics of its surface and intense cold."*

Lack of ice was not the only inhibiting factor that limited ice hockey back from England. The purchase of expensive and essential gear like skates, effectively barred the ordinary Englishman from participation. With easier access to playing fields and less costly equipment, mass affection for sports was directed particularly toward soccer but also towards rugby and cricket. It is no surprise then, given the prevailing conditions, that ice hockey was a game for the wealthier classes that had both the time and income to play. Yet gradually, more rinks were built. Prince's Club, which stands near the famed

71

department store Harrods in London's Knightsbridge district, replaced a roller skating rink with an ice surface showing the growing interest in the sport and making England the ice hockey epicenter of modern 20th century European hockey.

By the late 19th century Oxford University emerged as a base for British ice hockey. The Oxford Blues "officially" date their formation back to their first game against their traditional rivals from Cambridge in a match played at St. Moritz, Switzerland in 1885. It is believed to be a 6-0 Oxford victory although no written accounts of this game exist. The harsh winters of 1891 and 1895, offered a chance for the Oxford student body to effectively participate in ice hockey giving us the earliest known photograph of English hockey as it was being played on a frozen and flooded piece of Christ Church Meadow in the winter of 1895. Ironically, evidence exists in the form of published illustrations and a law library building blueprint implying that an outdoor rink existed three decades earlier on the exact spot. This evidence would seem to imply that ice hockey dates to at least 1865 at Oxford. For the average person, the advent of 19th century industrialization resulted in a rising standard of living and a shorter workweek. With the shorter workweek came an increase in personal leisure time. As a result, new artificial ice arenas sprang up throughout England and Continental Europe and by 1885 competitive British ice hockey had taken root. By the 1890's, matches were being held in London at the Prince's and Niagara rinks as well as on the frozen ice surface of the lake at St. James Park across from Buckingham Palace. During this time, the National Skating Club built a rink on the site of what is now the famous London Palladium theatre. It would be called Henglers Arena. Later, the rink would be home to two clubs, the Henglers and the Argylls, and would exist until 1909 when it was torn down to make way for the Palladium.

In 1897, Major Peter Patton received formal permission from Admiral Maxe, the founder of Prince's Skating Club, to create the Prince's Ice Hockey Club. By 1903, the Prince's, along with Cambridge University, Argyll, Henglers, and a team called the London Canadians, had formed the English League. The league was to last only two seasons, but it marked an important step in establishing competitive hockey in Britain.

France joined the ranks of enthusiastic pursuers of the ice sport when, in 1892, Paris opened its first ice rink - the Pole Nord - at the Porte de Clichy. A year later the city would be home to a second rink, the famous Rond Point des Champs Elysees, a circular rink that still exists as an indoor theatre. Though the French had played an organized form of hockey for two years it was not until the 1894 arrival

72

of Canadian George Meagher, with an updated rulebook and detailed coaching instructions, that the finer points of the game were introduced to the French. Meagher's efforts led to the formation of the first official club in the capital, Le Hockey Club du Paris, followed a short time later by the creation of Le Club de Patineurs de Paris. By 1904, the first hockey club outside of Paris was formed in Lyon.

Throughout Europe, hockey was beginning to develop into an organized sport. On May 16, 1908 hockey representatives from England, France, Belgium, Bohemia (today's Czech Republic), and Switzerland met in Paris to form the Ligue Internationale de Hockey sur Glace (LIHG), the forerunner of today's International Ice Hockey Federation (IIHF). In 1909, the Ligue Internationale would meet in Chamonix, France, establishing its own rules while deciding to organize an annual European championship, set to start the following year. In September 1908, the LIHG added Germany to its membership, paving the way for future conflict and rivalry between the Germans and the Bohemian Czechs.

Bohemia had been only a province of the Austro-Hungarian Empire at the time of the Ligue's formation. However, the people were keen players of the game (the area had historically been a home to primitive hockey for centuries) and the region had been allowed to join the organization due to its sporting reputation. In 1890, Josef Rossler-Orovsky "officially" introduced bandy to the Bohemian Czechs with hockey becoming popular in 1905 when a Canadian, Ruck Anderson, demonstrated the game in Prague. It was, however, Professor Joseh Gruss of Karlov University who was seen as the real founding father of modern Czech hockey, as it was he who had translated the rules into Czech. In 1908, Gruss had persuaded members of some of Prague's leading sports clubs to found the hockey teams known as *Slavia* and *Sparta*. In November of the same year, he helped institute the creation of the Czech Hockey Union and its entry into European ice hockey. On October 1, 1907, Scotland's first rink, the Crossmyloof ice rink, opened in Glasgow eventually staging their first hockey matches the following year. England played Scotland for the first time in March 1909 defeating their northern rivals 11-1 at the Prince's Club. Britain was the leader in European ice hockey in the years leading up to World War I. This pre-eminence was largely due to the Canadian influence in the mother country. British club teams would become the instrumental driving force for the further development of European hockey. One of these teams, the Oxford Canadians, an all-Canadian team of Rhodes Scholars attending Oxford University, would transform the European game.

In a country where sports was nurtured by the elite as a training field for future leaders, Canadian expatriates were able to sow their passion for ice hockey. The Canadian Rhodes Scholars (or "the Rhodies" as they were called) would form a team called the Oxford Canadians in 1906, and enter into English League competition, winning the championship in 1907. With their success, the Oxford Canadians would receive an invite from tournament organizer, Louis Dufouras, to participate in the European Championship of 1910. Held at the French Alpine resort community of Les Avants, the Oxford Canadians would participated as a non-official competitor playing against teams from Bohemia, Belgium, Germany, Switzerland as well as a second team from Great Britain. The Canadians would be the class of the tournament, winning all of their games, but it would be the gentlemanly Prince's Club team who would be declared the inaugural European Champion. In all, the Oxford Canadians would play a total of 17 matches in 21 days winning each one and outscoring their competition by 204 to 17 margin. Their influence would lead to the LIHG decision to adopt "the Canadian rules" of ice hockey for the 1911 championship.

The following year, the Canadians would find the competition to be greatly improved. Oxford Canadians goaltender, Gus Lanctot, in a 1913 article he wrote for *The Montreal Daily Herald*, stated that now *"Each game had to be fought to the very end. Even more, the Canadians met with two defeats at the hands of France and Germany."* Lanctot rationalized the defeat to Germany and France in part due to the inexperience of the officials and the presence of Canadian hockey star Quigg Baxter of Montreal, playing for France.

Later that year, at the age of 24, Baxter would perish on the *RMS Titanic*. Born in Montreal, Baxter had joined the Montreal Amateur Athletic Association when he was 17 and quickly earned a reputation as a star hockey player. He played hockey with the Montreal Shamrocks until he was blinded in one eye by an opponents stick a 1907 game. No longer able to play competitive hockey in Canada, due to his handicap, Baxter relocated to Paris where he was instrumental in organizing early French hockey.

During a trip to Brussels, Belgium, in the winter of 1911, Baxter met a young female cabaret singer and the two became lovers. He was determined to bring his love back to Montreal with him, and booked her into a stateroom on the *Titanic* under an assumed name. His bride-to-be would survive the sinking. However, Baxter would perish, his body would never be found. The woman later returned to Europe and resumed her career as a singer in Paris. She never married.

By 1911, Czech-Bohemia had eleven hockey clubs in existence, more than any country in Europe including England. As a result of their rapid growth Bohemia would become the dominant continental team winning the 1911 and 1912 European Championships. The political tension of the day manifested in the hockey arena in 1913 when Germany filed a protest against Bohemian-Czech participation, at the European Championships, on the grounds that as Austria was now a member of the LIHG and that the Bohemian-Czechs, being a province of the Austro-Hungarian Empire, should not be permitted to participate. In the end, the Germans were quietly persuaded to drop the protest, but the incident exposed the bitter rivalry between themselves and the Bohemian-Czechs. Such was this growing animosity that even after the breakup of the Austrian Empire following World War I, the fundamental divide between the Czechs and the Germans was still present. In time this anti-German sentiment would become a seething hatred made worse by the emergence of Czech nationalism.

On the British domestic level, 1913 would be a pinnacle year for hockey as five clubs came together to found the British Ice Hockey Association. The teams were Oxford University, Cambridge University, the Prince's Club, the Manchester Club and the Royal Engineers (a British army unit based in Chatham in Kent). The Association's first president was Major Peter Patton of the Engineers, the man who founded the Prince's Ice Hockey Club in 1897 and who, in 1914, would serve briefly as president of the LIHG.

Chapter Eight

False Gods and Profits

In the book *Halifax: Warden of the North*, one of the finest books ever written on Canadian history, the author Thomas H. Raddall, citing a British military diary from 1749, credits the Mi'kmaqs with an early influence on the Canadian game of hockey. He writes:

> *It is a fact little known in Canada, but a fact none the less, that ice hockey, Canada's national game, began on the Dartmouth Lakes in the eighteenth century. Here the garrison officers found the Indians playing a primitive form of hurley on ice, adopted and adapted it, and later put the game on skates. When they were transferred to military posts along the St. Lawrence and the Great Lakes they took the game with them and for some time afterwards continued to send to the Dartmouth Indians for the necessary sticks.*

In 1888, Reverend Silas Tertius Rand, a devoted missionary who had spent a lifetime among the Mi'kmaqs of Nova Scotia, published the *Dictionary of the Language of the MicMac Indians*. For four decades Rand had recorded the tribal language in an attempt to preserve their words for future generations. Rand was aware of the cultural difficulties facing these and other natives. In the end, his work was an amazing accomplishment. He had identified 40,000 Mi'kmaq words and their meanings. The Dictionary stands today as one of the few examples of the 19th century where a religious leader actually tried to preserve native culture rather than destroy it. Even more remarkable, the printing of the book was paid for by the Canadian Government in Ottawa who themselves were enlightened enough to understand the importance of Rand's work. Today, the Dictionary, though reprinted in the 1970's, remains one of the rarest works in existence. Few anthropologists, historians or philologists have even seen a copy. What makes the Dictionary timeless is its reference to words associated with Mi'kmaq sport. Though the words hockey, shinny, or bandy are never mentioned, it is apparent by language terminologies that such a game did exist among the Mi'kmaqs.

Rand was an expert of the Mi'kmaq language. He was also a master of ancient Greek, Hebrew, Syriac, Latin, French, Italian and English. Throughout the Dictionary he points to examples where the

Mi'kmaqs have borrowed from the French and English languages. This subtle technique allows one to differentiate the ancient words from the modern. It creates, in effect, a timeline between the ancient pre-European past and the present (1800s). It is important to note there are over 20 words or phrases, all of pre-European origin, which could be associated with Mi'kmaq hockey and ball games. These words are the proof to Mi'kmaq claims to have played a form of hockey prior to the arrival of the English. It also shows the Mi'kmaqs did not need to adopt English and French words in order to describe hockey as they already had ample descriptions to describe its play. Nowhere, among these words, is a Rand reference or linkage to a word of French or English origin. The best-known, and most widely reported word is the reference to a stick used to play shinny. It is called an *Oochamakunutk.* Since Oochamakunutk and the other Mi'kmaq words represent the first language of Canadian hockey they are worthy of mention. The following is a list of key Mi'kmaq words and phrases that are or could be attributable to hockey:

1. A Ball Stick - Oochanakunutk.
2. A Stick - Kumooch; Nebesokun.
3. To Skate - Elnogumaase
4. A Skate - Elnogum.
5. Sport - Papimk.
6. Athletic - Melkigunei.
7. To Challenge - Telooemk.
8. Champion - Kenap.
9. To Cheat - Kespoogwadega.
10. To Come On The Ice - Wechkoogomae.
11. On Each Side - Edoowu.
12. One On Each Side - Edoogooeek.
13. A Foot-Ball - Alchamakum (kicking the ball with the foot was allowed in Mi'kmaq hockey).
14. To Play At Foot-Ball - Alchamei.
15. Foul - Mejega.
16. To Foul - Mejegaadoo; Mejegaaluk; Mejegaluse.
17. A Pass - Chijiktek Owte; Weegadigun Usedadegemkawa Oochit Seoweadimk.
18. The Game - Uksuboodakun; Nedoogoolimkawa; Kedantegawemkawaal; Weisisk Ak Sesipk Tanik Etlekedankoosooltijik.

Unfortunately, there is a darker side to the Dictionary. By examining the words and definitions closely one discovers that Rand's work has been sabotaged. The Dictionary was printed at the Nova

Scotia Printing Company in Halifax, Nova Scotia. At the time of its printing, few Haligonians shared the same sense of enlightenment and appreciation of the Mi'kmaqs and their language as did Rand or the Canadian Government. Certain words, and their so-called Mi'kmaq equivalents, cannot be ignored. At first glance one is left with a sense of bewilderment followed by disbelief. Given Rand's expertise in language, and the sincerity and commitment of his work, it becomes apparent that someone took great care to discredit the translations. Among the more notable or notorious 'rewrites' found among Rand's work is: 1) Brothel - Badwoomuneeskwogwum (Bad Woman's Screw Wog Wum); and 2) To Fornicate - Winaasa (Win A Assa). It is said that Rand died within a year of the Dictionary's release. The question one must ask is whether or not he lived on to see his translations published or died in part as a result of discovering the vicious actions of some unknown person who tarnished his work and his years of effort?

The vandalization of the Rand Dictionary is an example of the contempt that many within Canadian society had towards natives during the later half of the nineteenth century. Therefore, it is no wonder that when it came to crediting the Mi'kmaqs with the origins of Canadian hockey their legacy was conveniently overlooked. Nothing apparently was sacred. Not even the writings of a dedicated clergyman.

In a letter to the *Halifax Herald Newspaper* on December 27, 1940, Joe Cope, an elderly Mi'kmaq native residing on the Millbrook Reservation near Truro, Nova Scotia wrote with regards to the origin of hockey:

> *I believe the honor and credit belongs wholly to the Micmac Indians of this country, for long before the pale faces strayed to this country the Micmacs were playing two ball games, a field and ice game, which were identical in every way. Each had two goals which the Indians called forts and were defended by the owners. I do not believe any white man living today ever saw an Indian field game played because it was suppressed by the priests about 100 years ago on account of the somewhat cruel nature; a good second to a prize fight. My father, who died in 1913 at the age of 93, saw . . . Indians of the old Ship Harbor Lake Reserve playing a skateless hockey game before the Reserve was abandoned about 100 years ago. When the Micmacs left the Ship Harbor Lake Reserve they came to Dartmouth, and camped on what was then known as Buston's Hill. Father said they played their old games in Maynard and Oak Hill Lakes long before they moved up to the Dartmouth Lakes. I was born in*

*a birchbark wigwam near the old Red Bridge on April 24th
1859, so I am no longer a papoose. The old Indian field
game should be studied and revived by some sports
enthusiasts for a change. It is a 20 man game - 10 on each
side . . . All this is sketchy, I know, but it throws some light
on the descent of the game from Indians to whites in the
region about Halifax.*

Disease and poor living conditions had, for over a century, taken a toll on the Mi'kmaqs of Nova Scotia. By the mid-1850's there were only 237 Mi'kmaq families remaining in the colony. These were the survivors of a tribe that had once numbered in the thousands. By 1917, many of the Halifax-Dartmouth area Mi'kmaqs that remained had resettled along the shoreline of small community of Dartmouth, across the harbor from the City of Halifax. There they lived with their families with most still residing in native teepees or wigwams. The men worked the docks as low paid laborers or fishermen while the native women tended to the children and sold Mi'kmaq baskets and other items to the area whites.

On December 6, 1917 an explosion occurred in the harbor when two ammunition ships bound for the war effort in Europe collided. The event would be known in the history books as the Halifax Explosion, the greatest man-made explosion prior to the dropping of the bomb on Hiroshima. The explosion and concurrent tidal wave swept across the harbor killing thousands and destroying the village. How many natives perished remains unknown, as there was no complete record as to the size of the Dartmouth community. What is known however is on that day the true heirs of Canadian hockey perished leaving few survivors to refute the established elitist claims of hockey's origin. Today one of the great fallacies of Canadian history is that it continues to permeate the false myths of hockey's origins. Today there is no monument in Dartmouth, Nova Scotia or the lakes regions around Halifax-Dartmouth crediting the Mi'kmaqs their contribution to Canadian hockey.

The first written record of hockey being played by Euro-Canadians in Canada occurs between 1802 and 1810 when English students at King's College School in Windsor, Nova Scotia, strapped on skates and played hurley-on-ice. Reference to this fact is found in the 1843 autobiography of Thomas Chandler Haliburton entitled *Sam Slick in England.* He writes: *"Boys let out racin', yelpin', hollering and whoopin' like mad with pleasure . . . hurley on the long pond on the ice."*

Later, as hockey's popularity grew, many attempted to claim credit for the game's origins. In Canada, where shinny on ice had been reshaped by merging aspects of Mi'kmaq hockey with the 1813 *Boys' Own Book*, a number of English and Canadian individuals conveniently announced themselves as the game's originators. Some went as far as to write and publish their own versions of the so-called "official rules" in order to aid in their questionable declarations.

In the decades that would follow, historians and writers, unfamiliar with the game's past history, and basing their research on faulty historical references, qualified these claims, creating a ridiculous myth of origin that ignored the game's early development and conveniently erased all traces of influence associated with the Mi'kmaqs. So successful was this rewriting of history that to this day many of these falsehoods persists in the official historical records of Canadian hockey.

The earliest recorded use of the term *"hockey,"* in Canada, is found in written accounts of the famous Arctic Explorer and British Explorer and Naval Officer, Sir John Franklin. After a failed attempt to reach to North Pole in 1818, Franklin began the pursuit in 1825 of finding the Northwest Passage. Franklin's expedition would be a partial success, as he mapped over 500 miles of previously uncharted territory, but, in the end, it would fail to find the passage. It was during this 1825 attempt, that *"hockey sticks"* were brought along, not only for enjoyment during the long periods of waiting for ice to recede, but, if need be, for firewood, as trees are a scarce resource in the extreme Arctic. In Henry Duff Traill's book *The Life of Sir John Franklin, R.N.,* in 1896, he cites a November 1825 letter from Franklin to the British geologist, Sir Roderick Murchison. In it, Franklin writes of crewmembers playing hockey in the North West Territories. The letter states:

> *We have, as yet, had no severe weather, nor do I think we are likely to have the temperature so low as at Fort Enterprise. We are, in fact, much less elevated in this secondary formation than when in its vicinity, where the rocks are entirely granitic. Until the day before yesterday we had comparatively little snow, and this is the first day that our dogs have been used in dragging sledges. Four trains of two dogs each were dispatched for meat this morning. We endeavour to keep ourselves in good humour, health, and spirits by an agreeable variety of useful occupation and amusement. Till the snow fell the game of hockey played on the ice was the morning's sport. At other times Wilson's pipes are put in request, and now and then a game of blind*

80

*man's bluff; in fact any recreation is encouraged to promote
exercise and good feeling . . .*

Born in 1786 AD in Spilsby, Lincolnshire England, Franklin,
was educated for two years at the St. Ives Grammar School in 1796 AD
to 1797 AD before attending school in Louth, England. Coincidentally,
St. Ives is one of the areas where the first parish-sponsored bandy
league had originated. It is this area and church where the deeply
religious Franklin's first exposure to the game of hockey would have
taken place, as his father had begun to groom the young boy for the
priesthood. Against his father's wishes, Franklin rejected the idea of
becoming a priest and at the age of 15 joining the Navy in 1800. In
1805, he fought in the Battle of Trafalgar against Napoleon Bonaparte's
France, serving as a signal-midshipman on the *HMS Bellerphon*. Later,
he would come to Canada to fight in the War of 1812 as second
lieutenant on the ship *HMS Bedford*. In January 1813, he wrote in his
diary about the war and his first experience with ice hockey in
Kingston, Ontario:

> *. . . While so many of my relations are dying around me.
> Shall I be permitted to finish this year? It is a question that I
> dare hardly ask, for I know that I am not fit to die. Still I
> hope this year to go home, and again see my dearest Father
> & Mother. What a happy meeting it will be, at all events I
> think it will be happy; I hope I may not be disappointed . . .
> Began to skate this year, improved quickly and had great fun
> at hockey on the ice.*

It is important to note that there exists a question as to the
exact year of the above-mentioned passage. The diary entry, which is
found on a single piece of paper and is housed at the National Library
of Canada in Ottawa, appears to be written in 1843 (the National
Library of Canada indicates it as being such) but upon closer
examination, and given the way Franklin wrote his the number "1" it
could only have been penned in 1813.

If we were to believe the Canadian National Library's
January 1843 interpretation, then Franklin would have been 57 years
old at the time of this account. A curious age for this portly aristocrat
to take up the sport and to "quickly" improve, especially in light of
noting his play in the Northwest Territories 18 years earlier. If, as he
stated, he did begin to learn to skate in Kingston, then it certainly must
have been in Kingston, Tasmania since, at this supposed time (1843)
Franklin was beginning his seventh year as Lieutenant-Governor of

Van Diemen's Land (later renamed Tasmania). It is on this South Pacific island, where Franklin would live until his release from duty on January 12, 1844. In addition, if it was 1843, it must have come as quite a disappointment to Franklin, when upon his return to England, he found out his father had not lived to the ripe old age of 105 and that his mother was not preparing to celebrate her 90th birthday. Instead, all "happy events" must certainly have been cancelled for time of personal reflection, upon hearing the astonishing news that his mother had died over thirty years prior and likewise his father nearly twenty years before his arrival in 1844. Although Franklin's grievous feeling must have been somewhat subdued as he could take condolence in prospect of knowing his own life was in safety. Since, of course, Franklin had just escaped the death-defying experiences of trying to establish Tasmania's first state educational system, along with other stately affairs, during a period where *so many of his relations were dying around him.* The prospects of freezing to death in the Arctic must have seemed quite utopian to him in light of the terrors of governing the former convicts of Tasmania.

By the time Franklin had been dismissed from his Lieutenant-Governor post, only approximately 200 miles remained to be charted in order to find the elusive passage. Leaving Greenhithe, England on May 19, 1845 he set sail for the Canadian Arctic with two ships, the *HMS Erebus* and *HMS Terror*, a crew of 143 men, and enough provisions for three years. Unfortunately, the 8000 tins of food that was brought along had been sealed with lead. It is believed lead poisoning would become a major contributor to the expedition's disastrous results. It would be proven later, through testing of some of the dead men's remains, that the crew was suffering from lead poisoning. Lead poisoning can affect virtually every system in the body resulting in damage to ones nervous system while causing digestive, memory, and concentration problems. This was only compounded by the harsh climate and conditions of the arctic. During one of the rescue missions looking for Franklin and his crew, Inuits reported seeing survivors from the two ships eating the remain's of dead crewmembers. The Eskimos claim they had encountered a group of 40 men dragging a small boat southward down King William Sound, and who had stated their boats had been crushed by ice. In Fergus Fleming's book, *Barrow's Boys*, he writes that when thirty dead men were eventually discovered *"many of the bodies had been hacked with sharp knives and the cooking pots contained human remains."*

Although credited with discovering the Northwest passage, Franklin, and the remainder his crew, were never found. It is unclear if the heavy-set Franklin met his fate in a cooking pot. What is known

82

is the first successful navigated voyage through the passage would come until 1905, therefore, possibly making Franklin's most significant contribution being his early accounts of hockey in Canada.

Strange and incredible as it sounds, today, some still argue that on Christmas Day in 1855 soldiers of the Royal Canadian Rifles, stationed at the British Garrison in Kingston, Ontario, were the first to play modern ice hockey. As the previous Franklin diary note shows, Kingston was home to hockey at least 42 years earlier than the "official" account. Halifax, Nova Scotia also lays claim to the origins of Canadian and modern ice hockey as British soldiers reportedly played the game there in 1867. The Province of Quebec also claims the origins of this ancient game, citing the "first ever" organized hockey game reported to be played at the Victoria Skating Rink in downtown Montreal on March 3, 1875. Almost two years later, McGill University would organize a hockey team and within a month they would print the "official" rules of ice hockey, a seven-paragraph text remarkably similar to those long in existence for English field hockey. Six years later, McGill would proclaim themselves the Canadian and World Champions after a two-team exhibition series in 1883, at the Montreal Ice Carnival. Today, McGill proudly claims to be the oldest hockey club still in existence. Many even believe that it was student's from Montreal who, in 1885, founded the Oxford University Ice Hockey Club, which lays claim to being the second oldest club in the world - next to McGill.

All these fraudulent claims do nothing but promote a ridiculous timeline of ice hockey origin in Canada.

While the interest in modern ice hockey was continuing to spread across Western Europe, developments in the basics of the game were continuing in Canada. In 1885 the practice of seven-man aside ice hockey was "officially" adopted by McGill and two years later the five team Amateur Hockey Association of Canada (AHAC) was formed. By 1890 the game was evoking great emotion not only from its players, but from spectators as well. The hard fought play was an attraction. As the *Toronto Globe* reported after a match at the Granite Club:

> *It is greatly to be regretted that in a game between amateur teams some players should forget themselves before such a number of spectators, a good proportion of whom on occasion referred to being ladies, as to indulge in fisticuffs, and the action of some spectators in rushing on the ice is also to be deplored.*

It was an Englishman, Lord Stanley of Preston, the sixth

83

Governor General of Canada and the 16th Earl of Derby, who gave the Canadian game its most sought-after prize. In 1892, being familiar with the sport through the participation of his sons, Lord Stanley sent his aide, Captain Charles Colville, to England to purchase a trophy which would suffice as an annual challenge cup to be awarded to the recognized amateur champions of Canada. For a mere 10 pounds, Colville purchased what would become one of the oldest and most prestigious trophies in North American sports. Within a season, the first Challenge Cup Championship of Canada, later nicknamed the Stanley Cup, would take place.

With Lord Stanley of Preston immortalized today by the trophy which bears his name, it is particularly interesting that it was his sons who were the motivating factors behind the trophy. In fact, Stanley never played the game. Later, the Stanley brothers, would return to Britain and play a key role in the advancement of late-1890's British ice hockey. It was the Stanley boys who reintroduced ice hockey to the British Royal Family in hopes that the Royals would serve as the role models for all of England's youth to emulate. Lord Stanley's concepts on sport were in keeping with his time. During the 19th century, it had been the English who had introduced the concept of competitive sports to much of the world. In an age of the Victorians and Victorian ideals, sports were regarded as models of teamwork and fair play.

Inadvertently, by recognizing Canadian hockey Stanley had accomplished something more. He has given the game royal acceptance removing its status as a game of the lowly masses and creating a tiered sport based on club elitism and commercialism. It was no secret that the Stanley Cup was only to be competed for by select teams within Canada. At the time of its presentation, it was a symbol for self-promotion all-the-while serving a supposed need. In time, those who controlled the Challenge Cup controlled hockey, effectively creating a "bourgeoisie" sport.

The growth and interest in ice hockey had also developed in the United States. By the late 1850's the first record of hockey being played in the United States appears in the *Journal* of the naturalist Henry David Thoreau. Writing on April 24, 1859, Thoreau proclaims:

> *There is a season for everything . . . Boys fly kites and play ball or hawkie at particular times all over the state. A wise man will know what game to play today, and play it. We must not be governed by rigid rules . . . but let the season rule us.*

It is important to note that the origins of Euro-American hockey dates to the 17th century. New Amsterdam, later renamed New York City, was the location of the Dutch colonists in North America. Many of these individuals were familiar with the sport of Kolven and likely played the game during winters. To assume that hockey in this primitive European form did not exist at New Amsterdam is to ignore the obvious. Kolven would have been played around the current-day Battery Park, Wall Street, and former World Trade Center areas of lower Manhattan. It would have also existed out on Long Island in and around Maspeth and Flushing, Queens.

By the early 1890's, there was a social movement among the American social elite to find and proclaim a birthplace for American hockey. Even though evidence existed of hockey being played by lower working class immigrants for decades through the New England States, and teams and leagues were already well established in Minneapolis, Detroit, and Baltimore, such facts were conveniently overlooked. In 1893, Yale University in New Haven, Connecticut, would declare themselves the birthplace of American hockey. Not to be outdone, Johns Hopkins University, in Washington D.C. followed, proclaiming themselves "the seedbed of American hockey."

Within two years, as hundreds of amateur and recreational hockey leagues came into existence across the United States and Canada, the first international contests in hockey were held as a steady stream of Canadian and American teams crossed over the Canada-U.S. Border to compete against their respective rivals.

On December 14, 1894, the first indoor ice rink in the United States opened on the corner of Lexington and 101st Street in New York. Known as the Ice Palace, it was home to the New York Hockey Club, the first hockey team established in New York City. Early in 1895 the first official Manhattan ice hockey games would be played using New York League ice hockey rules subsequently published (in the *Hockey Rules Revised*) by the local East 60th Street Saint Nicholas Club. A year later, the first officially recognized American Amateur Hockey League was established in New York City comprised of four men's teams from the St. Nicholas Skating Club, the Brooklyn Skating Club, the New York Athletic Club and the Crescent Athletic Club of Brooklyn.

The Crescent Athletic Club of Brooklyn had originally been founded in November 1884 as a football club. Two years later it had expanded to an athletic club and by 1888, it was a corporation, incorporated under the laws of the State of New York. The clubhouse was located on Clinton Street, Brooklyn. In addition, a country club house with its boat house and grounds was located on New York Bay between 1st Avenue and 83rd and 85th streets - the region known today as Bay Ridge. In order to ensure that no "riff-raff" could afford to attend the games, an admission fee of $1.00 per person was implemented.

The developments in New York City did not go unnoticed. One hundred miles west, in Philadelphia, Pennsylvania the local press embraced the game espousing it as the sport of the future. On December 22, 1895, *The Philadelphia Press* printed the following:

Hockey the Coming Winter Game

It Combines Many of the Requirements
Of a Successful Outdoor Sport.

How and Where to Play It

Details of a Once Humble Game
Which Promises to Surpass Golf
in the Affections of the Fashionable Set.

Hockey will boom this winter. The golfers and foot ball players who find themselves cut off from their favorite sports by the rough weather will have an opportunity to combine the elements of both in this increasingly popular game. For hockey once looked upon as a mere schoolboy's game, and commonly called 'shinny on the ice' is to be dignified by the approval of New York's fashionable set. It will also be one of the popular college games this season.

In the past, hockey players have been too dependent upon the vagaries of Jack Frost for their favorite sport; but now, in several Northern as well as Southern cities, rinks are being built for all kinds of skating, and especially for hockey. One of these is being constructed at Sixty-Sixth Street and Columbus Avenue, New York. It is to be 80 feet wide by 180 feet long, and it will be covered with ice generated by a huge freezing apparatus in the under part of the building.

In Baltimore a similar rink of somewhat smaller dimensions is in active operation, and the society ladies of that city take regular morning lessons in the novel art of flying on wings of steel - for all who have ever worn them will agree that skates, on good ice, give the nearest attainable approach to the delights of flying.

It is the enthusiasm of the hockey clubs that has caused this recent boom in the skating rink enterprise; and it is likely also, that the encouragement afforded by a sheet of ice ready for players at all times and in all weather will have a strong reaction upon the lovers of the sport. In New York hockey clubs are being formed in the Seventh Regiment Athletic Club, the New York Athletic Club and the Crescent Club of Columbia College, Harvard, Yale, Cornell, Brown and Princeton Universities are also organizing teams.

By 1897, aside from New York City, established teams and leagues were in existence in the eastern American cities of Pittsburgh, Philadelphia, Chicago, Washington, D.C., and Baltimore - a city reputed to be the *"most enthusiastic hockey city in America."* In 1898 in Newark, New Jersey, the Thomas Edison Company recorded the earliest known moving film footage of a hockey game showing young boys playing on the ice of a local lake.

Around the same time, hockey was coming into its own in the British colony of Newfoundland. Though not as well developed in play and popularity as in the case of Eastern Canada, the game held promise in the small, isolated, harbor communities and towns that lined the island's shoreline. Of all the places where hockey had taken root, Newfoundland was perhaps the most unique. The island's population at the turn of the century numbered less than 200,000. Outside of the provincial capital of St. John's, the island boasted only three communities with populations exceeding four thousand. Isolated and scattered fishing outposts were the norm, stretching the length of the island's rugged 6,000-mile coastline. The island population, for the most part, was of Irish and Scottish descent and no strangers to the games of hurley and shinny.

By the late 1890's, ice hockey was becoming a mainstream sport. In the wake of its growth, it attracted entrepreneurs and speculators who were eager to develop professional hockey. The first professional hockey league was the creation of Dr. Jack L. Gibson, a Canadian-born star hockey player and a dentistry graduate of the Detroit Medical School. While practicing dentistry in Houghton, Michigan in 1903, Gibson and a small group of local businessmen began to import Canadian hockey talent into the United States for the purpose of establishing an International Professional Hockey League (IPHL). Within a year, teams had been established in the Michigan communities of Houghton, Calumet, Sault Saint Marie, as well as Pittsburgh, Pennsylvania, and Sault Saint Marie, Ontario. The league adopted a six-man format and in turn created a faster and more spectacular game. With fewer men on the ice, the players could skate faster, and create more offensive action. The format worked and the crowds came in droves. For a while, Canadian hockey talent was in great demand and salaries paid to hockey players eclipsed those of American baseball greats. By 1905, Canadians such as Fred "Cyclone" Taylor were making in excess of $5,000 a year - even more than the baseball's immortal Ty Cobb.

Hockey had become a game which gripped the interests of a growing segment of North America. So it was not surprising that ice hockey was both a source of recreation and entertainment for the gold prospectors who had swarmed the northern territory of Canada, known as the Yukon, after gold was discovered in 1896. Complete cities numbering tens of thousands of prospectors existed from Alaska to the Yukon with the largest of these communities being Dawson City, a city that boasted a population of over 150,000.

In 1904 the Stanley Cup Champions were the Ottawa Senators (known as the Silver Seven) captained by the famous "One-Eyed" Jack McGee. Late in the year they received a letter from a group of hard-bitten gold rush miners from Dawson City, challenging the Silver Seven to a three-game, winner-take-all match for the Stanley Cup. It was a wonderful piece of bravado and great publicity for the game. The Senators agreed to the series and by doing so ensured a great story for sporting history for the miners would have to undertake a perilous journey which would take twenty-three days and cover 4,400 miles in order to get from Dawson City to Ottawa.

The Yukon challengers were sponsored by 37-year-old Joseph Whiteside Boyle, a native of Woodstock, Ontario, and one of the most successful men to emerge from the Klondike gold rush. "Gentleman Joe" Boyle was the self-proclaimed "King of the Klondike" and had a history of involvement with sporting ventures. In fact, he had been serving as the business manager of Australian boxer Frank Slavin, the so-called "Sydney Cornstalk," when word of the gold rush had drawn him to the Yukon and financial success. Boyle had always been a risk-taker when it came to hockey. As a child he had tested the limits of his abilities. Once during the 1870's while skipping school in favor of a game of shinny-on-ice, he almost drowned in a local pond when he fell through thin ice. He was rescued by his childhood friend, Joe Spice, who pulled him out of the water by lying flat on his belly and extending his shinny stick to the drowning Boyle.

In 1884, at the age of 17, Boyle left his home in Woodstock, Ontario, and headed for New York City to live with his older brothers. However, New York City was too confining for the lad and he would spend hours walking the walkways of Battery Park watching the sea vessels as they made their way in and out of lower Manhattan. That year Boyle himself would leave New York onboard the cargo ship *Wallace* as a deck hand headed for India. While docked in South Africa the young man would see first hand the excitement and unpredictability of the gold and diamond mining rush that was underway. He would never forget what he saw. It was likely this experience that helped convince him to travel north to the Yukon in 1897 to participate in the Klondike Gold Rush.

On December 19, 1904, the eight-man Dawson City Nuggets hockey team, led by the flamboyant Boyle, set out on their epic journey to Ottawa. All along their route they were met by groups of miners and local residents who lined the frozen expanse to cheer on their heroes. The season was far from the best time of the year for travel from the wild north and the group suffered many hardships in temperatures that plummeted to 20 degrees below zero Fahrenheit. Some of the men developed blisters on their feet. So painful were the sores that a few could no longer wear shoes, and were forced to proceed bare-footed through the snow. As the men progressed towards Ottawa the American and Canadian press carefully recorded their journey. The *Ottawa Journal* reported:

> *The first day the Klondikers covered 46 miles, the second 41.*
> *The third day saw them struggling to cover 36 miles.*

Delayed by the injuries and temperatures, the Nuggets missed their boat connection at Skagway by two hours, and sat idle for five days before embarking for Seattle. While waiting to leave Skagway, the team held one practice in a makeshift ice rink measuring 40 feet by 50 feet. The poor condition of the rink and the haphazard way the ice surface had been prepared (as half of the rink consisted of nothing more than a sheet of frozen dirt) only served to dull the minds and the skates of the players.

On December 31, 1904, the team boarded the steamship *Dolphin* and four days later they arrived in Seattle. At Seattle, amid large crowds of well-wishers and supporters, the team boarded a train and traveled 170 miles north to the Canadian-U. S. Border crossing over to Vancouver. In Vancouver, again amid a large crowd of well-wishers, the men boarded an eastbound train for Ottawa. While en route the men exercised in the train's smoking lounge sharing eight square feet of floor space. The limited area meant the only form of exercise that could be performed was push-ups, sit-ups, and rope-skipping with only one man exercising at a time.

When the team reached Brandon, Manitoba, Boyle and the men sensed they were not prepared for the upcoming series. They had suffered serious injuries and had faced unexpected training difficulties and so, needing an input of healthy talent, they recruited Lorne Hannay, a former team player who had returned home from the Klondike some months earlier after spending at least one season playing in the local Dawson City League.

When the team arrived in Ottawa on January 12, 1905, Boyle, serving as team spokesman, requested that the series be postponed for a week to give his men time to recover from the journey and to allow them an opportunity to practice. However, the Silver Seven refused insisting the first game in the series take place as scheduled the next day. It was hardly a sporting response but then the Nuggets did not appear to take the impending game too seriously spending the night partying well into the small hours of the morning.

During the first game, it became clear that by the end of the first-half, the style of play was becoming more and more physical as both teams battled along the boards. Early in the second-half the Ottawa's player, Arthur Moore tripped Dawson's top player, Norman Watt, resulting in a brawl. During the altercation, Watt would spear Moore in the mouth with his stick. The worse for wear, Moore skated back to his bench followed by Watt who subsequently broke his stick over the head of the already injured Ottawa player. Watt received a fifteen-minute penalty causing the Nuggets to play a large part of the second-half one man short. Though bleeding from the mouth and having been knocked out for roughly 10 minutes from the head blow, Moore continued in the game.

At the time of the altercation the Nuggets were down only by a score of 3-1 and were, by most accounts, taking the game to the Ottawa Seven. After the Nuggets were penalized, Ottawa reportedly scored six goals on their way to a lopsided 9-2 win. The win was not indicative of the true level of play that had been displayed by the Dawson City club. Later, P. D. Ross, the Challenge Cup (Stanley Cup) custodian would state:

> *Up to the time the Ottawans were leading 3-1 it was anyone's game and the Yukon men had the most of the play. . . It was only when the Yukoners tired and showed the effect of their long journey that Ottawa began to pile on the score . . . Add also that for a major portion of the game Yukon were playing a man short, and sometimes two, and it looks a bit better.*

Unfortunately, this reference has been overlooked by sports historians who tend to mock the Yukon team and their efforts; preferring instead to concentrate on the end scores rather than the true nature of the game in order to enhance the reputation and skill levels of the Ottawa Seven.

Three days and party nights later, One-Eyed McGee (the game's most famous star) scored 14 goals as Ottawa humiliated Dawson City in a second game with 23-2 defeat. He was, however, one of the best forwards ever to play ice hockey - the game's first real star. McGee finished his career with 71 goals in 23 games, with another 63 goals in 22 playoff encounters, and scored five goals in a game seven times during his career.

As for the Nuggets, no team in Stanley Cup history had journeyed farther, partied harder, nor taken a worse beating. The one bright spot for the defeated challengers was their goaltender, Albert Forrest. Despite letting in a record high 32 goals in two games, the seventeen-year-old French Canadian from Trois Riviere, Quebec, was praised by the Ottawa sportswriters: *"Forrest was sensational . . . Without him the score would have been double what it was."*

After the series the Nuggets continued their eastern journey on to Nova Scotia where they participated in a number of exhibition games against regional teams. In Amherst, Nova Scotia, they defeated a local select All-Star team 4-2. Later the Nuggets moved on to Cape Breton losing 4-0 against a tough squad of players comprised of working class coal miners. In the five games that would follow, the Nuggets would post four wins and one tie record as they crossed over the island provinces. From Nova Scotia, Boyle and the boys moved to Quebec and later Ontario for a series of games against local Quebec and Ontario university squads. By early March the Nuggets had made their journey south to Pittsburgh, Pennsylvania, playing a three game series against Dr. Jack L. Gibson's newly formed IPHL. The Nuggets would win two of the three matches against the IPHL's top team. From Pittsburgh they returned north to Canada ending their tour in Brandon, Manitoba, the home of Lorne Hannay, and playing an exhibition match against the Manitoba Provincial Champions in which the Yukoners won 9-1. After the Brandon game, the Nuggets were dismantled and the players went their separate ways, each holding a small token share of the revenue obtained from the tour game receipts.

Overall, the challenge did not provide the promised spectacular win for the Yukon underdogs. It did, however, emphasize the spirit of determination and endeavor characteristic of both the gold rush and Canadian hockey. The Klondike Challenge had been one of the wildest moments in hockey history. The excursion had cost Boyle

$3,000 and had made him and his team household names in Canadian sporting circles, although in time only Boyle would be remembered.

In the years following the series, and marked by the events surrounding the Great War, Boyle emerged again. This time as the leader and financial source behind an all-volunteer Canadian machine gun detachment that saw action on the European front. Awarded the rank of lieutenant colonel by the Canadian Army, he would later go to Russia in an attempt to aid the Russians in the rebuilding of their railroad system. Before war's end, he would be decorated for his service to the Allied cause by the governments of Russia, France, Romania, and Britain and would be rumored to have had a romantic relationship with Queen Marie of Romania. In 1923, Boyle died and at the time of his death, he was fifty-six.

1907 would be a turning point for ice hockey, one that would set the moral outlook for the sport for the 20th century. For it was in 1907 the sport lost its innocence, claiming its first official fatality. The game's increasing popularity brought an increase in the level of violence on the ice, particularly in Canada. It had become commonplace for players to have their faces sliced open by skate blades, heads cracked by sticks, and bodies and limbs broken by the impact of brutal body hits and violent assaults.

On March 6, 1907 in Cornwall, Ontario, Owen McCourt (Cornwall's leading scorer) died after being hit on the head with a stick by the Ottawa Victoria's player, Charlie Masson. During a scuffle between McCourt and Art Throop, Masson attacked him with a stick. McCourt left the ice bleeding profusely from a head wound and was rushed to the local hospital where he passed out. Later he fell into a coma and died from his injury. Masson was charged with murder. At the trial, witnesses testified that Masson had not been the first person to hit McCourt with a stick, that another nameless Ottawa player had hit McCourt on the head before Masson had swung. Unable to determine whether or not Masson had been responsible for the fatal blow, the Judge acquitted him.

Later that same year in Montreal, another violent incident occurred. The press dubbed the event as, *"an exhibition of brutality,"* and again the judicial system turned a blind eye to the offences being perpetrated in the name of sport. This effectively laid a foundation for Canadian ice hockey to become a bastion for thugs and social misfits, a place to settle old scores, where violence would go unchecked and be perceived as being above Canadian laws.

Such an attitude allowed men like Sprague Cleghorn to thrive. This was a player who, during the span of his career, sent more than fifty men to hospital on stretchers and served jail time in 1918 for severely beating his wife. Yet he and players like him were rewarded for their brutality both financially and sometimes, as was the case with Sprague Cleghorn, by being immortalized in the Hockey Hall of Fame. Cleghorn and others represented a breed of athlete the likes of which were seldom seen in other sports. These players were little more than 20th century Neanderthals whose only purpose in the sport was to wield a stick like a weapon, and to inflict pain and damage upon players of superior skill and ability. In other words, men like Cleghorn were nothing more than demons on ice in search of a sporting prey; hunters in search of the hunted.

The following year, in 1908, North American hockey continued to undergo monumental change. In the same year that Lord Stanley died the Stanley Cup was used for the first time as the championship symbol of professional hockey in Canada. The Allan Cup, donated by Sir H. Montague Allan, would in turn become the emblem of excellence for the Senior Amateur Championship of Canada. It would be the Allan Cup Champions who would later represent Canada in World Championship competitions.

Throughout this period, Canadian professional hockey struggled financially. In January 1910, the country's top hockey league, the Canadian Hockey Association, folded without concluding the championship. Its teams quickly amalgamated into the newly formed National Hockey Association (the "NHA") for the 1910-11 season - the forerunner of modern day professional-level National Hockey League ("NHL"). The NHA, eager to attract bigger crowds than its previous counterparts, (especially in Canada's largest city of Montreal) organized and founded the Canadien Athletic Club on December 4, 1909, which would later became the Club de Hockey Canadien ("CHC") in 1917. This newly formed Athletic Club's permitted only French Canadians to play for the squad. Later nicknamed "the Flying Frenchmen," the Montreal Canadiens would one of the greatest and most successful sports franchises in North American sports history - second only to baseball's New York Yankees.

At the time, however, they were simply created to serve a need - as an NHA promotional ploy, a dumping ground for French Canadians allowing English city teams a way to rid themselves of French-speaking Catholic players. Aside from giving Quebecers and Catholics a team of their own, the Canadiens would become the focus of pervasive English Canadian anti-French/Catholic sentiments – fueling controversy as well as ticket sales.

By 1911 professional hockey was being played on the west coast of Canada. With the founding of the Pacific Coast Hockey Association ("PCHL") by the Patrick Brothers, Frank and Lester (hockey stars in their own right), the Canadian cities of Vancouver, Victoria and New Westminster joined the list of professional hockey cities. The PCHL invigorated hockey becoming the first league to put numbers on players' uniforms for identification. They were the first to tabulate assists, and taking a lesson from a lesser-known league in Nova Scotia, the first professional league to allow goalies to flop to the ice to make saves. Borrowing from English rules of bandy, they painted blue lines on the ice. They also allowed forward passing and introduced penalty shots, again borrowing from the Nova Scotian hockey. In addition, they also created a playoff system. In time, the league would expand both east through the Canadian prairies and south into the United States. Eventually, the Canadian cities of Edmonton, Calgary, Saskatoon, Regina, and Winnipeg as well as the American cities of Seattle, Spokane and Portland would all become homes to the PCHL.

Although 1907 had seen the collapse of Gibson's International Professional Hockey League in the United States, its failure had been, at least in part, due to the very high player salaries rather than a lack of local public interest. Ice hockey was continuing to emerge and grow as a major sport of interest in the United States. One reason for the American growth was the emergence of an American superstar, the Pride of Princeton University Hobart Amory Hare Baker.

Born on January 15, 1892 in Wissahickon, Pennsylvania, Hobey Baker was perhaps the greatest hockey player of his generation. A one-man-wonder, he had captained Princeton University to two collegiate championships and, along the way, gained national and international attention for his skill and scoring abilities. A man who could do no wrong, Baker was idolized by those who witnessed his athleticism and soft-spoken manner. At 5'9" tall and weighing only 160 pounds, he was not a physically imposing man. His handsome features and blonde hair made the Ivy League graduate a favorite of the ladies. His ability to endure the physical punishment inflicted upon him by opposing players, without retaliating or showing anger, earned Baker the admiration from the toughest foe.

After graduating he had moved to New York City, taken a job as a clerk at the Morgan Bank in the heart of Wall Street, and immediately signed to play for the St. Nicholas Hockey Team. Baker was an immediate New York sensation. Fans clamored to watch him play. The newspapers ran stories on him akin to a modern day movie idol. Following the St. Nicks defeat of a highly touted Canadian hockey team, the Montreal Stars, a Canadian journalist wrote: *"Uncle Sam had the cheek to develop a first-class hockey player [Baker] who wasn't born in Montreal."* A year earlier, *The Boston Journal* had written that Baker was *"without a doubt the greatest amateur hockey player ever developed in this country or in Canada."*

By the spring of 1914, the popularity and growth of ice hockey in Canada was well established. With a national population of less than 8 million, there were almost 4,000 amateur men and boys' hockey leagues throughout the country. From the Yukon in the far northwest to the American border in the south, and from the Atlantic to the Pacific, hockey was the one common thread that bound Canadians together. Unbeknownst to all, the frozen ponds and ice rinks of Canada would begin to fall silent as a generation of boys and men marched off to a distant war in Europe. At the time, no one could imagine the horrors that lay ahead. Over the next five years, Canadian hockey players would find themselves wearing a new team uniform and playing a different type of game - the game of their lives.

Chapter Nine

The Gods of Ice and War

It has been said that the Battle of Waterloo was won on the playing fields of Eton. If that holds true then it must be equally true that World War I had been won - at least in part - on the hockey arenas and frozen ponds of Canada.

On the social and political front, 1914 was a busy year. In North America the Canadians were celebrating the end of the War of 1812 (which of course didn't actually end until 1814) in remembrance of the one hundredth anniversary of the victory over their neighbors, the United States of America.

For a century two sworn enemies, Canada and the United States, had enjoyed an often uneasy peace. Although the two North American countries shared the same continent and their pioneering quests to the Pacific had run parallel lines, they were both historically and culturally quite different. For much of their existence, these two nations, both former European colonial entities, had been enemies and their wars among the most bloody and vicious in recorded history. On two occasions, the United States had attempted to conquer Canada, only to be beaten back. And, although the United States military had often promoted a myth that *"they had never lost a war,"* the fact that they had failed in two attempts to invade Canada was a point of pride that had not been forgotten by their self-professed *"peace-loving"* northern counterparts. Canadians, though welcoming American business and tourism, did not wish themselves to be incorporated into the American melting pot. For Canadians were an integral part of the British Empire, proud of their connections to the mother country, and firm in their loyalty to the Crown. At the turn of the 20th century, the Canadian Dominion was rapidly emerging as an industrial jewel within the British crown.

For all their ties to the empire, Canadians for the most part paid little attention to the political and military developments taking place in Europe. The old continent was an ocean away and though Canadian foreign policy was inextricably bound to, and mandated by, the British government in London, few people in Canada had any grasp of the consequences of such a political reality. By 1914 Europe was in political ferment as Germany continued to flex its political muscle, looking for an opportunity to increase its influence and power. Britain watched the German actions with increasing alarm and her concern was made manifest when on Sunday, June 28, 1914, Archduke Franz

Ferdinand, the heir to the Austrian throne, and his wife, were assassinated by a Serbian nationalist during a visit to Sarajevo.

Convinced that the Serbian government was behind the assassination, Germany seized upon the opportunity to urge the Austrians to take an aggressive stance, promising them full military support should the Serbs fail to acquiesce to Austrian demands and make reparations for the murders. The Austrian demands were harsh, and the Austrian Government secretly believed the Serbs would never accept them. Both Austria and Germany knew war was inevitable as both countries had an agenda beyond recompense for the assassinations. Austria needed a military victory to bolster its aging empire, which was on the verge of collapse. Germany had eyes upon the territories it could gain by force of arms. With Russia and France promising to aid Serbia should a military conflict occur, the stage was set for what was to become the bloodiest and most devastating war in human history. On August 4, the German Army moved against Serbia's ally France by invading France via neutral Belgium. Britain and her Empire, as treaty guarantors to Belgium neutrality, was drawn into the escalating conflict following Germany's refusal to withdrawal.

It was seen as a great adventure. The war, it was said, would be over in six months. For its part, the British War Office in London had asked the Canadian Government to supply them with 10,000 troops - ample enough men to meet the expected needs. Eager to impress, Canada instead promised 25,000, an impressive commitment given the fact Canada's full-time army numbered only 3,110 men. Almost immediately recruitment had begun. Within a month, following a more than successful recruiting drive, one hundred troop trains were on the move across the country loaded with high spirited young volunteers in search of travel and adventure. Their destination was Valcartier, Quebec, a new military camp specifically organized to house the 25,000 troops anticipated. Upon arrival, and to the pleasure of the Canadian commanders overseeing the task, 32,655 men were counted.

Within two months, the first contingent of the Canadian Expeditionary Force, was sailing to England in the largest convoy of men ever to cross the Atlantic. In total, 30,617 men, 7,697 horses, 127 field guns and equipment had been loaded onto 30 ships. Off the coast of Newfoundland the convoy was joined by 550 men from the British colony of Newfoundland sailing aboard the *S.S. Florizel*. It had been one hundred years since Newfoundland's sons had been involved in any military undertaking, underscored by the fact that the men were being sent to England without weapons and adequate uniforms. It was hoped that the "*Newfies*" would obtain the needed supplies once they arrived at their expected destination in Scotland. Crossing the Atlantic took ten days. By October 14, the convoy had arrived at the British Port of Plymouth. Nine days later, the unloading of the troops was complete and the Canadians were moved to Salisbury Plain where most would spend the next four months training in the rain and snow of winter.

Canadian professional hockey players were very prominent among those answering duty's call. One-Eyed Frank McGee enlisted with the Canadian Expeditionary Force despite the fact that he was legally indeed blind in one eye. The 32 year-old was determined to serve, regardless of his handicap, and assumed the rank of lieutenant. Other famous recruits followed. The NHA's great right-winger, Scotty Davidson of Toronto; Ottawa Senators unbeatable goaltender, Percy LeSeur; the NHA's Hamilton Tigers Captain Shorty Green; Talbot Papineau, the French Canadian star of the 1908 Oxford University Blues; Toronto's Queen's University great George Richardson; and the NHA's Duke Keats were just a few of the many Canadian hockey elite who hung up their skates and put away their sticks in their determination to serve a greater cause.

December saw the first units of Canadian troops crossing the English Channel and landing in France. By February 1915 the complete First Canadian Division had landed and had been given brief trench warfare training. They were assigned to a four-mile line of trenches in the Armentieres Sector. Almost immediately, hockey began to lose its stars. On February 9 in a brief engagement between Canadian and German troops, George Richardson, the star of the 1909 Canadian Amateur Senior Champions Queen's University, was reported killed. He was 27. By 1916 Frank McGee was dead, a casualty of the Battle of Courcelette, and a year later Talbot Papineau would die as well. Prior to his death, Papineau, having obtained the rank of major, wrote to a French Canadian newspaper:

> *At this moment as I write, French and English Canadians are fighting and dying side by side. Is their sacrifice to go for nothing, or will it not cementing the foundation for a true Canadian nation?*

By now the war had ground to a halt with horrendous number of casualties claimed on both sides. Defensive zones dominated a six hundred-mile front of trench works, barbed wire and gun emplacements - a seemingly impregnable killing ground of destruction, mud and death.

In mid-April, Belgian sources in Ghent informed the French that the Germans had placed a rush order for *"20,000 mouth protectors to protect men against the effects of asphyxiating gas."* The Belgians feared that the Germans were preparing for an all-out gas attack and military assault along the trench works opposite the German 26th Reserve Corps - an area held by Algerian troops of the French African Light Infantry and the Canadian First Division. The French had concluded, without further investigation, that the idea of gas warfare was absurd and that the Germans, fearful of the consequences of such actions would never dare use gas as a weapon. The French inaction would be one of the greatest blunders of the war, subsequently leading to one of the most important and crucial battles in human history.

On April 22, following an intense artillery bombardment, the German 26th Corps released 60 tons of chlorine gas into a light northeast wind blowing south over the Allied trenches near the Armentieres Sector. The thick clouds of yellow-green chlorine - fifteen feet in height - drifted over the trenches effectively blocking out the sun, and killing every man in its path. In the panic that proceeded, two entire French colonial divisions dissolved as the Algerian and French defenses crumbled, and troops fled in horror. In their wake they left behind a gaping 4-mile-wide hole in the Allied lines exposing the Allied flank and leaving the road to Paris virtually undefended. As the German advance moved forward, it threatened to sweep behind the Canadian trenches and encircle fifty thousand British and Canadian troops. Canadian field commanders, in desperation, ordered their men to close the gap and initiated a series of counterattacks against the enemy advance. What happened next was one of the most dramatic moments ever recorded in the annals of war. Canadian troops, outnumbered ten to one, walked unprotected towards the mountain of gas clouds and the hidden German enemy, effectively becoming the first army in modern history to bear the brunt of a chemical warfare attack. As Leslie Hudd, a Canadian soldier, would state years later:

> *We saw this stuff coming over, it was sort of mist. The wind was blowing our way, towards the trenches. So next we knew it was gas, chlorine gas. The only thing we could do, we covered our mouths. So we took a piece of shirt, anything we could get, and wet on it. I don't know if I should say how we wet on it, but we wetted it, anyway, and wrapped that around our faces, and we had to take a chance with our eyes. Anyway, it worked some, but we lost a lot of men over that. It was hell, that gas . . . we did what we could.*

John Carroll, a Machine-Gunner of the 3rd Brigade, Canadian

Expeditionary Force wrote in a letter to his mother:

It was a screeching of shells, men falling on all sides, Frenchmen retreating in disorder, yelling all kinds of things we could not understand. . . We drove the Germans back, a few hundreds of Canadians against thousands of Germans. But I don't think they knew there was only such a small number of us. It was getting dark . . . You would hardly know me now. I have aged quite a bit in looks, also in feelings, and got very thin. It is all with the continued hardships and nerve-racking things we have to endure. Well, dear mother. I will close, hoping I am alive to receive your answer to this letter.

With no protection from the deadly gas, the Canadian troops used whatever they could to cover their mouths and faces, the most common solution being handkerchiefs soaked in water or human urine. Already dire, there appeared no conceivable way the situation could get worse - yet it did. The Ross rifles that the Canadians were issued continuously jammed when engaged in rapid fire. With a useless weapon, the Canadians were forced to face the German advance with little more than bare hands and bayonets. Eleven thousand Canadians advanced into the gas clouds - six thousand died. Of the five thousand who were to survive the first round, it is estimated that one-third had been forced to abandon their rifles during the heat of the battle.

The Germans had not expected the Canadian action. Because of the fierce Canadian resolve the German advance was temporarily halted as the German commanders, unable to gauge the battle, assumed that they were facing a greater force than was the case. Regrouping two days later, they tried again. Once more the gas came, once more the Canadians held. The Germans were dumbfounded. Their commanders could not explain the actions of the enemy. Who were these men?

In the heat of battle, when all appeared to be lost, the Canadians did the impossible and engaged the enemy in a fierce, unforgiving, self-sacrificing manner, which sent shock waves through the German military. Prior to the Battle of Ypres the Germans had assumed that only seasoned, professional soldiers could perform well in battle. And yet, they could not explain how it was that their well-prepared troops had been stopped so close to victory by such an unlikely force as were the Canadians. Perhaps, in the end, the Germans needed only to look at their own history for the answer.

After the military humiliations of the Napoleonic Wars, the

Prussians (the driving force behind the future Germany) turned to theorists to devise a plan to "regenerate" their army and improve the soldiering abilities of their men. One of the theories espoused at the time was the doctrine of Friedrich Jahn, a leading proponent of sports and human physical fitness. Jahn argued that in order to succeed in war it was necessary to create a singular national sports movement designed to *"strengthen the military bodies and abilities"* of his fellow countrymen, creating a soldier capable of achieving *"teutonic thoroughness."* Only through a universal and demanding sports program could they create the ultimate army.

In the early days of World War I, few realized the significance of Jahn's theories especially in the context of Canadian sports and society. For almost one hundred years Canadians had channeled their militaristic spirit and energy into the sport of hockey - a sport whose origins and concepts were based on the ideals of physical endurance, tribalism, and warrior cults. In doing so, Canadians had inadvertently proven Jahn correct by creating, through hockey, an example of a so-called teutonic thoroughness. If one assumes Jahn's theories are valid then hockey in Canada was a training ground for warriors.

The parallels between Canadian ice hockey and militarism were startling. Both demanded teamwork over individualism, loyalty and unquestioning self-sacrifice. In Canadian hockey, a player was expected to endure pain and injury. He was expected to face the opposition regardless of the task and to never accept defeat. He wore his uniform with pride, never allowing himself to be shamed by an opponent. His uniform was more than a simple form of identification. It was who he was, whom he represented, his unit, his team, and his heritage. Few sports expected such commitment, few were as demanding. In the end, it would be these conditional factors that shaped the character of Canada's youth. Ice hockey gave the Canadian male the social conditioning necessary to produce a soldier, the social conditioning necessary to succeed in war; for hockey in Canada had always been a controlled form of warfare. Or, as the Soviet writer Maxim Gorky would later argue, hockey was nothing more than *"a bourgeoisie sport designed specifically to produce cannon fodder."*

On May 7, 1915, three weeks after the infamous battle of Ypres, word of the German sinking of the passenger ship *RMS Lusitania* with a loss of 1,195 lives reached the Canadian troops. Among the victims were one hundred Canadian women and children en route to England to be with their husbands and fathers who were serving in the Canadian Expeditionary Force. Though the world's attention had been concentrated on the loss of American lives and the impact the sinking had on U.S. and German relations, the slaughter of the Canadian civilians only hardened the Canadian troops' resolve, in the end ensuring that for the duration of the war, the German soldier's greatest and most feared enemy would be the Canadian soldier. Later in his *War Memoirs*, British Prime Minister David Lloyd George summed up the hatred between the Canadian and German troops by stating: *"Whenever the Germans found the Canadian Corps coming into line they prepared for the worst."*

By the summer of 1915, there was little humanity remaining between the Germans and the Canadians. Following the Battle of Ypres and the sinking of the *Lusitania*, the Canadians openly boasted that they did not take German prisoners. The Germans, of course, reciprocated in kind escalating the growing hatred. In four years of hard-fought battles, the Germans would claim 3,842 Canadians as prisoners of war, a ratio of less than 1 in every 200 Canadian soldiers - the lowest ratio of any Allied force. Of these, most had been taken during the early stages of the conflict. A further indication of the hatred between the two groups could be seen in a recorded example of a German interrogation of a Canadian soldier captured at the height of the war. When the Germans asked the man why he had come so far to kill Germans? The man replied: *"For Fun."* Later, when trainloads of Canadian prisoners were transported through Germany, it became a common practice for the German guards to open the doors of the boxcars whenever the trains stopped in a German community and to allow angry German citizens the opportunity to beat the men.

Of the 3,842 Canadians held by the Germans, 377 were Canadian pilots shot down over German lines while serving in the British Royal Flying Corp. Among the pilots held captive was a 22-year-old Canadian hockey player from Toronto named Conn Smythe.

Constantine Falkland Cary Smythe was born on February 1, 1895 in Toronto to Albert and Amelia Smythe, a pair of Northern Irish immigrants who had arrived in Canada in 1889. Albert Smythe was a devoted member of the Theosophy Sect, a religious movement whose ideas of spiritualism and reincarnation were based upon the books of Madame Helene Blavatsky. The Smythes were not wealthy, though Mr. Smythe became editor of *The Toronto World* newspaper. His father ensured that Conn would mix in the best circles of Ontario society, having him educated at the elite private school, Upper Canada College, and then at the University of Toronto. Conn Smythe was an outstanding schoolboy and athlete, excelling at hockey.

In 1915, as a high scoring center, he led the University of Toronto to the Ontario Junior Hockey Championship. After winning the championship on a Friday they all volunteered for military service the following Monday. Commissioned into the 2nd Ottawa Battery of the 8th Brigade, he trained at the artillery school in Kingston, then managed to secure a transfer to the famous 40th Battery (the so-called Sportsman's Battery) put together by publishing magnate Harry Southam under the command of his son Gordon.

The 40th Battery was to be more than just a military outfit. With several top amateur players on the squad, the Battery entered the OHA (Ontario Hockey Association) competitions. However, for some reason, the Battery was not overly welcomed by the OHA, and so its members were placed in a division with the Riversides, the Argos, and the Toronto Rowing and Athletic Association. They were also forced to play all their games at the old Mutual Street Arena.

Managing the team, Smythe's inexperience was used against him. The Battery was required to play at the old Mutual Street Arena as the "home team" for the first part of the season and the "away team" in the second half. Financially this meant that the 40th would get the lion's share of the receipts for the first half of the season. It was well known that hockey crowds grew throughout the winter, meaning 40th Battery got the lion's share of the small early season crowds, missing out on the big gates. As Smythe would later remember:

> *The old hockey men, I was told later, laughed at how they'd put one over on the kid but the joke was on them. They misjudged the patriotic sentiment in Toronto, plus our good players were starting to make us crowd favorites. As a minor piece of retribution, this meant that the guys who had conned me in the scheduling weren't going to get the home-team break in gate money from us at all.*

Smythe would play his last game as a player in the team's opening game against the Riversides. His team lost 8-3, and one of the reasons according to the *Toronto Telegram,* was Conn Smythe's inability to back-check effectively. Smythe decided to concentrate on coaching and the team started to play well. However, on January 26, 1916, Major Southam received orders that his outfit would soon be heading overseas to France. Southam and Smythe decided these orders could be turned to their advantage. The team's entire gate receipts were bet on a game with the Argos. Prior to the start, Smythe informed his players that $2,800 was riding on the game. The 40th Battery players did not let their officers down, winning 8-3, and earning just under $7,000 in all including gate receipts for the game. The money was subsequently put to good use, giving the troops some comforts as they fought in France. The 40th Battery would eventually fight at the Somme and later at Vimy Ridge. Several of the hockey players, including the team's star rover Jack Petnick, would not survive the war.

Smythe's religious convictions gave him a fatalistic view of life, so much so that he may actually have been welcoming or even seeking death. Theosophy taught him that all things were preordained and that life was continual based on the concepts of reincarnation and that death was simply a transitional step to the next higher level of being. In 1917 Smythe made a bid to part this realm when he made a single-handed charge at a German position only armed with just his service revolver. He recalled that as he ran down a German trench, he met a German with a rifle and bayonet: *"I put the pistol in his stomach and fired, and he cursed me all the way down to the ground."* Smythe kept on shooting until his pistol was emptied. His rash act would win him the Military Cross.

Following the death of his commanding officer, he transferred to the even more hazardous service of the British Royal Flying Corp. In November 1917, while flying over the battlefield of Passchendaele, spotting for the artillery units on the ground, he was shot down. For several months he had been engaged in a philosophical debate with a comrade on what happens to the soul at death. He was later to recall that as his plane spun earthwards:

> *I frantically tried to get her out of a flat spin, I remembered that I should have been scared to death, because here was the World coming up to me, upside down and inside out, but the only thought I had at the time was this: 'In about ten seconds I'm going to prove that Bill O'Brien was wrong and I was right.*

Smythe was to survive the crash, and was imprisoned as a POW at Schweidnitz in Upper Silesia. He would twice attempt to escape, being recaptured both times and would be released after the Armistice. The First Great War would be a defining experience for Conn Smythe, and later it would not only help shape his life but also shape the sport of hockey in the years ahead.

Though Canada had no air force during the war, active recruitment of Canadians for the British Royal Flying Corps had been extensive, resulting by war's end, in one-half of all Royal Air Force pilots being Canadian. In the early days of the Flying Corps the British believed that hockey players, on account of their ability to tolerate cold, as well as their ability to balance on skates, made for ideal pilots. Thus players, such as future Toronto Granites star Harry Watson and William Duncan of the Pacific Coast Hockey's Victoria Cougars (credited with six and five kills, respectively) were members of the Flying Corps. Led by the likes of Watson and Duncan, complete squadrons of Canadian pilots flew under the banner of the British Royal Flying Corps. In total, by war's end, 25,000 Canadians would serve in the Corps. Of the eleven highest scoring World War I aces of all nations, four would be Canadian.

So prevalent was the Canadian presence that by 1917, Canadian pilots were being killed in training accidents at a rate of two a day. For many, the Flying Corps became an immediate death sentence. By 1917, the average life expectancy of a Canadian pilot was less than three months. In one six-month period alone, the death rate of Canadian airmen over the Western Front reached 92 percent. In the end, 1,300 Canadian airmen would die.

For ten months after arriving in Scotland, the Newfoundland battalion did little more than train. At the time of their enlistment, and believing that the war was to last only six months, the men had only volunteered to serve one year. As the battalion's enlistment deadline approached, British military officials feverishly searched for a solution to what was quickly becoming an embarrassment. The last thing anyone wanted was to have the men return home. Following an inspection by the King and Lord Kitchener the men were advised that they were exactly the men Kitchener required to support the Allied initiative at Gallipoli and the men would extend their contracts and sign on for the war's duration. Fearing the humiliation of returning home, most agreed to extend their service. Within a week the battalion was on its way to the Dardanelles in support of the Australian, New Zealand and French troops already there. Over the next four months the battalion would be decimated, as the men became victims of Turkish snipers, disease, and exposure to the elements. Of the 500 men that would land at Gallipoli, two hundred and seventy would die. For the remaining Newfoundlanders there seemed little hope; few expected to leave the peninsula alive. In the end when all seemed lost, the Allies abandoned the Gallipoli peninsula and the men returned to Britain to be reassigned to the European battlefront.

By the spring of 1916, following an effective recruitment drive in Newfoundland, the battalion recorded 753 men among its ranks with 40 percent under twenty years of age. Given the tragedy of Gallipoli, and the small male population of Newfoundland, the rebuilding of the battalion had been extremely successful. Part of the reason for the recruiting success had been socio-economic. The military was a way for Newfoundlanders to enjoy a better life and the promise of a regular paycheck.

A Newfoundland boy's childhood was one of hardship. At six

years of age, many a youngster had to forego schooling and instead worked alongside his father helping to tend to the family fishing nets. It was a simple case of survival. By ten, the boy would have learned the secrets of fishing. By fourteen, he would be considered a man - his hands callous and face weathered beyond his years. In winter, when the fishing boats were brought ashore for repairs and preparation for the spring fishing season, the island youth would turn their attention to hockey. It was one of the few pleasures they could claim. It is unknown how many teams or leagues existed in this barren island outpost but by all accounts, hockey was a game rooted in the fabric of Newfoundland life.

By June the men had been moved from England to the Western Front and the British-controlled area near the Belgian town of Maricourt by the River Somme. They were to be part of the 100,000-man British force being gathered and prepared for an attack against German positions along an 18-mile front. General Sir Douglas Haig, Commander of the British Forces, believed this was to be the pending battle which would ensure a deathblow to the German Army and hasten the end of the war.

In the days leading up to the start of the major British attack, Haig, no fan of colonial troops, had developed a dislike for the Newfoundlanders. During a series of limited engagements against the Germans he had questioned the men's fighting abilities and had even implied during one diary entry that the men were cowards. Though he would have preferred that the battle be fought with only British troops, he accepted the involvement of the Newfoundlanders and other colonials as the price one pays for waging war, thus seeing the men as nothing more than an adventurous lot of riff-raff which war attracts.

The British plans for the Battle of the Somme called for the Newfoundland battalion to capture the village of Beaumont Hamel. On July 1 at 9:15 a.m. the order was given and the men of the Newfoundland Regiment, each of them weighed down with sixty pounds of equipment, slowly climbed out of their protective trenches and began a steady walk into no-man's-land towards the cut barbed wire that divided the British from the German lines. Almost immediately the German machine guns opened up on the advancing columns of men who scrambled desperately to free themselves of the German gunner's sights. In less than twenty minutes, it was over. Of the 753 men of the Newfoundland battalion who had gone into battle that fateful day, only 43 would answer the call the next morning. In a matter of minutes, a generation of men, the pride of Newfoundland, had ceased to exist.

The Battle of the Somme would prove to be a failure. In the

106

aftermath, Haig, the man who had only weeks earlier questioned the Newfoundlanders' courage, would travel to Newfoundland to dedicate a war memorial to the battalion. Men who had, only days earlier, been considered useless and expendable in life were now heralded by the same critical British officials as heroes in death-a timeless example for those still living who were now being urged to follow in the dead men's footsteps.

By war's end, the male population of Newfoundland had been decimated. In what would be four years of war, 5,482 Newfoundland men would go overseas to fight. Of these, 3,814 would be killed or wounded, a casualty rate in excess of 72 percent. Complete groups of boyhood friends, "pals", in many cases, the males of entire families as well as the entire male population of small Newfoundland fishing communities had ceased to exist.

The legacy of World War I on Newfoundland is haunting. Communities of nothing more than widows, small children and the elderly were left to fend for themselves. With few men to fish or support families, the living standards fell, as more and more families slipped into the ranks of the impoverished. In the early 1920's, a life-sized bronze monument of a caribou was erected overlooking Beaumont Hamel to pay tribute and in remembrance to the men who had perished. Impressions are important. The caribou stands proud and pointing to the sky. Its mouth is opened as if it were bellowing an anguished cry. The longer one stares at the figure, the easier it is to sense the anger. The easier it is to understand the sense of loss. It is as if nature was questioning the gods, asking why? The beauty of the monument lies in its simplicity. What better symbol of Newfoundland than a lone caribou against an endless sky. Man is small. The world with all of its pain looms large. Nature is limited in its power and sense of understanding. Prior to WWI, Newfoundland was a region of peace - a society unaccustomed to war. When war came, this small island had answered the call. Her youth had marched forward into the unknown. In terms of overall numbers, Newfoundland's contribution to the British Empire and the war was small. However, those few were all that Newfoundland had. Following the Battle of the Somme, Commander-in-Chief Sir Douglas Haig sent a telegraph to the people of Newfoundland. In it he wrote:

The heroism and devotion to duty they had displayed on the 1st of July has never been surpassed.

Slaughters seldom are.

In 1949, the people of Newfoundland voted to join Canada as the 10th province. During that same period, over 2100 Newfoundland communities were abandoned. At the time, the Newfoundland government cited the tremendous loss of men, during the First World War, as one of the main reasons for the abandonment. With their passing, the social infrastructure of communities had been destroyed, as was much of the island's hockey playing tradition, with the result that Newfoundland didn't produce a professional hockey player until Alex Faulkner in 1961. Even today, more than ninety years after the birth of professional hockey, scantly more than two-dozen Newfoundlanders have ever reached the professional level.

Throughout the war, Canadian hockey did more than could be expected to support the war effort. The dedication to the cause was seen in the message issued on December 30, 1915, by James T. Sutherland, President of the Canadian Amateur Hockey Association and Captain of the 146th Overseas Battalion:

In this my first official note as president of the Canadian Amateur Hockey Association, I take the greatest pleasure in sending out to all officers and players in the many provincial associations connected with our governing body the heartfelt wish that the coming year of 1916 will bring to one and all the greatest amount of happiness and prosperity possible. I feel, however, that I have a greater responsibility and duty to perform at this time and that is to point out to the great army of hockey players and officials scattered throughout our beloved Canada, from coast to coast, how great and urgent the need is for men to come forward and rally to the defense of the common cause, and strike a blow for liberty and justice that will re-echo around the world. Canada's athletes have responded nobly to the call in the past, and will, I am sure, continue to do so. In a few short weeks, our hockey season will be over, and if there are any who have not made up their minds regarding their future course of action, let me say that, in my opinion, there should be only one conclusion, and that should be to exchange the stick and puck for a Ross rifle and bayonet, and take your place in the great army that is being forced to sweep the Oppressors of humanity from the face of the earth . . . It takes nerve and gameness to play hockey. The same qualities are necessary in the greater game that is now being played in France and on the other fighting fronts. The thousands of hockey players throughout the Dominion of Canada have all the necessary

108

qualifications. Therefore, I strongly urge all such to rally around the flag. With every man doing his bit, Canada will raise an army of brains and brawn from our hockey enthusiasts the likes of which the world has never seen. The bell has rung. Let every man Play the greatest game of his life. Over to center!

At the start of the conflict, the Canadian Amateur Hockey Association believed that there had been almost 4,000 established hockey leagues in Canada. By 1916, with the demand for replacement troops in Europe, almost all the leagues had shut down as a gesture of support for the war effort and to encourage hockey players to enlist. Robert Service, the famed Scottish poet and newsman, who had made a name for himself writing newspaper stories and poetry on the Klondike Gold Rush of 1898, had enlisted with the Red Cross as a stretcher bearer following the death of his brother. His brother had joined up with the Canadian Army early in the war and had died on the Western Front. Shortly after arriving in Europe Service penned a poem that epitomized the Canadian hockey player in military uniform. He wrote:

And when I come to die, he said,
Ye shall not lay me out in state,
Nor leave your laurels at my head,
Nor cause your men to speech orate;
No monuments your gift shall be,
No column in the Hall of fame;
But just this line ye grave for me:
'He played the game.'
So when his glorious task was done,
It was not his fame we thought;
It was not his battles won,
But of the pride with which he fought;
But of his zest, his ringing laugh,
His trenchant scorn of praise or blame:
And so we graved his epitaph,
He played the game.

In Manitoba, the Winnipeg 61st Battalion team that starred future Hockey Hall of Famer 'Bullet Joe' Simpson would win the Allan Cup in 1916 before being sent overseas. They were, however, not the only Winnipeg military team to prove their worth in both war and peace. The Winnipeg Falcons enlisted *en masse*, and, with Hall of Famer Frank Frederickson, played for the 223rd Battalion in

Manitoba's Patriotic League. Their players were doing their military training in Portage la Prairie and would return to Winnipeg for games. The 223rd Battalion was sent to Europe in May 1917. Olie Turnbull, Buster Thorsteinson and George Cumbers all laid down their lives in the greater game.

As the need for men at the front increased, Canadian soldiers began to carry an expanded role as Allied "Storm Troops." As a result, the symptoms of shell shock among the Canadians increased. At the time, the diagnosis carried a stigma associated with cowardice and even homosexuality and almost always went untreated. If the soldier was not fit to return to battle he faced humiliation. To prevent shell shock incidents among troops, the men were told that they would receive no pension or medical support that the symptoms were nothing short of "a manifestation of childishness and femininity." In reality, shell shock was a condition resulting from the bruising of the nerves due to a violent concussion brought on by being too close to a shell explosion. Raymond Massey, a Canadian volunteer, and later Oscar-winning actor, wrote of his experiences:

> *There were other shell shocks in the ward - four or five, I think. In the bed next to mine was a young . . . officer whose hair was completely white. It looked odd with his young face. His eyes stared and didn't seem to focus. I remember this man clearly. He never spoke to anyone . . . In the morning (he) was dead. Heart failure, they said. I did not think so. I think he was scared to death by his dreams.*

On Monday April 9, 1917, one hundred thousand men of the Canadian Army crawled out of their trenches into the face of a driving snowstorm and moved forward in an attempt to dislodge the Germans from the highest grounds overlooking the Western Front, an area known as Vimy Ridge. Vimy Ridge was the strategic key to the entire German defensive system. It was the center point of the Germans' Hindenburg Line and the network of German defenses running north to the English Channel. Rising 200 feet above the Douai Plain, it commanded a ten-mile view of the French countryside in all directions, and had been in the hands of the Germans since 1914. In a series of failed attempts to capture it, the British and French Armies had sustained over 200,000 casualties.

It would be the greatest Allied victory of the war and marked the first time that the Canadian Army had fought as a separate unit. Later, a British officer who had witnessed the battle wrote of the Canadians that he *"had witnessed the birth of a nation"* as men from all corners of Canada had fought side by side for the first time ever.

By the summer of 1918, with the entry of the United States into the war, and the subsequent first arrival of American troops to Europe, the Allies were once again on the offensive. Again, the Canadian Army along with their Australian counterparts would play a disproportionate role. On August 8, Australian and Canadian troops attacked Amiens. They would smash the German lines and create a breakout leading to the largest Allied territorial gains of the war. Within three days the Australian-Canadian attack had penetrated 12 miles causing panic among the retreating Germans. Over the next two months, the Canadians alone would advance eighty miles capturing 32,000 German prisoners, 623 field guns, 3,000 machine guns, and 350 mortars. Canadian casualties exceeded 50,000. Though American ground troops did not see action in Europe until the summer of 1918, that did not stop war fever from affecting many American young men, as several of them, during the period of 1914-18 had enlisted in the armies of Canada, Britain and France.

In the summer of 1914 Hobey Baker, America's greatest hockey star of the time, had left New York for a quick vacation through Western Europe. When the war erupted, Baker was in London. Caught up in the feverish events, he had considered enlisting in the British Army. However, at the last moment he was talked out of doing so by a group of New York friends who had journeyed to Europe with him. He returned to New York and resumed his hockey career.

By 1916, he had grown restless of hockey and seeking excitement and a purpose hung up his skates and enlisted with France's volunteer all-American squadron known as the Lafayette Escadrille. For the next two years, he would sit behind a desk and serve as little more than a filing clerk. In April 1918, as casualty rates of Allied pilots continued to climb, Hobey Baker was relieved of his desk responsibilities and assigned to the combat air squadron. By May he had recorded his first official kill. By war's end, in November, he would have three confirmed victories.

By all accounts, Hobey Baker was not happy with the announcement of the war's end. Following the word of the Armistice, Baker had become depressed, to some, even suicidal. No one knows for sure why this may have occurred though one possiblity is worthy of mention. In order to be considered a 'Fighter Ace' one would have needed to record five confirmed kills. Baker's record of three meant that the man who had been considered 'above all others' was by fighter pilot standards only average. Less famous men had achieved more. On December 21, 1918, five weeks after the war had ended, and the same day Baker was scheduled to return to the United States, he decided to

111

take one last flight, his so-called final farewell. His ground crew, sensing something was wrong, advised him not to go. They told him he was testing fate. Too many times, as the stories went, the last flight of a pilot was just that. Baker ignored their pleas and climbed into the cockpit of his Spad fighter and flew away. At 1800 feet the engine suddenly shut off. Almost immediately the plane plummeted to the earth. Though his friends feverishly fought to rush Baker to the hospital and keep him alive they were unsuccessful. Hobey Baker, the greatest hockey player in American history, was dead. He was twenty-six. During his time, he had been proclaimed a god - a star above all others. In the end he had reached for the heavens only to crash to earth a fallen mortal. The life and times of Hobey Baker had been the modern day equivalent of a Greek tragedy. Icarius had fallen, and with it too had the American public's interest in ice hockey. With no heroes to emulate, American hockey was relegated to the shadows of Canadian hockey. It would be 62 years before American hockey would regain its lost glory.

By the end of the war Canada, with a population of only eight million, had succeeded raising an Army of 620,000 men in addition to the tens of thousands of others who had served in other military branches. Boys as young as ten and men as old as eighty had served in the Canadian Expeditionary Force. Every single corner of the country had been impacted by the war. In total, 425,000 Canadian troops had fought in the trenches. Of these, 66,000 had been killed and over 200,000 wounded. Of the dead, 25,000 had no known grave. Uncounted for were the tens of thousands of men who had suffered severe psychological injuries.

Within days of the armistice, as the victors congratulated themselves on a war well fought, largely and conveniently forgotten was the role played by the Canadians. At Versailles, the American delegation, attempting to have the U.S. war contribution recognized to a greater extent than had actually been the case, lobbied to have the Canadian delegation removed as treaty signatories arguing Canada was not, by definition, a nation and her participation in the war had been minimal. The other Allied countries refused to go along with the American effort. For four years Canadians had held firm on the Western Front ensuring that Germany, with its great land army, was held in stalemate. Without the Canadians, the Germans in all likelihood would have emerged victors long before the United States had ever entered the war. Even to this day the reality of this fact flies in the face of the American myth that "the United States won the War" conveniently ignoring the fact that the greatest victories on the Western Front had been achieved by Canadian and other British Empire forces.

Never fully recognized for their achievements, the Canadian troops returned home embittered by their experiences and expressing a subtle anti-Americanism. This anti-Americanism would solidify in Canadian cultural and military circles years later, following a series of published American press articles that criticized the war efforts of the Canadian military declaring Canadian military accomplishments as insignificant in comparison to American.

With the Great War ended, Canadian Ice Hockey took time to record the dead and injured. Many players who were notable in Canada for their hockey excellence had paid the supreme price; men like Frank McGee and Scotty Davidson. In the end, a complete generation had been destroyed or changed forever. In time, this generation of men, hardened by war, would return to the hockey arenas and frozen ponds of their youth. They would bring with them a new sense of identity. A new sense of nationalism, self-pride, as well as the belief that they were unique and unbeatable. In time they would teach their children the rules of the game and instill in them a concept of Canadian nationalism, self-pride, and identity unknown prior to the Great War. It is these concepts, which are the cornerstones of Canadian hockey to this day. The Ice Men had cometh. The game of hockey would never be the same again.

The Third Period

Chapter Ten

The Undeclared War

By 1920, the game of ice hockey had taken on a more complex form as teams representing nations began to compete in international play. Cultural differences, political ideologies, and blind nationalism supplanted sportsmanship. Pride and emotion replaced reason. What was intended to be annual displays of international goodwill became instead a test of human endurance. From South Africa to Nazi Germany and beyond, what were intended to be games became battles. The Great War was over; the longest undeclared war of nations in modern history was about to begin.

Though World War I had been a major setback for the infant sport of professional hockey, the newly formed National Hockey League had been able to survive. Now with the conflict ended and with the return of hundreds of thousands of Canadian men from overseas, the NHL was given a new lease on life. It was now possible to recruit from a much larger pool of talent, as hockey returned to its former civilian footing. Play in the game became bruising and tough as players, hardened by long years of war, returned to resume their careers in the sport.

Throughout the four-year conflict professional hockey continued to be played in Canada in a limited form, providing the population with entertainment that held reminders of pre-war enjoyment, allied to the promise of a return to normalcy once the fighting ended. In this period of war, civilian players built reputations that carried forward into the new era of peace when their compatriots returned to do battle once more on the field of ice.

During the 1918-19 NHL season 'Bad Joe' Hall, Montreal's old man of hockey, continued to be a league leader in penalty minutes. His roughhouse style and brutality made him one of the most feared competitors in the NHL. At one point during the season, when asked by a reporter if he felt that he was too old for such a punishing style of play, Hall replied: *"A fellow is just as old as he feels and right now, I feel I am good for at least 10 more years of hockey."*

Leading the Canadiens to the Stanley Cup Final, Hall and his teammates moved west to do battle against the Pacific Coast League Champion Seattle Metropolitans. At the time of the series the Spanish influenza was sweeping the world and concerns of having five thousand fans confined in one arena caused the Seattle Health Department to issue cotton surgical masks to all spectators. With five thousand masked onlookers in attendance the series was permitted to go on. It was a spectacle never seen before, or since, in the annals of sports.

With the series deadlocked at 2-2-1, the Stanley Cup Championship had to be cancelled as five Montreal Canadien players, Joe Hall, Newsy Lalonde, Billy Couture, Louis Berlinquette, Jack McDonald, and Manager George Kennedy were rushed to the hospital, victims of the influenza virus. Though four of the players would recover, Joe Hall would not. On his fifth day in Seattle's Columbus Hospital, Hall succumbed to his illness and died. The toughest man in hockey was dead at the age of 36.

In a historical sense, by 1920 the concept of sport had evolved into four distinct classes or categories. The first was sport simply for the purpose of exercise, the second as an outlet for the very human vice of gambling and the third for entertainment and spectacle. Then there was the fourth, a newly defined form of controlled modern warfare where athletes represented regions, peoples and nations in competition against others; a war without the killing and a quest for international dominance without the changes of boundaries. It was this concept that was the fuel of victory for the hearts and minds of those whose own self-doubt and inadequacies were epitomized by concepts of nationalism and the need to feel better than other people they did not consider to be their equals. It was a concept of war and hate that harkened back to the simpler days of warfare when armies could live to fight another day. A reenactment of World War I played out without the finality of death. A genteel display of what war should be. The perfect war, where nationalism and arrogance were allowed to fester and where nations could remain supreme. It was the same ideal that was behind the origin of the modern Olympic Games.

With the war over, the Olympic Games, the brainchild of French baron Pierre de Coubertin, were again reinvented with the new idea of having both summer and winter spectacles. This contest of nations and the growth of professional sport would be the proving grounds for the emergence of the first generation of battle-hardened Canadian athletes. Pierre de Coubertin was a nobleman who had been affected greatly by the French defeat in the Franco-Prussian War in 1870–71. He viewed the defeat as a challenge to French pride and turned attention to the concepts of international competition and sport as a way for France to regain its former glory. Studying the English and their sporting history, de Coubertin concluded that their mental abilities in sport had helped them develop the necessary mental and physical skills to establish their empire.

For the French nobleman and his quest for French prestige, the

116

Olympics would be France's new empire - an empire of the mind, where Frenchmen could display their elitism through the triumph of human skill and physical mastery. In sport, the fields of battle would be leveled with neither side having a technological advantage. It would be a forum for chivalry, honor, and national pride - elements sacred to the French and their interpretation of their own history. The Olympics would be de Coubertin's gift to France, an international spectacle that would bestow upon the French their rightful place among the elite nations of the planet. However, it was a legacy based on concepts of hidden hatreds, prejudice and elitism. Prior to the Great War, de Coubertin's Olympics had struggled. The games had been virtually ignored by the world press and had drawn even less attention from the international sporting community or national governments. Then, in 1904, the dreams of French elitism were essentially crushed during the St. Louis Olympics when American athletes dominated all events, taking 238 of the 284 medals, effectively turning the Olympic Games into an American orgy of self-love and nationalism. Even worse, in 1908 in London, biased judging and outright fraud tainted the competitions creating more international strife than goodwill.

The 1912 Stockholm Games received the first taste of "yellow journalism" through extensive coverage by the American press - a press transfixed with its love for all things American. The writers used the Games to expound on homegrown nationalism at the expense of international goodwill, the birth of a tradition of using the Olympics as a forum for self-motivated nationalism and the promotion of racial elitism. In the end, the only thing that truly mattered was the number of gold medals won.

After an eight-year absence, the spirit of Olympic competition was renewed in Antwerp, when Belgium played host to the 1920 Summer Games. Determined to leave the memories of total war behind them, twenty-nine countries represented by 2,669 athletes and competing in 154 events, would mark the return of sports to the international stage. For the first time ice hockey would be included on the list of sports even though the Winter Olympics would not come into existence until 1924. Played as a trial sport only five nations would compete - the United States, Czechoslovakia, Sweden, Switzerland, and Canada as European hockey powers, Germany, Austria, and Hungary, were among the nations to be excluded from the Olympic competition.

Representing Canada would be the Winnipeg Falcons hockey team, a group of Canadian veterans who had played together in the Manitoba military leagues during the First World War. Comprised of Canadians of Icelandic origin, the Falcons had proven themselves both on the field of battle as well as on the field of ice. Unfortunately, three of their original players, Ollie Turnbull, Buster Thorsteinson and George Cumbers, had been killed during the war.

In 1919, the team, with the addition of goalie Wally Byron (the only non-Icelander on the team), defeated the University of Toronto to claim the Allan Cup Championship as the top senior amateur hockey team of Canada and thus was given the right to represent Canada in Antwerp. The Falcons were led by 25-year-old Frank Fredrickson, a former Royal Flying Corps pilot and a man of proven endurance and courage. During the war, while en route to a fighter squadron base in Egypt, Fredrickson's troop ship had been torpedoed. For two days, he had floated in the Mediterranean holding on to a piece of the ship's wreckage, awaiting rescue. Later, because of his excellent piloting skills, he was assigned to pilot training and spent the rest of the war preparing young recruits for combat. Now with the war over, he would lead the Falcons into battle - this time as the captain of the Canadians. In the first game, Canada defeated the Czechoslovakians 15-0. They would follow up with a hard-fought 2-1 victory over the United States, a team comprised of four former Canadians as well as four players from the St. Paul, Minnesota, Athletic Club, including team leader and American World War I veteran, Francis 'Moose' Goheen. A defenseman, Goheen was the master of the on-goal rush - a defensive style of hockey that would not be seen again until the arrival of Eddy Shore in the 1930's and later by Bobby Orr in the 1960's. A man ahead of his time, Goheen led the Americans in their quest for a medal with a 7-0 victory over Sweden, a 16-0 defeat of Czechoslovakia, and a 29-0 whitewash of Switzerland.

With Canada winning the gold on a 3-0 winning record, and a goal differential of 29-1, the United States would claim second place with a 3 and 1 record and a goal differential of 52-2. In the end, the American achievement would go unrecognized back home, for, as had been the case in the spirit of the ancient games, few celebrated a second place finish. The silver medal, according to popular American sentiment, was akin to stealing a kiss from one's sister.

Later, during the first official Winter Olympics at Chaimonix, France, in 1924, both the Canadian and American representative teams would again finish first and second, respectively, with a string of victories that clearly showed the superior levels of talent of the North Americans in relation to their European counterparts. The Canadian team, the Toronto Granites, would post six wins, no losses, and outscore their opponents by a combined total of 132-3. The USA was almost as dominant, keeping a clean slate except in their final 6-1 loss to Canada. The United States would claim four victories and one defeat at the games, with an end score of 73 to 6.

The subsequent Winter Olympics at St. Moritz, Switzerland in 1928 saw the Canadians led by Team Manager Conn Smythe. The team representatives, the University of Toronto, would continue Canada's string of victories by posting a 3-0 winning record with 38 goals for and none against. In three Olympic tournaments, the Canadian amateurs would outscore the competition 199 to 4, an average of almost 50 goals to one - dominance unseen in any other sport to this day.

The 1920's marked a major period of hockey development in the United States. With the advent of radio, Americans could now listen to weekly radio telecasts of hockey games in Canada with play-by-plays delivered by the likes of Foster Hewitt, the first modern hockey sports announcer. In 1924, the NHL crossed over the Canada-United States border and established the Boston Bruins Hockey franchise. That same year, the league added a sixth team, the Montreal Maroons, while increasing its hockey itinerary to a 30 individual team schedule.

The year 1925 saw the Hamilton Tigers finish atop the NHL and the firm favorites to win the Stanley Cup. Despite their success, the Tigers' players were far from happy. The players had signed contracts for seasons of twenty-four games and had seen their schedule increased to thirty games without their salaries being raised in compensation. The Tigers demanded to be paid an extra $200 each to play the NHL championship series against either the Canadiens or Toronto, and threatened to strike if their demands were not met. NHL President Frank Calder was indignant about the demands of the Hamilton players and he announced that the victors of the Montreal vs. Toronto series would be declared NHL champions. On April 17, 1925, the NHL suspended the Hamilton players and fined them $200 each.

On September 22, 1925, the NHL met and dropped the Hamilton franchise, assigning the Tigers' players (who were, officially, still suspended) to a new franchise to be based in New York's Madison Square Garden - the New York Americans. However, there still remained the question of settling the fate of the striking players. Although the league initially demanded payment of their fines, after the players apologized for their actions they were quietly reinstated and the fines forgotten. After that, new franchises were awarded to Chicago and Detroit, and by 1927 the NHL would boast ten professional teams with both American and Canadian divisions made up almost entirely of Canadian hockey players.

Following the war, Conrad Smythe returned to Canada and established himself as a successful businessman. Among his successes was a company that supplied crushed gravel for the Toronto area's construction industry. In the post-war period, he had also been busy building a reputation as a shrewd hockey man at the University of Toronto, and in 1926 he was offered a $10,000 contract to build a new club, to be called the Rangers and to be based in New York. For a total of just $32,000, Smythe assembled a squad of thirty-one players for a team that was to be good enough to win the Stanley Cup within two seasons. However, Smythe was not destined to be the man at the helm for that triumph. Rangers' owner, Colonel John S. Hammond, fired Smythe before the club even played its first game claiming a big club needed a big game coach. Therefore, Lester Patrick was employed and it was he who received the plaudits as the Rangers won the cup with the team Smythe had built.

Smythe took the $10,000 the Rangers had been forced to pay him and bet it all on a football game, backing his alma mater the University of Toronto, to win. The bet paid off and Smythe then wagered his winnings on the Toronto St. Pats to beat Ottawa in a hockey game, winning once again. The money he won allowed Smythe to go into a business partnership.

During the 1926-27 hockey season, the Toronto St. Patrick's Hockey team of the NHL was sold to a managing company controlled by Hugh Aird and Conn Smythe. Almost immediately, Smythe changed the team's name from the Toronto St. Patrick's to the Toronto Maple Leafs, as a tribute to the wartime memory and heroism of Canada's soldiers. As Smythe would later explain:

> *Now, the Maple Leaf to us was the badge of courage, the badge that meant home. It was the badge that reminded us all of our exploits and the different difficulties we got into and the different accomplishments that we made. It was a badge that meant more to us than any other badge that we could think of, so we chose it, hoping that the possession of this badge would mean something to the team that wore it, and when they skated out on the ice with this badge on their chest, they would wear it with honor and pride and courage, the way it had been worn by the soldiers of the First Great War in the Canadian army.*

To further inspire his new warriors, Smythe hired as the club's first president Canada's greatest wartime Flying Ace and recipient of the Victoria Cross William George Barker, a man credited with 71 combat victories. Barker had served along with another Victoria Cross recipient, the legendary Billy Bishop, one of the many Canadian fighter pilots who won glory in the skies over the Western Front.

Born in 1894 in Dauphin, Manitoba, Billy Barker had played

hockey as a youth before enlisting in the Canadian Mounted Rifles at the outbreak of war in 1914. By 1915, he was serving with his regiment in the Canadian trenchline near Flanders, Belgium, and within days of his arrival at the front found himself fighting in the horrific second battle of Ypres. The British Royal Flying Corps was, at this time, very short of aircrew and Barker, seeing a way out of the carnage on the ground, applied for a transfer. Initially he served as an observer/gunner but in 1917 he became a pilot, rapidly becoming recognized as one of the best Allied pilots on duty.

Wounded several times, he was awarded both the Military Cross, with two bars added for further acts of gallantry, and the Distinguished Service Order, with a bar added for other acts of heroism. In the dying days of the war on October 27, 1918, he won the Victoria Cross, the British Empire's highest award for bravery, for courage shown when, despite being wounded three times and fainting twice from the pain, he brought down a German Rumpler two-seater and three Fokker D VII fighters before crash-landing his plane behind British lines in the Foret de Mormal, in France.

After the war, Bishop tried to start a fledgling air service flying out of Toronto, but that quickly went bust and he was forced to sell his aircraft. In 1920 he entered the new Royal Canadian Air Force doing much of the work organizing the new body before retiring from the military again in 1924. Like many other returned soldiers, Barker had a hard time adjusting to life in peacetime. His wounds left him in considerable pain. He was subject to long bouts of depression, and he drank heavily. To Conn Smythe and his fellow investors, however, Barker seemed to embody the spirit of the Canadian fighting man that they wanted to be the example for their new hockey club. Barker became the Maple Leafs first president, but the old hero was not content to be merely a figurehead, and after a series of clashes was quietly dismissed from his post.

Barker tried to farm tobacco from 1924 through 1929, but after catching pneumonia in 1929, he was forced to quit another unsuccessful business. In January 1930, he became president of Fairchild Aviation and died in March of that year after crashing a plane he was demonstrating for the Department of National Defense at Ottawa's Rockliffe Aerodrome. Many people have speculated his death was not an accident but in fact suicide.

By the mid-1920's, the center of American hockey had shifted from the Northern Great Lakes states to the most unexpected location of all - New York City. Home to two professional teams, the Americans and the Rangers, New York was now the greatest hockey center in America. In the New York Public Schools Athletic League, nine high school hockey teams competed in an all-out battle for the title of "Best of New York." Teams comprised mostly of the sons of Jewish and Irish immigrants represented regions of the city where hockey had only a few years earlier never existed. From Jamaica, Queens, to Stuyvesant, Bronx, and on through to Erasmus Hall, Brooklyn, young men played the game with a dedication and determination seldom seen south of the Canadian border.

Men's leagues also existed, with the first school teams emerging in New York as early as 1906. At the same time, city recreational leagues of men from the outlying regions of Flushing, Queens, and Brooklyn's Coney Island sprung up with an ebb-and-flow manner of seasonal play determined more by the availability of indoor ice surfaces than by the popularity of the sport. By 1927, so popular was amateur hockey amongst New York's Jewish population that the management of the New York Rangers franchise played with the idea of changing the names of some of the team's star hockey players in order to make them appear to be Jewish. It was a short-lived plan, but one which received serious consideration and a degree of implementation at the time.

The New York Americans and the New York Rangers were two teams that epitomized professional hockey in the 1920's. They were among the toughest teams ever assembled, led by men who were unyielding in terms of competition and seasoned beyond their years in life experiences and hardships. Teams of Canadians who had spent their youths playing the game of hockey and their teens enduring the realities of war. Men like Red Dutton, star of the New York Americans.

Born in 1898, Dutton, at the age of 16, had joined the Princess Patricia's Canadian Light Infantry at the outbreak of war. He lied about his age in order to enlist. In his twentieth month on the frontline during the Canadian assault on Vimy Ridge, he was seriously wounded when a mortar shell exploded within a few feet of him, ripping open his buttocks, thighs, and calves. Not expected to survive, the doctors had considered amputating both his legs in order to save him. At the last moment, they decided to try to keep him intact, and worked feverishly to save his limbs. He was lucky to survive, and struggled afterward to regain his walking, and later, skating skills. At the time of his injury he was eighteen. Amazingly, considering the wartime injuries Dutton had to endure, he was able to rise to the ranks of professional hockey. In his ten years of playing professional hockey he would become a team leader and one of the most popular sports figures in New York. Among his teammates were 'Bullet' Joe Simpson, a veteran of the Battles of the Somme, Passchendaele, and Amiens; Harry 'Punch' Broadbent, another Canadian military veteran and one who had been awarded a military medal for valor on the battlefield; and Wilfrid 'Shorty' Green, who had, at the age of twenty, been a victim of a German gas attack at the Battle of Passchendaele while serving with the Canadian Expeditionary Force on the Western Front.

At the other end of town, the New York Rangers were led by the likes of Ivan 'Ching' Johnson, a tough-as-nails defenseman who had also served with the Canadian Expeditionary Force as a teenager. His style of hockey was one of punishing hits, fearless skating, and energy. In 436 professional games he would amass 808 penalty minutes and numerous injuries including a broken leg, a broken collarbone, and a broken jaw.

These were the men of professional hockey, men who represented a generation of athletes unlike any seen before. Men who had been raised in the cold and baptized in fire, men who set the standard of Canadian hockey, a standard that all Canadians who were to play the game would aspire to achieve. A level of skill above all others and an ability to endure pain, injury, and anguish second to none.

In Canada, the great rivalry between Toronto and Montreal was nurtured. Throughout his life, Conrad Smythe had been no fan of French Canadians. With his acquisition of the former St. Patricks, he now had the perfect vehicle to extend his hatred - a hatred that grew more hostile as the rivalry between Smythe's Maple Leafs and Quebec's professional hockey representatives, the Montreal Canadiens, intensified. In public speeches, Smythe would often begin his opening remarks with the words, *"Ladies, Gentlemen, and Frenchmen"* - words that won him few friends in Quebec. He was, however, astute enough to realize that the great English Canadian/French Canadian rivalry was good for business.

Smythe's anti-French Canadian viewpoints were not unique. In almost every corner of English Canada one could, if one looked close enough, see the outline of anti-French racism. Even the most patriotic of English Canadian songs expressed a one-sided concept of Canada, a perception not lost on the people of Quebec. A case in point, the often sung song *The Maple Leaf Forever!*

First composed in 1867, it had been a standard of many an English Canadian classrooms. The lyrics spoke volumes on English-French Canadian relations.

> *In days of yore, from Britain's shore,*
> *Wolfe, the dauntless hero, came*
> *And planted firm Britannia's flag*
> *On Canada's fair domain.*
> *Here may it wave, our boast and pride,*

And joined in love together,
The Thistle, Shamrock, Rose entwined
The Maple Leaf forever!

Chorus -
The Maple Leaf, our emblem dear,
The Maple Leaf forever;
God save our Queen, and Heaven bless
The Maple Leaf forever.

One of the great ironies of hockey is the symbolism of the Maple Leaf. Unbeknownst to Smythe, in the purest form the Maple Leaf is a symbol of Quebec. The first reference to Maple Leaf symbolism occurred in 1836 when, during a speech at the St. Jean-Baptiste society in Montreal, society official Denis B. Viger told the crowd:

This tree - the maple - which grows in our valleys . . . at first
young and beaten by the storm, pines away, painfully feeding
itself from the earth, but it soon springs up, tall and strong,
and faces the tempest and triumphs over the wind which
cannot shake it anymore. The Maple is the king of our
forest, it is the symbol of the Canadian people.

During the 1930's Smythe's passions were sealed by two violent encounters, a 1938 fight in the stands with Montreal owner Ernest Savard and an earlier fistfight with Montreal Player-Coach Sylvio Mantha. These incidents, along with the leadership style of Smythe, would in turn help elevate the Maple Leaf making it seemingly a visible symbol of English Canada. For the French, the Montreal Canadiens and their nickname 'Les Habitants' or 'Habs' (a reference to the original French-speaking colonials of Quebec and represented with an 'H' in the middle of the larger 'C'), become in turn a symbol of the French Quebecois. The English-French rivalry, for generations an undercurrent of Canadian history, was made even more symbolic as the two teams seemingly played out a modern sporting version of the c.1759 AD Battle of the Plains of Abraham every time they met on the ice. As Toronto journalist Jeffrey Simpson would write years later:

For a very long time, the Canadiens were Quebec's only
entry into North American sport. Tucked into a corner of
the continent, speaking a different language and feeling
sorely looked-down-upon by English speakers, especially in
the rest of Canada, the Canadiens showed vicariously what

124

Francophone Quebeckers could accomplish.

Years later Smythe would sum up his sentiments towards the Montreal Canadiens by stating:

> *I went to the Somme in the First Great War; the Van Doos were there, and they never gave an inch. Great fighting men, those fellows were, and every one of them was French. Then you have the Montreal Canadiens. When I was with the Maple Leafs, it seems like I battled with the Canadiens for a hundred years and it was tough all the way. Those French players were great, but remember, they always had some English on the team, Harvey or Elmer Lach and this Ken Dryden fella today. Know why that is? Because the English may not be able to rise as high as the French, but they never sink as low, either.*

Representing over 30 percent of the Canadian population, the French were the weak link in the dominion's allegiance to England. Long abandoned by France, and victims of English chauvinism, they did not need to be reminded that force and economic suppression had imposed upon them their position in Canada. If there was ever a social underclass in Canada it was the French Canadians. Their standard of living was the lowest in North America. Repressed in their own land, these self-professed *"white slaves"* had the highest percentage of unskilled workers and poor farmers of any Canadian province. By the late 1930's, because of substandard living conditions, Quebec City earned the dubious distinction of having the highest diphtheria rate in the world. The Quebec community of Trois Riviere had an infant mortality rate of 297 per 1,000 births, which placed it well ahead of Bombay and Madras, India.

In an article written for the American magazine *New Republic* in 1940 entitled *"Province of Quebec,"* the writer Maurice Lenoir summed up the status of French Canadians by addressing the historic plight of the people. Lenoir made special mention that on top of English domination and conquest, if this were not enough, French Canadians also had to deal with the Quebec Catholic Church at the time said to be the most authoritarian, non-military organization in the world. Void of Gallicanism, a movement originating among the French Roman Catholic clergy who favored restrictions on papal control and universal self-determinism, the Quebec Catholic Church had succeeded in creating a type of Frenchman ignorant of Descartes, Montesquieu, Rousseau and the French Revolution. Quebec universities promoted the safe classical works of Corneille and Racine. They had no time for the humor of Voltaire or the anti-religious undertones of Victor Hugo. In the 1930's the local provincial government, at the urging of the Church, had banned the literary works of Mark Twain and Robert Louis Stevenson, claiming they were both anti-religious and pro-Communist.

Decades earlier, the American writer Goldwyn Smith had remarked that the French Canadian was *"a relic of the past preserved like a Siberian Mammoth in ice."* Smith agreed with the assessment given two centuries earlier when Voltaire wrote in *Candide*, that Quebec was nothing *"but a few acres of snow,"* the only escape for many Quebecois being found in the pursuit of part-time sports, particularly the game of hockey.

If the pride of Quebec was the Montreal Canadiens hockey team, then the pride of the Canadiens was Howie Morenz. He was the NHL's first recognized superstar. In fourteen seasons of playing professional hockey, he had spent eleven of those years wearing the Montreal uniform. This so-called *'Babe Ruth of Hockey'* electrified the game and gave the NHL the recognition it needed to ensure press coverage and the respectability it needed to survive in the United States.

Howie Morenz was born into an English-speaking family of Swiss descent that lived in the area of Stratford, Ontario. A standout player in the junior ranks, he came to the attention of the Montreal Canadiens in 1923. Former Montreal player Ernie Suave recommended the young player to his old team after officiating at a game in Stratford. Canadiens boss Leo Dandurand consulted Toronto sports writer, Lou Marsh, who raved about Morenz and urged Montreal to sign him quickly. Dandurand sent Riley Hern to Stratford in the spring of 1923 with a $2,500 check in his pocket and orders to sign Morenz. Hern reported back that Morenz wasn't interested in turning pro, that he had a good job, and was happy playing intermediate level hockey.

Dandurand decided to let Morenz wait, but a long distance phone call from Lou Marsh in July to Dandurand's summer home in the United States prompted the Montreal owner to act. Marsh told him that the Toronto St. Pats were suddenly really interested in Morenz and that Marsh had found out Morenz had some small debts he needed to pay off. He then suggested that a cash-on-the-table payment might secure a signature on a contract. Cecil Hart was dispatched to Stratford with $850 in cash, and the sight of the cash spread on a table persuaded Morenz and his father to sign the contract. Morenz's decision to sign with Montreal caused a minor firestorm. St. Pats accused Montreal of *"kidnapping"* a player from their area. Morenz's minister read scriptures on the wickedness of the Montreal people luring such a fine young man away to a life of tawdry professionalism in their sinful city and the newspapers were full of editorials criticizing Morenz for deserting Ontario.

On August 10, Dandurand received in the mail a check for $850 and a letter from Morenz begging to be released from the contract he had signed. Dandurand saw the hand of the Toronto club in what was going on and warned, *"If Morenz doesn't play for us, he'll play hockey nowhere else."* He also reportedly threatened to reveal that Stratford was paying Morenz $800 a season, with the accompanying threat that this would expose the whole sham nature of Ontario Amateur hockey.

Morenz reported to Montreal but a stream of letters and calls from home kept him unsettled. He pleaded to visit home, which Dandurand agreed to only on condition that he went with an escort who was under orders to *"bring him back bound and gagged if necessary."* Morenz remained unhappy until the season started, but once he was on the ice he quickly settled down and rapidly became the idol of the Montreal fans and the whole Quebec population.

In 1934, he had been traded from Montreal to the Chicago Black Hawks. A year later, he was playing in New York with the Rangers. By season's end, he had been reacquired by Montreal. Sadly, on January 28, 1937, while skating in a game against his old Chicago teammates, and during an all-out rush on the Chicago goal, he had crashed into the boards breaking his ankle and leg in four places. As he was rushed to the hospital it was apparent to most that Morenz's career was over. At thirty-four years of age, the injury was simply too great, and he was simply too old to recover and return to the professional ranks. In the subsequent days ahead, Morenz boasted from his hospital bed that he would skate again, but in time, the reality of the situation began to take a toll on him. He fell into a severe depression. Trying to uplift his spirits his teammates had visited the hospital, often bringing him alcohol to comfort his depression. The alcohol complicated his recovery by not allowing the injuries to properly heal. On March 8, 1937, after being visited by some of his teammates, Morenz fell into a deep sleep and died. The official reports claimed that he had died of a coronary embolism to the brain. His teammates, ignorant of the impact the alcohol had had on his recovery, claimed that he had simply died of a broken heart. When his body was returned to Montreal, an estimated crowd of 250,000 fans lined the streets to pay final tribute to the man who had elevated French Canadian hockey to a level of excellence never before seen in the history of the sport. In the four hours prior to his funeral services, more than 50,000 mourners filed by his coffin, many in tears. Six months later, the NHL would hold their annually sponsored all-star game to raise funds for his family. Morenz had been the hero of Quebec - the man all Quebec children wished they could be. And like so many heroes, he had died suddenly and at a young age leaving his family penniless.

While the Maple Leafs and the Canadiens maintained their traditional rivalry throughout the 1930's, Toronto actually found greater competition in their repeated tussles with the Boston Bruins. The Leafs and the Bruins met five times in the Stanley Cup playoffs between 1933 and 1939.

Conn Smythe and Boston Manager Art Ross were mortal rivals and refused to speak to each other for more than twelve years. The relationship soured in December 1932 when Ross argued a call with referee Cooper Smeaton in the second period of a game with Toronto. All the players quickly became involved and, in the resulting melee, Ross hit Toronto's star defenseman King Clancy. Following a report from Smeaton, Ross was fined $50 but the incident served to make a bad relationship worse as Smythe aired his contempt of Ross to the press. A year later, tempers still had not cooled and on December 12, 1933, when the Leafs visited Boston for the first time that season, the press was in full speculation that there would be trouble in the game.

The game between Toronto and Boston in December 1933 was to be an explosive affair, showing just how dangerous and hard the sport could be, as well as highlighting the elements of thuggery that were prevalent. The first period of the match turned out to be relatively quiet with just one minor penalty going to Toronto badman Red Horner. In the second period, things began to warm up and a string of four penalties were given to the Leafs. Bruins defenseman Eddie Shore, who had been playing his usual tough game, was then knocked unceremoniously to the ice following a forward rush. When he regained his feet, Shore proceeded to either slash the skates of Ace Bailey or shoulder him to the ice. Few witnesses actually saw the incident, which happened behind the play, but the result was that Bailey fell to the ice hitting his head becoming unconscious.

Seeing Bailey lying still on the ice, Red Horner chased after Shore and, after exchanging a few heated words, hit him with a clean punch to the jaw that knocked Shore to the ice cutting the Boston man's face. The referee tossed Horner out of the game and gave Shore a major penalty as Bailey was carried from the ice. Conn Smythe then hit a man who impeded his efforts to reach Bailey and was later charged with assault and battery, which was dismissed in court when a judge accepted Smythe's plea that he'd been under great stress.

Bailey was taken to a hospital where it was found he had a

fractured skull. For the next ten days he was close to death as surgeons twice operated to try and save him. Eventually he recovered consciousness and was pronounced out of danger. President Calder suspended Horner until January 1 but the punishment of Shore awaited Bailey's full recovery. Shore was not allowed to play during that time, but in January, with Bailey's life now out of danger, the NHL announced that Shore would still remain suspended until January 28. This meant he actually missed sixteen games. Smythe was irate, claiming that the punishment was woefully inadequate. On February 14, 1934, a game was played at Maple Leaf Gardens to benefit Bailey, whose career was obviously over. Later, Toronto played against the very first NHL All-Star team that drew two players from each of the other NHL clubs. One of Boston's two representatives was Eddie Shore. Despite the potential for more trouble, all sides agreed to forgive and forget and Shore was treated well by Toronto fans as the Leafs won the game 7-3.

Hockey in the 1930's was a hard, physical sport. During The Great Depression, the worst economic crisis of the 20th century, players fought tooth-and-nail to keep their jobs or to reach the NHL. In this era of hardened men, perhaps the toughest player of them all was Eddie Shore.

Shore was born in Qu'Appelle, Saskatchewan, and came into the NHL in 1926 when the Western Hockey League folded. He would spend thirteen years with Boston as a first team all-star seven times, winning the Stanley Cup twice and earning the Hart Trophy as the league's most valuable player four times. Shore was also the first player of the modern era to hold out for more cash. He had long feuds with the Bruins over money, forcing NHL President Frank Calder to have to intervene and finally settle the dispute in November 1933, with a $7,500 contract award.

While Canadians and the Americans worked towards a North American dominance of the game, Europe struggled to overcome the destruction that inevitably followed in the wake of the WWI. Ice hockey had a fairly low priority in the minds of most Europeans. Few even thought about it. However, as Europe began to recover interest in all sports began to pick up.

During the Great War, the presence of Canadian servicemen's hockey leagues in Britain had enabled the game to both survive and take a step forward. The English gentlemen players at the clubs were amazed by the speed and skill of the Canadians and were quick to try to emulate what they had seen. By the 1920's, Canadian scholars began to return to the university campuses of Europe. They would bring with them the skills of hockey and, in time, would help propel the sport to a higher level. One of these men would be Lester Pearson.

Lester Pearson was born on April 23, 1897, in Newton Brook, Ontario. His upbringing had been shaped by the fact that his family held strong religious beliefs and a desire for learning. The son and grandson of Methodist Ministers, the young Pearson had learned early a love of history as well as an appreciation of sports. As a child he had spent hours in the pursuit of hockey and baseball. During the Great War he had served as a Lieutenant with the Canadian Army Medical Corps and later as an officer with the Royal Flying Corps.

His physical conditioning and intellect had served him well. Following his graduation from the University of Toronto in 1919 he returned to England and enrolled at Oxford University. While at Oxford he joined the Oxford Blues Hockey and Lacrosse Clubs. Though he was not large in stature, he was quick on his feet and possessed strong hockey skills. It has been said that he was an excellent puck-handler and had great offensive speed, which helped make the Blues one of Europe's top teams. Upon his graduation, Pearson returned to the University of Toronto to pursue graduate studies. For five years he worked as an adjunct professor within the History Department as well as a part-time coach of the school's intercollegiate men's hockey team. In 1928, he was offered a job in Foreign Service through the Canadian Department of External Affairs in Ottawa. By now married, he accepted the position - a move that would years later have profound implications for both Pearson, Canada, and the World. Years later, Pearson would reflect on his hockey successes at Oxford:

By European standards, which were modest, we were magnificent and indeed unbeatable. Swiss and other European teams were eager, but not very skillful as yet, while Cambridge had of course no Rhodes scholars. The varsity match which was played at Murren in Switzerland was, in consequence, very one-sided - so much so that it was called off at the end of the second period with Oxford ahead 27-0. Our matches with the European clubs were also easy victories, so we thought, naturally, that we were better than we actually were by Canadian standards.

Comprised of a squad of young Canadian scholars, the Oxford Blues had taken their play to the European continent recording the first of a long series of victories over mainland opponents. In the winter of 1921 they beat the Swiss National Team 9-0 before recording even more lopsided wins over the club teams Davos and St. Moritz en route to winning the tournament that was the forerunner of today's

Spengler Cup. This Oxford team was a featured draw wherever they played in Europe. Led by Pearson as well as star center and former Canadian Royal Flying Corps pilot Dick Bonnycastle, the team dazzled spectators all-the-while laying waste their European competition. Pearson, in particular, caught the eye of the German newspapers and was nicknamed *"Herr Zig Zag"* because of his skating style.

In February 1922, five members of the Oxford team were part of a Great Britain international squad that won a tournament in St. Moritz. The Oxford Blues of the 1922-23 were perhaps the most successful team of athletes and representatives in the annals of amateur sport, ironically, not because of their on-ice performances, but rather due to their off-ice career accomplishments.

One member of the team was Roland 'Rollie' Mitchener. In later years he would become the Governor General of Canada - the Queen's Parliamentary representative in Canada. Other members were equally successful, including Dick Bonnycastle. In 1925, when he was just 23, Bonnycastle joined the Hudson's Bay Company as an accountant and in the following years he made many trips north. He recorded his observations in a diary. His diary was eventually published in book form under the title *A Gentleman Adventurer: The Arctic Diaries of Richard Bonnycastle*. In 1945, he left the Hudson's Bay Company to pursue a career in the Canadian book publishing industry. He would go on to co-found Harlequin Books, a publisher of romance novels. Later, became the first mayor of Greater Winnipeg.

Even with all the on-ice success of Oxford, the British game was not in good shape domestically. In 1923, only the Manchester ice rink was actually staging hockey in England and the British Ice Hockey Association, which had been dissolved during the war, had only just been re-founded that year. It would not be until three years later that England would end a 16-year absence reentering the European Championships in 1926. Oxford University had ensured that British hockey remained alive, even if its pulse was faint. Despite all this, at the Olympic Winter Games in Chamonix, France, in 1924, Great Britain would surprise many by fielding a team good enough to better all its European continental rivals taking home the bronze medal behind Canada and the United States. This gave hope to the dedicated English hockey enthusiasts that eventually the game could obtain greater success in England. But it would be a long road.

London would once again have a working ice rink with the opening of the Ice Club at Westminster, in 1926. That year also saw the first visit to Britain by a top Canadian amateur club when the Montreal Victorias gave a series of exhibition games, culminating in their 14-1 victory over the English National Team. The year 1928 brought the sport a major boost with the opening of new indoor rinks at Richmond in London and a new rink at Crossmoyloof in Glasgow.

By 1930 there were sufficient nations playing hockey for the first World Championships to be held independently of an Olympic games. These games took place in Chamonix, France, and for the first time ever in a major competition, a team from outside North America or Europe began play as the Japanese entered the world stage. However, warm weather and bad ice forced the final games of the tournament to be moved to Berlin. Canada, represented by a Toronto-based team sponsored by the CCM sporting goods company, had been given a bye to the final. Although they were a little game-rusty, they still had no trouble winning yet another title easily handling the European Champion German team by a 6-1 margin. Great Britain had not played well in the Chamonix World Championship, finishing in tenth place. Despite the poor showing, hockey in Britain was beginning to emerge from the doldrums with the 1929 formation of the English Southern Ice Hockey League followed by the 1931 formation of the English League.

The English League consisted of Oxford University, who won the first championship; Cambridge University, a combined team from the Prince's and Queen's sports clubs; and the London Lions of Manchester and Sussex. It also included a team called the Grosvenor House Canadians who played at a rink at the Grosvenor House Hotel in London's ostentatious Park Lane. The Canadians played in front of dinner-jacketed guests in what is now that grand hotel's banqueting hall. Despite the gentlemanly appearances, this team was a radical new departure in British Hockey because the Canadians were openly paid "expense money", introducing professionalism into the British game for the first time. Despite the Grosvenor House's imported Canadian players, Oxford University continued to prove itself to be the best club in Britain and Europe. Larry Bonnycastle (the younger brother of Dick Bonnycastle) was a pure goal-scorer who terrorized defenses in Britain and Europe along with C. H. 'Herbie' Little who was thought of by many as the best goalie seen in European hockey to that date. Upon leaving Oxford, Little would turn down an offer from the Toronto Maple Leafs deciding instead to retire from the sport. After winning the English League Championship, Oxford would defeat the German National Team in Berlin - the same German team that had claimed the European Championship and had lost in the World Final the year before to Canada. The winter of 1931-32 would be Larry Bonnycastle's final year at the university and the last of Oxford's domination in European Hockey.

On February 6, 1932, Oxford and Cambridge played their

annual match in the new indoor rink in the London suburb of Richmond. The Blues would easily win another English Championship defeating Cambridge 7-0 along with, once again, winning the top European honors. At a reception in the spring of 1932, the Mayor of Oxford presented the Blues players with gold medals and as the team captain, Larry Bonnycastle gave a speech on behalf of the team thanking the city. In the late spring of 1932, Bonnycastle graduated and Oxford's golden era of hockey passed into the history books with him. The Oxford team, which had done so much to popularize the game, in the end had shown the country's rink owners and promoters that there was money to be made from hockey. English ice hockey was about to enter the major leagues.

Despite the economic hardships of the period, the 1930's were the golden age for sports in Britain and Europe. Hockey was first broadcast on British radio in 1932; a year after the Streatham rink was opened in London. Though it never held much more than 3,500 fans, Streatham was the first major rink to be built. It would be eclipsed in 1934 when the Empire Pool opened at Wembley in North London with a capacity of 10,000. Wembley was a big venue, and when similarly sized rinks were opened in London at Earls Court in 1935, and at Harringay in 1936, the sport had the arenas needed to hold the large crowds that flocked to see what promoters had dubbed *the fastest game on ice.*

With good money to be made in Britain, often on par with or better than that of the NHL, many top young Canadians crossed the Atlantic to play in England. During the early 1930's, as many as thirty top Canadian players turned down opportunities to play in the NHL in order to play in the English League. Among those to cross over were Tony and Albert LeMay, members of the 1935 Amateur World Champion Winnipeg Monarchs.

The big rinks were not the only event of significance to happen in British hockey in the early 1930's. In 1933, John F. 'Bunny' Ahearne, an Irish travel agent living in London, was appointed Secretary of the British Ice Hockey Association. He was to become a dominant figure in British and later international ice hockey for the next forty years. Though few could have guessed it in 1933, Ahearne's and British ice hockey's greatest moment was rapidly approaching.

Emigration from Britain to Canada was particularly strong in the years leading up to World War I, and picked up again rapidly after the war ended in 1918. These British emigrants took with them a love for sports they had known at home, but their young children, growing up in a new land and a new culture, would learn and play the games of their new homeland. In Canada, that meant hockey and many of these

English-born children, while living in Canada, had often developed as youngsters into fine hockey players. Together, Bunny Ahearne and Philip Vassar Hunter, the president of the British Ice Hockey Association (BIHA), had determined that they wanted Great Britain to make a serious challenge for Olympic glory at the 1936 Winter Olympic Games. They ruled that each club in the British League should have to play at least four British-born players giving, theoretically, the BIHA a pool of 28 good quality British-born, but Canadian-trained players. They also knew they needed a great coach if their Olympic dream was to be achieved. They settled on the Winnipeg-born Percy Nicklin, who had just guided the Moncton New Brunswick Hawks to back-to-back Canadian Amateur Championships winning the Allan Cup in 1933 and 1934. Nicklin had been engaged to coach the Richmond Hawks in London while also recruiting players for the newly formed Brighton Tigers. He was contacted to take the Great Britain national team job and asked to find as many good British born players as he could. Nicklin did his job well. His goalie at Moncton had been the Glasgow native, Jimmy Foster. Foster was certainly the best goalie in the world not playing in the NHL and, in view of many observers, was probably better than most goalies playing in the NHL.

The captain of the Great Britain team was, however, a throwback to the gentlemanly era of the 1920's. Carl Erhardt was born in 1897, partly of German decent he learned to play hockey at exclusive schools in Germany and Switzerland. Being the oldest player in the tournament at the age of thirty-nine, he was still a fine rushing defender. Erhardt usually played the game by an old-fashioned, gentlemanly code, though he could still take out a menacing adversary with one good solid hit.

The 1930's became a time when the relationship between Britain and her dominions were being reassessed. The new dominions had lost the lives of hundreds of thousands of their best and brightest young men in the horror that was World War I. However, they also gained a strong sense of their identity as nations and not merely as British colonies. This new assertive nationalism caused severe strains between the mother country and her offspring nations throughout much of the 1920's and 30's, though these strains did not manifest themselves on the diplomatic front.

In 1932, the official relationship between Britain and Australia nearly broke irreparably over, of all things, cricket. The controversial tactics of the English team touring Australia (the ball was apparently being deliberately bowled at the opposing player's head and upper body, the so-called "bodyline") threatened, at least for a while, to destroy the imperial fabric. The 1936 Olympic Games were to cause a smaller, but similar, rift between Britain and Canada.

F. A. Gilroy, the president of the Canadian Amateur Hockey Association (CAHA), was a man with problems in the winter of 1935-36. Canadian custom had dictated that the Allan Cup winning team of the previous year would represent the country in international play the following year. In 1935, the Halifax Wolverines had won the Canadian senior championship. However, when it was discovered that five star Halifax players and their coach were going to play elsewhere for better pay in 1936, the CAHA decided to offer the Olympic berth to the Port Arthur Bearcats who had lost the Allan Cup Final to Halifax. This produced howls of protest from the Montreal Royals, who claimed they had played better in losing to Halifax in the semi-final than Port Arthur had in the final. In the end, seven players from Port Arthur, two from Montreal, and a sprinkling of top players from other clubs were formed into the 1936 Canadian Olympic team.

Just days prior to the opening of the Olympics, Gilroy did his best to disrupt British plans to field a contending team. He claimed the British and the French teams were using ineligible players. Gilroy argued two British Olympic players, Alex Archer and Jimmy Foster, and 16 others currently playing in the English League should be declared ineligible for the Olympic Games because they did not have permission to leave the jurisdiction of the CAHA. As for the French, the Canadians argued their entire talent base should be disqualified from participation. Initially, the International Ice Hockey Federation (IIHF) ruled on the side of the Canadians. Both the British and the French threatened to withdraw from the tournament prompting negotiations to continue into the start of the Olympics Games. The issue of player eligibility would finally be resolved when the British declared that top Canadian goaltender, Jimmy Haggary, be declared ineligible because he had also played in the English League and also had not received permission to leave the jurisdiction of the CAHA. Faced with the prospects of losing one of their own star players, the Canadians withdrew their protest. The French were so incensed over the ordeal they almost did not play in the Olympics choosing to do so just before their first game.

The 1936 Winter Olympic Games were held at Garisch-Partenkirchen in Adolf Hitler's new Germany. For Hitler, the games were an opportunity to promote his shameless concepts and notions of Aryan supremacy and German glory, as he would subsequently do during the 1936 summer games in Berlin. It was the ultimate culmination of Nazi ideology and German sports excellence. For *"handsome Adolf,"* as he was affectionately referred to by his ideologically blinded followers, was to be the star of the ceremonies.

The man who rebuilt Germany in the face of a global depression, and from the ashes of war, had high hopes riding on the success of his German National Hockey team (even though one of the team's star players was a Jew - a fact conveniently overlooked for the greater glory of Germany and the Aryan ideal).

For years the German state had secretly funded their hockey program. Ice hockey was the most visible team sport of the Winter Olympics and was, therefore, the ultimate German prize. Yet, in order for the Germans to obtain mastery of the game they would have to first defeat their great enemy - the Canadian hockey player. The Germans hoped that their hockey team would achieve the improbable feat and use their Aryan abilities to defeat the Canadians and bring glory to the Third Reich. It was to be a coming out party for Hitler - a glorious moment in the annals of Aryan youth. For years the Nazis had marveled at Canadian hockey and, in the early 1930's, German writers had analyzed the sport in an attempt to determine the Canadian hockey secrets.

During the 1920's, the Germans embraced Canadian-style hockey. The hockey power Berliner SC, under the coaching of Canadian Dr. Blake Watson, had been the leading club in Europe after Oxford University winning the Spengler Cup in 1924, 1926, and 1928. The German National Team, made up largely of these Berlin players, won the European Championship in 1930 and 1934. The Germans entertained high hopes for their prospects on the ice at the 1936 Olympics, and the new Nazi government channeled both cash and other forms of support to the national team.

For the Germans, winning wasn't just a matter of national pride; it was also a matter of racial pride. As early as 1933, the German Nazi Minister of Propaganda Joseph Goebbels had seen in sport the necessary ingredients needed to create the perfect civilization. On April 23, of that year he wrote:

> *German sport has only one task: to strengthen the character of the German people, imbuing it with the fighting spirit and steadfast camaraderie necessary in the struggle for its existence.*

By developing sport to a higher form, Goebbels believed that the Aryan youth could be strengthened and, in the end, be better prepared for war. This was in keeping with earlier German theorists and the concepts of Nazi Aryan doctrine. Arguing that the Olympics could be used for propaganda purposes as well as a showcase of Aryan supremacy, he convinced Hitler (himself, no great fan of the Olympic

136

movement) to make available state funds for the development of athletes for the sole purpose of ensuring international sporting victories.

In 1936, Germany's greatest hockey player was Rudi Ball. Considered by many to be the reason for the Germans obtaining the bronze medal in the 1932 Olympics, Ball was half-Jewish and had only one month prior to the Games fled to France for fear of Nazi persecution. Desperate to defeat the favored Canadians and to show the International Olympic Committee (IOC) that they could curb their anti-Semitism for the Olympics, the German organizers had asked Ball to rejoin the team. Having been promised that his safety would be guaranteed, Ball returned from Paris making him the only Jew to represent the German state during the 1936 Winter Olympics. In the months prior to the Winter Games, opposition to growing Nazi anti-Semitism had escalated with international groups calling for a boycott of the German-hosted event. Nowhere was this opposition more pronounced than in the United States. In a letter to the International Olympic Committee, the American IOC President and Representative Ernest Lee Jahncke wrote on November 25, 1935 to the President of the IOC, Count Henri Baillet-Latour:

Neither Americans nor the representatives of other countries can take part in the Games in Nazi Germany without at least acquiescing in the contempt of the Nazi's for fair play and their sordid exploitation of the Games.

Jahncke's concerns were ignored, as the International Olympic Committee was more interested in seeing the Games staged than worried about where the event would take place or about the political motives of the host. In the end, instead of addressing Jahncke's letter, the IOC instead voted to remove him from their organization and replace him with Avery Brundage, a man less likely to criticize or embarrass the Olympic movement. Jahncke would be the first member in IOC history to be ejected due to his moral stance. Later, Avery Brundage would proclaim: *"No nation since ancient Greece has captured the true Olympic spirit as has Germany."*

In the end, though Nazi Germany did indeed win 136 Olympic medals, the German hockey team failed to meet the expected goals of their country, losing to both Canada and Great Britain in semi-final rounds, and failing to advance to the medal round. From the start, the Garmisch-Partenkirchen Games had been unusual in terms of hockey. Britain had fielded its strongest team in years. Of the twelve members that comprised the squad, nine had been born in Britain, but had moved to Canada as children where they learned to play the game alongside their Canadian counterparts. A tenth player, Gordon Dailley, was in fact a former Canadian national and military veteran. During their first game, Britain opened with a defensive struggle against Sweden and owed their 1-0 victory largely to the brilliance of Foster between the pipes. They then beat Japan 3-0 to progress as winners of Group D into the semi-final round. It would be Japanese goaltender Teiji Honma who would become the third goalie to wear a facemask in competitive ice hockey. The first being a Swiss goalie named Wylemann in the 1920's. Followed later, in 1932 by Clint Benedict, the first goalie to wear a mask in the NHL. The idea that goalies wearing facemasks is a new concept is yet another example of a great hockey myth as American indoor hockey goalkeepers had been wearing facemasks at least as early as the 1890's.

Drawn in a semi-final group with Canada, Germany, and Hungary, Nicklin knew his men would need to play at the top of their form to progress. On the eve of the opening semi-final round game was against Canada, the team's best offensive player, Gerry Davey, was in bed with the flu. Davey, an experienced Streatham player, had learned the game when his family moved to Port Arthur, Ontario. Ashen-faced and clearly sick, he had refused to sit out the match and within 40 seconds of the opening period had put Britain in the lead with a shot from long range. Just over halfway through the period, Ralph St. Germain tied the game up. It stayed that way until 90 seconds from the end when Gordon Dailey intercepted a pass and skated in on goal. He shot and the goalie padded the puck away, but Edgar Brenchley got in quick enough to sink the rebound. Ten thousand spectators went wild as Britain celebrated an unlikely victory ending the Canadians 20-game winning streak. Next the British played a triple overtime game against Germany that finished in 1-1 tie. They followed it up with a 5-1 victory over Hungary, advancing to the medal round.

Both Britain and Canada qualified for the same pool and, under the rules of the tournament, Britain's 2-1 victory over the pre-tournament favorites would be counted in the medal round standings. In Pool B, the United States and Czechoslovakia had both advanced. With the European Championship officially up for grabs, Davey would again lead the English to victory scoring a hat trick on route to their 5-0 defeat of the Czechs. In the end, the tournament came down to the final game. If the U.S. could defeat Canada without conceding a goal, or by 5-1 or more, they could snatch the gold medal on goal differential. However, the schedule was not kind to the American team as they had played a long game with the British a day earlier finishing in a 0-0 draw. Tired, and without injured captain Johnny Garrison, the

Americans never found their spark and were defeated 1-0 by Canada. A miracle had happened; Great Britain became Olympic, World, and European Champions and, with their games being broadcast over the radio back to England, the players instantly become national heroes back home. This would be British hockey's finest moment.

Fresh off Olympic victory, British ice hockey was on top of the world. With players able to make good money, many very talented Canadians were now flocking to England to play. In 1936, the English League expanded internationally adding two teams loaded with French Canadians playing out of Paris, France.

The Paris Rapides and the Francais Volantes opening amid a fanfare of publicity, but the ambitious project was doomed to failure. Reeling in an economic crisis worsened by American tariffs, the French government responded by devaluating the Franc by twenty-five percent, in September 1936. The move made travel costs for the two French teams prohibitive. The owners of the Paris clubs quickly gave up operating the teams from within France and in November the players were relocated to Britain, finishing the season as the Manchester Rapids and Southampton Vikings.

Hockey in the 1930's was being played against a background of economic and political turmoil. The Depression was in full swing worldwide and a growing militarism was sweeping across the nations. Conflict was in the air and poverty and despair were all around. For those who could afford tickets sports presented a momentary release, an escape into a different simpler world. At the arena there was conflict, there were fights, there were good guys to cheer, and bad guys to jeer. It was all seemingly harmless entertainment, though one which always showed signs of a dangerous undercurrent - the darker side of human sports. George Orwell wrote:

> *Sport is an unfailing cause of ill will, and how could it be otherwise? I am always amazed when I hear people saying that sports creates goodwill between the nations, and that if only the common peoples of the world could meet one another at football or cricket, they would have no inclination to meet on the battlefield. Even if one didn't know from concrete examples that international sporting contests lead to orgies of hatred, one could deduce it from general principles. At the highest-level sport is frankly 'mimic warfare'. Serious sport has nothing to do with fair play. It is bound up with hatred, jealousy, boastfulness, disregard for the rules, and sadistic pleasure in witnessing violence. In other words, it is war minus the shooting.*

In the 1930's, the old gentlemanly era of sports was coming to an end. Professionalism and nationalism had started to overwhelm what had simply been games of recreation. There were those who now saw in sports something more than just a game. The relentless rise of both Fascism and Communism was creating a climate where national strength was being linked to national pride and sports. Further Orwell observations,

> *There cannot be much doubt that the whole thing is bound up with the rise in nationalism - that is, with the lunatic habit of identifying with large power units and seeing everything in terms of competitive prestige. If you wanted to add to the vast fund of ill-will existing in the world, you could hardly do better than by a series of football matches between Jews and Arabs, Germans and Czechs, Indians and British, Russians and Poles, Italians and Yugoslavs - each match to be watched by a mixed audience of 100,000 spectators.*

Ice hockey, in the period between the two World Wars, was not enough of a mainstream sport to receive the attention from governments and fans that a sport like soccer or track and field did. However, in a period that saw ice hockey advance in Britain and Europe in stops and starts, the number of players and the standard of play increased dramatically. Still, the sport remained largely a minority even in such hotbeds as Germany and Czechoslovakia.

After a three thousand year absence, competitive hockey returned to the African Continent in 1936 when, at the urging of the Canadian Trade Commission to South Africa, the University of Witwatersrand formed the South African Ice Hockey Association. Although the heat of Africa was no place for natural ice, artificial ice rinks had existed in Johannesburg as early as 1910, when members of the sports-mad population of Johannesburg, enriched by the gold that lay literally beneath their streets, imported the latest in ice-making equipment.

The South African Ice Hockey Association immediately invited Oxford and Cambridge Universities to play some exhibition games as part of the British Empire Exhibition of 1936 on a rink at Milton Park in Johannesburg. This gave the sport just the boost it needed and local enthusiasts, who had learned to play roller hockey, started trying the ice version of the sport. In 1937 South Africa became the first, and still only, African country admitted into the IIHF and by 1939 a five-team senior league was in existence in Johannesburg.

In 1937, the World Championships were held in Britain for the first time. Great Britain had high hopes for repeating its triumph at the Olympics the previous year, but Canada, represented by the Kimberly Dynamiters of British Columbia, went unbeaten and restored Canada to what it considered its rightful place on top of the hockey world. Great Britain slipped to second place but was still crowned as European Champions.

Under the gathering cloud of war of the late 1930's , the popularity of hockey in Britain continued to rise and began to boom and on October 29, 1938, the English League game between Harringay and Streatham became the first hockey game to be televised anywhere in the world. Later that winter, Canada would win another world title with runner-up, Great Britain, claiming their fourth European Championship, in Prague, Czechoslovakia. It was to prove to be among the last major events staged in the Czech capital before Hitler completed his annexation of the nation.

The Trail Smoke Eaters, or 'Smokies' as they were affectionately called, would become Canada's representative for the 1939 World Championships held in Basil and Zurich, Switzerland. The Smokies were the pride of Trail, British Columbia, a community located in the southeastern corner of Canada's westernmost province, and had won seven consecutive Provincial titles before finally winning their first Allan Cup. It was a mining community founded in the early 1890's by two American mining speculators who had hoped to build a smelter operation that could process the mined ores from the nearby Rossland Mines. In 1896, the first smelter was completed. Throughout World War I the Trail smelter operations expanded and by 1920 the community was home to a growing population of working class Canadian miners and European, mostly Italian, emigrants. By 1938, the population of Trail had reached 10,000, making it one of the largest, hardest working, toughest, and most isolated towns in Western Canada. It was the perfect breeding ground for Canadian hockey - a place where men truly were as big as the mountains and among the best in athletics, emotional character, and work ethic.

Following a cross-Canada fundraising tour, the team would begin a 98-day, 46-game European tour through Great Britain, the Netherlands, Germany, Czechoslovakia and Poland. They would dominate their competition only losing one game to an English League all-star squad made up entirely of Canadians, representing Wimbley, England. Their success would carryover into the World Championships, as the Smokies would win all eight of their tournament games, outscoring their opposition 42 to 1. The only goal scored against them would be inadvertently shot into their own net by one of their own players during the game against the Czechoslovakians, a team coached by Trail native Mike Buckna. Such was their hockey domination that the European press would claim that they were the best hockey team that had ever played in Europe. In reality, they may have very well been the greatest Canadian Amateur Hockey team in history.

Chapter Eleven

Sons of the Fathers

On September 3, 1939, following the German invasion of Poland, Britain declared war on Germany. Canada, due to its still close political ties to Britain and the British Empire found itself facing the prospect of being drawn into another European war. Though English-Canadian newspapers were already announcing that a state of war existed between Canada and Germany, in truth, the decision to wage war on Germany would depend on the vote of the Canadian Parliament and not on the actions of Britain. Unlike World War I, there would be little Canadian celebration of anticipated future battles. The Great War had scarred Canada's national psyche and Canadians had seen themselves in the Great War more as victims than victors. Unlike Britain, France, and the United States, Canada had profited little from the financial demands of the 1919 Treaty of Versailles, while the heroic actions of her soldiers had been conveniently overlooked by foreign nations, historians and others self-motivated groups determined to manifest their own nations' accomplishments and sacrifice, regardless of whether or not a full and accurate story was being told.

On September 7, 1939, the Canadian Parliament convened and two days later, on September 9, Canada's Parliament officially declared war on Hitler's Germany. Again, Canadians would be asked to answer the call of war. Again, the defense of the country would fall on the backs of a generation of men and boys trained in the sport of hockey -- a sport specifically designed to instill the skills necessary to produce a successful warrior. A game that had, in the twenty years following the end of World War I, produced a newer, more resilient breed of Canadian hockey player, one molded in spirit and stamina by a generation of men who had witnessed the brutality of war firsthand.

With the outbreak of war, many of the Canadian stars of the English National League decided to either stay in Canada or join up with the armed forces. The league would only have just enough players to ice three teams, Harringay, Streatham and one of the Wembley clubs, to play out the 1939-40 season. After the completion of the season, the lights would go very dim on British ice hockey as the sport would be placed on hold for a period of five years as players and fans, not only in Britain but also around the globe, woke up to find that the world had fallen into yet another abyss.

On December 18, 1939 the first contingent of Canadian troops arrived by ship in England. Under a banner of celebration, the

Canadian commander General Andrew MacNaughton, confident that his forces would prove themselves as capable as those who had set foot on these shores two decades earlier, proclaimed that *"the Canadians were a dagger pointed at the heart of Berlin,"* a statement and message designed for the benefit of the German press. A subtle reminder that England and France were not alone and that Germany's most feared World War I adversary was again prepared to engage Germany's fighting forces on the continent.

In the summer of 1940, as the German Blitzkreig rolled through France, the French Government cabled the British seeking immediate troop reinforcements. On June 11, under the cover of darkness, the first Canadian soldiers began to land at Cherbourg, France. They were scheduled to receive support by a second Canadian force due to arrive on June 20. Armed with 72 field guns, the Canadians began their advance north towards Paris. On June 13, one week earlier than expected, the second Canadian force landed in France. Coming ashore at Brest, they quickly set up positions around Laval and Le Mans. As the force began a rapid move inland, with some units traveling over two hundred miles in an effort to link up with the earlier Canadian units, word came of the French surrender. What was to have been an aggressive move north toward the old World War I battlefronts and an expected all-out engagement with the German enemy, suddenly became a desperate race by the Canadians to the landing ports of southern France for an evacuation to England before imminent enemy capture. As the World watched the British and French situation unfold at Dunkirk, few noticed or were even aware of, the Canadian drama unfolding in the south of France. At the height of the confusion, amazingly, only six Canadian soldiers failed to be evacuated.

Back in England, with most of their equipment still intact, the Canadians were assigned to the southern coasts, the area most vulnerable to the anticipated German invasion. With the fall of France, Canada, with a population of only eleven million, was now the second largest military power opposing Hitler's Germany. As the seriousness of the situation began to be realized, attempts to mobilize the Canadian war effort increased. As had been the case in the Great War, legions of former and current hockey players were among the throngs of Canadian volunteers flocking to the recruiting stations, prepared and determined to do their part.

Among the more notable individuals to volunteer was the Great War veteran and Canadian actor Raymond Massey who would, by 1943, assume the rank of Major. Others were equally in the forefront. Conn Smythe, a commissioned Major, along with Rhodes scholar and former hockey player, Clarence Campbell, would be added to the swelling ranks of Canadian soldiers, along with a venerable who's who of Canadian National Hockey League talent. So complete was the Canadian nation's transformation from at peace to at war that, by 1945, they would boast an army of over one million men. Their Navy would be increased 500-fold, and would play a major role in supplying and protecting the North Atlantic Sea lanes, the lifeline of the Allied European war effort and besieged England. By 1945, the Canadian Navy would be the third largest naval power on the planet, with a fleet of ships numbering 700 -- the numerical equivalent of the United States Navy during the height of the Cold War.

In addition, by 1945, Canadians would once again command the air, with Charlie G. "Chubby" Powers, a former hockey player of the powerhouse team Quebec City Bulldogs from 1903-1909, serving as Canadian Air Minister, overseeing the creation of the world's third largest air force -- third only to the United States and Great Britain. For three months following the British defeat at Dunkirk, all that stood against a German invasion of England was the British Royal Air Force guarding the skies and the Canadian Army guarding the British coastlines.

Following the Battle of Britain and the diminished threat of a German invasion, the first signs of tension between the local British population and the now-seemingly restless Canadian troops began to show. At the time, the average Canadian soldier in England was only 19 years of age. Fewer than two percent of them had obtained higher than a sixth-grade education, with many from towns and isolated farm communities with populations of fewer than 4,000 inhabitants.

Aside from cultural differences between the two groups, part of the problem between the British and the Canadians was the Canadians' unfamiliarity with functioning in a tradition-bound, class-structured society. This problem was magnified tenfold by the fact that part of the high profile contingent of Canadian troops upon which the British relied for protection was not only so-called *"former colonials,"* but also a large contingent of French Canadians. The English High Command held little tolerance for the French Canadians and their proud nationalistic tendencies. What bothered the British generals even more was that much of the defense of England was in the hands of these perceived social inferiors.

In the weeks that would follow, discontent among the lower Canadian ranks would continue to grow, especially among the French Canadians, and by July 1941, foibles in discipline were reportedly widespread. Reports of increased assaults on officers by enlisted men, smoking while on parade, refusals to get out of bed at reveille, and insolence and absent-without-leave incidents became common.

145

Discontent and frustration were reaching a boiling point. In the twenty months from December 1940 to August 1942, a total of 3,308 Canadian soldiers were court-martialed. At the same time, civilian authorities in England reported 23,039 offenses committed by the servicemen of the Canadian First Division. In the case of the later-arriving Second Division, an additional 21,492 incidents were recorded. On average, by 1942, a Canadian soldier was being arrested in England at a rate of one every 18 minutes. Following a rash of Canadian soldier suicides, the Sussex Coroner remarked:

> These soldiers very unselfishly come to this country for the purpose of giving us aid. We are apt to forget because they speak our language, that they are to all intents and purposes, in a foreign country, just as much as we should be in Libya.

German propaganda sources even took notice of the problems. In a radio broadcast, an announcer remarked of their old foe:

> If you really want to take Berlin, give each Canadian soldier a motor cycle and a bottle of whisky; then declare Berlin out-of-bounds and the Canadians will be there in 48 hours.

In September 1941, Canadian Prime Minister William Lyon-Mackenzie King pleaded with Churchill to commit Canadian troops to battle, adding, *"I don't know how long I can go on leading my country while our troops remain inactive."* Churchill, not wanting Canadian troops to be seen in the forefront of the English war effort, refused, stating that he did not want to give the impression that the British were relying on Commonwealth troops to fight their battles, as had been the case in the last Great War. Later, Prime Minister King was forced to tour Canadian military bases in England under armed bodyguard; for fear that the troops he was to inspect would attack him.

Canadians sports and amateur hockey leagues were rapidly shutting down amidst the vast recruitment of young men. By December 1941, the buildup of Canadian troops in England reached 200,000, an incredible figure given the fact that in 1939 Canada's entire army numbered only 4,500. Prior to the December 7, 1941 Japanese attack on Pearl Harbor, the Canadian Government, responding to request made by Winston Churchill, had dispatched two battalions of soldiers for the protection of Hong Kong. What has often been overlooked and forgotten are the other Japanese attacks which occurred within hours of the attack on Pearl Harbor, the attacks on the Philippines, Malaya, and Hong Kong. For more than two and a half

146

weeks, two thousand Canadian soldiers, outnumbered more than ten to one, fought a gallant and desperate battle in Hong Kong in the vain hope of gaining time for Allied reinforcement. That help never arrived and 1200 Canadians were marched off to Japanese prison camps, many never to return.

As Western newspapers reported on the possibility of a Japanese landing in Canada, and amid the calls in Canada to remove the troops from England and send them to the Pacific Theatre, tensions in the Canadian camps were reaching the boiling point. Brawls continued to break out as soldiers refused to follow orders. After three years of inaction, the Canadian Army had ceased to be an effective fighting force. By 1942, the Canadian Overseas Army in England, the so-called "Army of the Ice Men," was on the verge of disintegration.

By the spring of 1942, even with the entry of the United States into the war, the Western Allies were on the threshold of military collapse. In January, General Erwin Rommel had gained the offensive in North Africa. By February, Allied shipping losses in the North Atlantic had reached the breaking point. On June 14, Tobruk, in Libya, fell to the Axis with thirty thousand British and Australian troops surrendering with little more than a few shots being fired. It was one of the most humiliating British military defeats in history, and one that sent shockwaves through British military circles that were fearful the British Army was no match for the enemy. Following the defeat of the British at the Battle of Knightsbridge, the English 8th Army was forced into retreat. The British were now pushed back into Egypt, ensuring their total defeat at the Suez Canal.

The Americans believed that the solution to the problem facing the Allies could be found through a staged military operation in Northern France, in a plan of action codenamed SLEDGEHAMMER - an operation designed to buy the Allies much needed time as they awaited American military reinforcements. Operation SLEDGEHAMMER called for the invasion of Northern France in either August or September 1942. Its purpose was to gain a foothold on the European continent, which would lead eventually to a full-scale Allied assault on Germany in 1943, called Operation ROUND-UP. In addition to securing a continental foothold for the Allies, SLEDGEHAMMER would also help relieve the embattled Russians and force the Germans to fight on as many as three fronts. At the very least, SLEDGEHAMMER would ensure Russian continuation in the war, since it would demonstrate the West's resolve to fight and aid the Russians.

The Americans made no effort to hide the fact that the landing, called for in SLEDGEHAMMER, would require ten divisions and be purely *"sacrificial"* in nature. The force would come ashore and remain through the winter, holding a beachhead against continuous enemy attack. Unlike Dunkirk, there would be no evacuation. If the plan were to go ahead, the bulk of the forces would be Canadian troops stationed in England. In the end, it would mean the deliberate sacrifice of the entire Canadian Overseas Army, a force almost equal to a quarter million men. A sacrifice considered by a number of political and military officials in Washington and London to be *"neither here nor there,"* and a small price to pay in order to keep Russia in the war. As it turned out, the plan did not go forward for the simple reason that there were not enough Naval and transport craft in England to carry the Canadians across the Channel. There were only enough landing craft to transport 6,000 troops.

On May 31, following meetings with Soviet Foreign Minister Molotov, Roosevelt cabled Churchill seeking the Prime Minister's support for a second front to be scheduled for August 1942. The President feared that the Russians would be knocked out of the war and be forced, as in 1918, to sign a separate peace treaty with Germany. All parties realized that something drastic had to be done. Operation RUTTER was a plan calling for an amphibious raid on the port of Dieppe. The operation, originally intended for British commandos, was instead assigned to elements of the Canadian Second Division in hopes that the operation would alleviate some of the pressures associated with having the Canadians standing idle in Britain. On May 20, Canadian troops were moved from their bases in Sussex to the Isle of Wight for amphibious training. Earlier, reports from the training grounds had indicated that the operation had all the markings of failure. Troops had routinely landed off target, security was a problem and the operation lacked the necessary naval and air power to provide adequate support. Most amazing of all, the plan ignored basic and tried amphibious military rules and lessons.

The Canadian writer Ralph Allen in his 1965 book *Ordeal By Fire*, wrote that the RUTTER plan made sense *"only if it were considered as an exercise with live ammunition aimed to kill (where) surprise was neither hoped for nor intended."* In other words, it was a plan intentionally designed for failure.

From the start, the Canadian military questioned the raid's logic and as this criticism grew amongst their ranks, orders from the British command came down to the Canadian leadership advising that all dissent was to be suppressed. Furthermore, Canadian commanders were advised that they would not be allowed to sit in at the Command Center during the operations, effectively separating the Canadian commanders from their own troops. Later, under protest, the British relented somewhat, granting the Canadians *"observer status"* during the operations.

On July 3, a force of six thousand men, five thousand of whom were Canadian, were loaded onto ships destined for Dieppe. However, the weather deteriorated and the operation was postponed. Five days later, with the troops still on board the ships, the operation was cancelled. Within days of the cancellation, efforts were secretly underway to reinstate the operation. The raid was renamed Operation JUBILEE and a new staging date, August 19, was chosen. Still, security had been jeopardized and all military logic was either ignored or deliberately vetoed. There were even reports that the Germans were anticipating an Allied attack.

On the evening of August 18, under a veil of darkness, an Allied armada of 237 ships left ports in Southern England heading in the direction of Dieppe. Among the men on board were five thousand-one hundred soldiers of the Canadian Second Division. Unknown to the men, the events about to unfold would mark a turning point in Canadian military history. In only seven hours of battle, the Canadians would lose more men at Dieppe than the United States had lost during the War of 1812, the Mexican-American War, or the Spanish-American War. Before the day would end, the Canadians would record a 70 percent casualty rate. Of the Canadians who landed at Dieppe, fewer than 1450 returned to England, many of whom were wounded. The first attempt to land a large force on the European continent since the evacuation of Dunkirk had turned into a horrendous slaughter.

For two days following the August 19, 1942 amphibious raid, bodies of Canadian soldiers, the once youthful pride of the Canadian Army, continued to wash up on French beaches. Not since the 1916 Battle of the Somme had so many Canadian soldiers been killed. At Dieppe, men had been killed, wounded or captured at a rate of one every five seconds. In four hundred minutes, the heart of Canada's Second Division had been riped out. In one single action, a force of men that had taken three years to equip and train had ceased to exist. It would take thirty years before an Allied account of the incident would be *"officially"* released.

Some of Canada's finest and most visible regiments had fatality rates of 96 percent. The Toronto-based Royal Regiment, for example, had numbered over five hundred men only days prior to Dieppe. After the battle, only two men were accounted for back in England. The Mont Royals of Montreal, the French Canadian Regiment that was the pride of Quebec, had landed square in the middle of the Dieppe beach front during the height of the battle - easy pickings for the murderous German machine guns. For all intents and purposes, the regiment no longer existed. For the people of Quebec, the slaughter of the Mont Royals was unconscionable, and just another example of British contempt for French Canadians.

At Dieppe, even the Germans had been shocked by what they had seen. On the morning of August 19, in the midst of preparing a documentary on the German's line of defenses known as *The Atlantic Wall*, a German film crew happened to be shooting footage of the cliff tops overlooking Dieppe. They would have a bird's eye view of the Canadian landings, allowing them to film one of the most tragic military events of the twentieth century. Their footage seems surreal as it captured the final moments of a group of men thrown to the wind by questionable military logic and opportunist political leadership.

The German General Conrad Haase, Commander of the German 302nd Division that defended Dieppe, wrote of the battle:

> *The fact that the Canadians did not gain any ground on the main beaches was not due to any lack of courage, but because of the concentrated defensive fire.*

Later, while some British officials attempted to cover up the slaughter by blaming the casualty rates on the poor fighting abilities of the Canadian troops, the official report of the German Fifteenth Army was even more direct in their assessments of the situation as it stated:

> *The large number of English prisoners might leave the impression that the fighting value of the English and Canadian units employed should not be highly estimated. This is not the case. The enemy, almost entirely Canadian soldiers, fought - so far as he was able to fight at all - well and bravely.*

Following the raid, with its many unanswered questions, as well as a series of questionable military actions using Canadian troops in Italy, the strains of distrust between the Canadian and British militaries grew even more apparent. Canadian military officials now accused British officials of using Canadian soldiers as sacrificial pawns for the sake of British politics.

By 1943, as discontent among the Canadians and their English allies continued to grow, the Canadian Government worked feverishly to improve the lives of the Canadian servicemen standing idle in England. Among the innovations was the establishment of military hockey leagues comprised of some of the biggest names in Canadian hockey. Rather than shut down the NHL, both the United States and

Canadian Governments allowed the league to continue, citing the need to sustain public morale. At the time, however, almost 40 percent of the players from the league were in military uniform. By 1943, so plentiful were former professional hockey players in the Canadian Army that complete military teams comprised of former NHL players were assembled to represent all branches of the Canadian military including the Air Force and Navy.

It was hoped that the teams would create the necessary distractions and entertainment required to ensure that Canadian troops would not continue their rampaging escapades throughout England. In the end, though the teams were successful, they were not without their criticisms or controversies. For in the haste to create a distraction, professional athletes had been given preferential military treatment, a fact that created even more tension within the ranks. Concerned by the developments, J. P. Fitzgerald, sports editor of the *Toronto Telegram*, wrote on November 10, 1943:

> *The Army is training soldiers and the very best material should be young athletes. When they stay athletes and are not turned into efficient fighting soldiers in the least possible time, there is something wrong.*

Embarrassed by claims that Canadian Military Hockey teams were little more than professional outfits making money for rink and arena owners, the adjutant general sent out the following telegram on January 8, 1944:

> REFERENCE HOCKEY stop EFFECTIVE TENTH INSTANT NO OFFICER OR SOLDIER OF THE ACTIVE ARMY MAY TAKE PART IN HOCKEY CONTESTS IN ANY ORGANIZED LEAGUES THE CHAMPIONSHIP OF WHICH WOULD QUALIFY THE TEAM TO PLAY OFF FOR THE ALLAN CUP OR MEMORIAL CUP stop ARMY HOCKEY TEAMS MAY PLAY IN INTERMURAL GAMES LOCAL GARRISON LEAGUES AND MAY ALSO PLAY EXHIBITION GAMES AGAINST TEAMS BELONGING TO THE OTHER ARMED SERVICES WHO ARE LOCATED WITHIN THE SAME GEOGRAPHICAL BOUNDARIES AS THE COMMAND OR DISTRICT TO WHICH THE ARMY TEAM BELONGS stop SUCH EXHIBITION GAMES WILL NOT BE HELD MORE THAN ONCE EVERY TWO WEEKS stop ENSURE ALL UNITS

The position was clarified on January 29th when a document under the signature of Colonel E. A. Deacon, the Director of Auxiliary Services, was circulated.

The idea behind the playing of hockey and all other games by Army teams was to maintain morale and create an *esprit de corps* in the units. As long as the interest created by such contests was primarily significant to the service, games and competitions, which involved civilians, were not discouraged. As matters proceeded, however, such competitions, and the service teams playing in them, were found to be in danger of coming under the domination of civilian organizations that were using the military teams for their own commercial purposes. Instead of the teams being organized in the interest of the armed services, the teams were becoming revenue-earning units for commercial corporations. When this trend was realized, several meetings were held by officers of the Navy, Army and Air Force responsible for the organization of sports in the services. The situation was explored in all details and, as a result of these conferences, it was decided that it was in their best interests to withdraw all service hockey teams from organized league competition. In the end, hockey would still be played in garrison and camp leagues with the three branches of the Armed Services organizing exhibition games with very satisfactory results.

During the 1938-39 tour of Europe, the Trail Smoke Eaters had never been issued Canadian national team uniforms, thus, they ended up representing Canada in their black and orange club jerseys. As a result, the Trail Smoke Eaters jersey became a recognizable symbol of Canadian hockey in Europe. In Murray Grieg's book, *Trail on Ice: A Century of Hockey in the Home of Champions,* he writes how Steve Saprunoff, brother of former player Sammy Saprunoff (who was killed in the European Theatre) was shot down in a bombing mission over Berlin in 1944 and wound up as a prisoner of war in a German concentration camp.

Steve Saprunoff had been a mascot and stick boy for Trail, and was given a uniform by Smoke Eaters player Mickey Brennan. He had worn his Smoke Eaters sweater uniform underneath his flight jacket that day, which turned out to be an unexpected blessing. In an interview with Grieg, Saprunoff stated:

> *. . . for the first couple of days in that cell I wasn't given anything to eat . . . Then on the third and fourth day this old guard comes to the cell and tells me to take off my jacket.*

When he saw that Smoke Eaters sweater he got all excited and started going on and on in German about how he'd seen Trail play in Berlin in 1938 and how he was a big hockey fan and loved the Canadian players, that sort of thing. He even mentioned Jimmy Morris, who was one of his favorite players. You can imagine how shocked I was to hear this old guy going on and on about the Trail Smoke Eaters!

Later that same day he came back to my cell with a package of bread and sausage. He actually smuggled it in for me. It was the first food I'd had in days, so I was grateful for that. The same thing happened the next day and the day after that. He'd come to my cell all smiles and talking about the Smoke Eaters, and then he'd give me a little bundle of food. I couldn't believe it . . . it was all because of Mickey Brennen's hockey sweater! After four or five days the Germans moved the whole gang of us by train to a camp outside Berlin, but before we left my old guard came in one last time and gave me some apples and sausage and bread to tuck under my hockey sweater. On the train I saw some of the guys from my own unit and they were really starving. When I took 'em aside and pulled out the food, they just about fainted.

On June 5, 1944, the greatest military armada in human history slipped out of the ports of southern England and headed east toward the French coastline. Over 7,000 ships and 11,000 planes would be part of an Allied invasion force determined to breach Hitler's *Fortress Europa* and liberate Western Europe. Among the armies that would land in France was the Canadian Army, led by the likes of men such as Major Conrad Smythe and the Commander of the 4th Canadian Armed Division, Clarence Campbell.

Following the war in 1945, Clarence Campbell would join the Canadian War Crimes Unit and play a role in the Nuremberg trials. A year later, he would become the president of the National Hockey League, a position he would hold for thirty-one years. He is credited with successfully expanding the NHL from a six-team league to a twelve-team league in 1967-68. He retired from hockey in 1977 and died on June 24, 1984 at the age of 79.

Fate had dealt Conn Smythe a different set of cards. Following the D-Day Landings, Smythe would be severely wounded when a German plane, dropping flares over a Canadian encampment, dropped a flare onto an ammunition truck. The subsequent explosion killed two men. Fragments of shrapnel pierced Smythe's spine, leaving him almost paralyzed. Even as he lay wounded, he is said to have continued giving his men orders, preparing them defensively for the anticipated German counterattack. Smythe would recover from the injuries and miraculously walk again. He would return home to Canada to rebuild the Toronto Maple Leafs. Years later, when asked by a reporter what was the secret to his hockey success, Smythe would claim that it was simply the same formula that had been the secret of the Canadian Army during World War II:

> *Youth is the answer to this game. Put the kids in with a few old pappy guys who still like to win, and the combination is unbeatable.*

Yet, all this was still in the future. In the early dawn of June 6, 1944, the vanguard of the Canadian Army began to land on the beaches of Normandy. Determined to avenge Dieppe, and to prove to all that they were one of the finest military forces ever assembled, the Canadians drove into the enemy with fierce resolve and brave determination. That day, the Canadians would record the greatest territorial gains of all the invading armies, all the while sustaining the lowest casualty figures. A feat made even more remarkable given the fact that they had run straight into two German Panzer Divisions.

In the months that would follow, in a string of continuous military victories that would send the German Army reeling, this Army of former and current hockey players would assist in the liberation of three countries and the conquest of a fourth. The Army of the Ice Men had returned to Europe. The world would never be the same again.

Chapter Twelve

Clash of the Ice Men

Lester Pearson had spent the war years as a Canadian representative in both London and Washington. In 1945, he was named Ambassador to the United States and attended the founding conference of the United Nations, in San Francisco. He helped draft the United Nations Charter and establishing the UNRRA (the United Nations Rehabilitation and Relief Agency), the first U.N. mandated agency charged with rebuilding the war-ravaged nations of the world.

In 1946, Pearson became the Deputy Minister of Foreign Affairs and was a key figure in the Canadian proposal for the creation of a Western military alliance that would counter Soviet Expansionism. Taking a concept from the charter of League of Nations, Canada had lobbied for the creation of a "collective security military alliance" among the Western Powers. In 1949, this concept would be realized with the creation of the North Atlantic Treaty Organization, a military alliance that would hold firm in the face of Soviet expansionism for over forty years.

After World War II, the Soviet Union entered the realm of international hockey competition determined to proclaim themselves the masters of the sport and to end Canada's dominance. For the next two decades Soviet and Canadian teams would engage in a series of fierce battles for hockey supremacy creating one of the greatest rivalries in sports history.

Almost immediately after the guns had fell silent in Europe, the Soviet sports leadership began to develop a hockey program in preparation for their international debut. On December 22, 1946, six teams began competing for the ice hockey championship of the Soviet Union. This is the date Russians officially recognize as the birth of Soviet ice hockey.

Traditionally, Russian athletes would play soccer in the summers, and in the winters many of the same players would play ball hockey. So when the different sports organizations began to assemble their teams for the new Soviet league they drew on the top players from both sports. One of these two-sport players was Vsevolod Bobrov, the star of the Moscow Dynamo soccer club and the captain of the Soviet Union's National Soccer Team. In November 1945, a year before the debut of the new hockey league, Bobrov led the Dynamo soccer team on a four game tour of England shocking the British with wins over the Cardiff City Bluebirds and Arsenal while achieving draws with Chelsea and the Glasgow Rangers.

Bobrov would also be named the first captain of their national ice hockey team. He would become Russia's first hockey star garnering the nickname the "Russian Rocket," due to his having a similar style of play to that of the great Montreal Canadians player Maurice "the Rocket" Richard. During the 1947-48 season, Bobrov scored 52 goals in Soviet league play, outpacing the nearest runner-up by 29 goals, while recording an astounding 89 goals in 59 career international matches. His most remarkable achievement would come in December 1951, when Bobrov scored 10 goals in a single league game finishing the 1951-52 season averaging 2.18 goals per game (In comparison, Wayne Gretzky holds the professional NHL record of 1.18 goals per game set in 1983-84).

In 1948, Europe's top team, the Prague LTC (Lawn Tennis Cercle), traveled to Moscow to play an assembled team of the Soviets' top players, Team Moscow. The LTC was made up of players who had earlier that year represented Czechoslovakia at the Olympics in St. Moritz winning the silver medal and becoming the first team to not win the gold after going undefeated in Olympic play. The Czechs had tied the eventual gold medal champion Canadian team 0-0 but had to settle for the silver due to their goal ratio.

With over 30,000 people attending each game, Team Moscow defeated the Czechoslovakian team in their first match 6-3 but lost the next 5-3 and finishing up in the third match with a 2-2 tie. The Soviets declared themselves the winners of the three game exhibition due to an 11-10 goal differential. The captain of LTC would be star forward Vladimir Zabrodsky, who had tallied 27 goals in seven games at the previous Olympic tournament. A veteran of international play, Zabrodsky was largely responsible for the Czechoslovakian National Team's success against the Canadians during the Olympics. The Russians impressive play and skating ability prompted Zabrodsky to boldly state afterwards, *"I do not have any doubt that the Soviet team will be able in short time to become the strongest team in the world."*

At a time when the rest of European hockey stressed defense, LTC's offensive orientated style stood out in stark contrast, influencing both Team Moscow Head Coach Arkady Chernyshev and Player-Coach Anatoli Tarasov. This style would have an impact on the future direction of the so-called *"Soviet hockey system."* The Czech's play had been the creation of Mike Buckna from Trail, British Columbia. Buckna, while visiting Prague in 1935, decided to offer his services as a player-coach to the Prague LTC club. At the time, LTC had already established itself as one of the top club teams in Europe and had gained respect in Canada with its 1-0 win over the World Champion

Saskatoon Quakers, in 1934. At the age of 21 the former Trail Smoke Eater had become one of the top players on the Prague club.

Czechoslovakian hockey was traditionally a very defensive style with defensemen rarely touching the puck in the offensive end and with the forwards dropping back to cover the net. Even with LTC's achievements, Buckna believed the defensive coaching philosophy adopted by the Czechoslovakians was stale and limiting the development and success of their hockey. Buckna later said:

> They either had old hockey players, who taught the same thing over and over, or coaches, who'd never played hockey at all, but soccer or tennis. The problem was definitely the coaching.

Buckna saw hockey as a game built on the offensive fundamentals of passing, puck-handling, and forechecking. By the end of his first season in Prague, Buckna had already begun holding coaching clinics. The following year, at the age of 22, he was invited to run the Czechoslovakian National Team program. Buckna would stay in Prague until 1939 departing only when all Canadian coaches and players were evacuated just ahead of the Nazi annexation.

Years after the war, Buckna would return to Czechoslovakia where he would rebuild the nucleus of a great team utilizing former juniors he had coached before the war. In 1947, he led the Czech's to their first World Championship and in 1948 he coached Czechoslovakia to the silver medal at the Winter Olympics. After the Olympic Games, Buckna returned home to Canada leaving a team and a system built largely on his techniques and philosophy. It would be the concepts used by Buckna's in Czechoslovakia, which the Russians would draw upon to create their own offensive orientated system. It was Buckna's theories on how the game should be played, evident in the success of his Czechoslovakian team, which largely shaped what would eventually become the European style of hockey.

Over the next twenty years, Arkady Chernyshev, the Soviet Union's first national team head coach, along with Assistant-Coach Anatoli Tarasov each would alternate as head of the Russian National Team, when one or the other would fall out of favor with Communist officials. Ultimately, it would be Tarasov who would be recognized as the genius behind the system, eventually becoming the most famous man in all of Soviet sports. Later he would be proclaimed the *"Father of Soviet Hockey."*

A graduate of the Moscow Institute of Physical Education, Tarasov was a product of the Soviet Union's program, which believed a competitive advantage could be created in hockey by approaching hockey in a scientific way. Prevailing Soviet philosophies stressed the development of higher educated athletes, believing the better educated a player, the better he would perform. The Soviets were the first to truly master the use of scientific monitoring of athletes in order to adjust training and enhance performance.

Prior to 1953, Tarasov had attempted to travel abroad and study Canadian hockey but was prevented from doing so. He believed by studying Canadian hockey he could aid himself in his efforts to develop a unique Russian style of play. He wanted to create a style that captured the strength of the Soviet character, something, he said, a foreigner unfamiliar with the nuances of Russian behavior would be unable to do. Later, Tarasov would write in 1969 in his book, *Road to Olympus*:

> *I am convinced that if countries, so well developed in their hockey tradition, such as Denmark, Holland, West Germany, and our neighbors the Fins, refused to imitate the Canadian manner of play, they would achieve much more marked successes. It is common knowledge that a copy is worse than the original . . . [But] all the European teams are only too glad to get a former leading pro to coach them . . . There is not a single country without a Canadian hockey specialist . . . After all, a coach from Canada would start building a team along his own lines, along Canadian lines, and this is why he would be eternally trying to catch up with the Canadians . . . I felt that a person from another country would find it more than difficult to teach us if he did not know our people, their character, their tendencies, their peculiarities of national behavior - simply their good points and their shortcomings as human beings.*

Tarasov's critical opinion of other countries reliance on Canadian hockey specialists is ironic, given the realization that his so-called "Soviet hockey system" was not the invention of Tarasov, nor any other Russian. Rather, it had been largely copied from Buckna and a Toronto-based Canadian sports exercise and sports conditioning expert, Lloyd Percival.

During the 1940's, Percival had published a series of handbooks on sports training, among which two were on hockey. The first book was entitled *How to Train for Hockey*, and later, he followed it up in 1951 with *The Hockey Handbook*. Percival's methods stressed conditioning and proper diet along with teaching balance, agility and lateral movement. He had studied track and field under Dean Cromwell, the great track and field coach who had led the University of Southern California to twelve national titles including nine straight from 1935 to 1943. Later he studied legendary University of Notre Dame football Coach Knute Rockne, who lost only twelve games in thirteen-year tenure. In addition, Percival had studied the innovative coaching tactics employed by Lester Patrick and his 1930's New York Rangers hockey teams. Patrick had stressed the basic fundamentals of the game along with the concept of hard, clean, play making the Rangers *"the classiest team in hockey."* Besides the Rangers, Percival examined the passing techniques and principles used by the Toronto National Sea Fleas, the 1932 Allan Cup Champions. Along with studying and observing the coaches, he sought out the best minds in sports psychology and physical education. From North America to Europe, he tried to learn from the best. He would become one of hockey's great pioneers, stressing the importance of mental practice and preparation.

Percival was the first to look at hockey through the eyes of a sports scientist. Though he understood the game in its entirety, he sought to find the game's strengths and weaknesses by studying aspects of the sport in isolated forms. He realized that the secret to hockey and game success lay in one's ability to skate. An average or typical Canadian hockey player would skate between 2 to 4 miles a game depending on the degree of substitution. To his surprise, Percival concluded that a great deal too much of Canadian skating was haphazard in style and lacking proper technique. He also concluded that through skating the Canadian hockey system could be defeated.

During 1949 and 1950, Percival conducted a hockey survey in which he studied the skating speeds, with and without the puck, of the best players in the NHL. His findings were revealing. The fastest players in the NHL appeared to be Max Bentley of the Toronto Maple Leafs, Norm Dussault of the Montreal Canadiens and Milt Schmidt of the Boston Bruins. Their rates of speed were between 22.6 and 23 miles per hour or the equivalent of 33.8 feet per second, or one hundred yards in 8.9 seconds. At the time, the world record in speed skating for 100 yards was 9.4 seconds. Typical professional hockey players were capable of traveling at a top rate of 22.3 miles per hour without the puck and 21.1 mph with the puck. During the games, the average speed dropped because of two reasons. First, the smaller Canadian style ice rinks meant there was less open ice for a player to skate unimpeded versus the larger playing surfaces found in European and International competition. Second, the North American emphasis on constant body checking also slowed down speed of a competitor bringing the average skating speed to between 16.9 and 18.8 mph. Such findings were significant. They seemed to imply that proper skating techniques, a larger ice surface, proper conditioning and less physical play would not only speed up the game, but also create a faster moving-more skilled hockey player.

The next area of study for Percival pertained to goal scoring. Though Canadians had long been known for their high scoring when they faced European competition, Percival discovered that here too Canadian hockey was underdeveloped. On an average, only one in ten shots on goal in Canadian hockey resulted in a score. Twenty-five percent of the shots were too close to the net to be effective. Another 24 percent went wide of the goal area. Twenty-percent were too weak, though one in four shots was of quality. The average Canadian goalie could generally be expected to prevent 60 percent of the "quality shots" from scoring, leaving approximately only 10 percent of all shots finding their mark.

Though the study was a glaring indication of the current level of Canadian hockey, it was not a condemnation. Percival's data revealed not only the weaknesses found in Canadian hockey but also its areas of strength. In terms of goal scoring, he found that the most successful shots were usually those that were low, as they were the most difficult for goalies to handle. In addition, success could be increased if the shooter forced a goalie to make his move by faking a shot in one direction, but aimed at another stick handler up to the time of the shot.

In the area of passing, Percival's research revealed additional points of interest and concern. He found that on average a total of 480 passes were attempted per NHL game. Of these, only 55 percent were completed. Twenty-five percent were incomplete due to poor technique and the opposition intercepted the rest. Percival concluded that further hockey success lay with the developing of a player sporting structurally sound skating and passing skills, thus creating a system less inclined to develop a physical slower-moving hockey style. He argued that such a style of play would create the best possible level of hockey and ensure its growth.

Percival's techniques, although written for the benefit of hockey players, could be, and were, applied to athletes in various sports. One of the men implementing his ideas was Bud Wilkinson, the coach of the Oklahoma Sooners football team from 1947 to 1963. Under Wilkinson, the Sooners set a NCAA Division I winning record of 47 consecutive games (a record still held today). Percival had approached the NHL and various Canadian hockey associations with his concepts only to have them rejected as being "too extreme." Ironically, only one NHL team would incorporate some of his methods, the Detroit Red Wings.

160

Gordie Howe said it did help the players, particularly him: *"I was into a lot of his stuff, running and aerobics. He was so far ahead of his time they all thought he was a little wacko."* The Toronto Maple Leafs were particularly scornful. The two sides feuded and Percival was moved to say at one point, *"NHL players are the most primitively trained of all major athletes."*

Percival's writings would become a cornerstone of the Soviet hockey program. Without the restrictions of work, Soviet hockey players could spend eleven months out of a year competing and training, with only a one-month obligation to attend to their civilian professional responsibilities. It was a schedule that would lend itself well to the Percival system. With a shortage of available ice arenas, so much of Tarasov's training was concentrated on off-ice activities, as ice time had to be shared with many other athletes. Tarasov adopted a rigid dry land training that included long-distance running, soccer, swimming and gymnastics, all based on Percival's sports science programs. This training resulted in Russian hockey players always being in peak physical condition.

Turning inward, Tarasov also adopted a widespread Russian coaching philosophy used in their youth soccer and basketball programs. Teenagers who played five-man soccer or basketball could be found on ice rinks being coached hockey by the very same coaches who were teaching them soccer and basketball. Generally, Soviet teenagers would move collectively as a unit from one level to another. This familiarity, learned over time, resulted in improved teamwork and a higher sense of collectiveness. Tarasov's national team would adopt this style becoming the first to use five-player units in international hockey in order to create an unprecedented cohesiveness with the forwards and defensemen. This was in contrast to the style being played by the rest of the world, in which players were teamed in separate forward and defensive lines. To develop this style even more, players trained on frozen soccer fields. Goalies trained using soccer goals as nets forcing the goalie to defend a much larger area than would be the case in ice hockey.

Tarasov's patterned philosophy utilized soccer techniques when it came to puck control and passing. Due to its generally low scoring nature, what is often lost to the casual North American sports observer is that soccer is an offensive game emphasizing strategic passing and positioning in order to create an attacking forward flow. This meticulous technique of ball control and possession creates a style featuring multiple combinations of passes in the hopes to create a high quality scoring opportunity. The thought being the more a team passes, the more opportunities for developing an attack, and, in the long run, resulting in more scoring. Adapted to hockey this means the center acts more of a soccer half-back conducting the play versus pushing forward towards the goal in the hopes of banging in a loose puck. This also minimizes the possibility of icing, by always forcing players to catch up to the puck carrier.

In the Soviet system, every attacking player had to cross the blue-line as quickly as possible, denying the opponent any chance of anticipating the plan of attack. To do this, Tarasov told his players:

> *Even if you're open - even if you can rush the puck yourself - keep moving it up ice by passing to a forward partner, just because he's ahead. And do it immediately.*

Drawing from Percival's hockey concepts, the Russian coach would count the number of passes made in a game. According to Tarasov, on average his national team made 270 passes per game versus his opposition's 150. Reasoning, the 120 extra passes potentially created 120 more offensive opportunities over their opponents. Not only did he view this as academically sound, but also philosophically, as it was in agreement with Marxist belief of being a "collective" brand of hockey. By the time Russia entered world play, Tarasov had created a system difficult to defend and unique enough that it would force their opponent to play a style they are not accustomed to seeing. Russian hockey had become a blended fusion of both skating skills learned from Buckna's hockey style, the game of soccer, and Percival's fitness and hockey techniques.

Before entering world competition, the Soviet Union would experience a setback with the tragic death of several members of the Military Air Force hockey club, *Voenno-Vozdushnye Sily* (VVS, later to be known as the *Wings of the Soviet*). Consisting of many of the best young players in the country, VVS had finished second in Soviet Elite League. On January 7, 1950, eleven of the VVS players were on a chartered military plane when it crashed during a blizzard en route to a hockey game in Sverdlovsk. In total nineteen people would die, among them the Soviet hockey star Yuri Tarasov, the younger brother of Anatoli. In the book *Total Hockey*, former Soviet sports journalist Igor Kuperman, writes:

> *. . . at the time, there was absolutely no information in the newspapers about the disaster. Even players' immediate relatives weren't informed right away and knew nothing about it for quite a few days. Very few people in Moscow knew either. The team's fans heard only rumors . . . A few*

162

days later, VVS started to play again, but the censors prohibited writers from even mentioning the names of the new players. Only when Vsevolod Bobrov and Viktor Shuvalov scored were their names even mentioned.

By chance, two star players happened not to make the flight. One of them was Bobrov. It would be three years before the Soviets would be able to recover the quality and the depth they had lost that tragic winter's night.

In 1952, Lester Pearson rose again to new heights when he became the President of the United Nations General Assembly. Pearson's political rise had begun in 1929, when he had transferred to Washington spending the summer overseeing the Canadian Embassy day-to-day operations. A year later, he was in London as part of the Canadian delegation to the London Naval Conference. By 1935 he was in Geneva as a Canadian delegate to the League of Nations. Pearson was a firm believer in the concept of the League of Nations. The idea of "collective security" whereas all nations came to the aid of another under attack by an aggressive power appealed to him. With the failure of the League to come top the aid of Ethiopia and China following aggressive moves by the Italians and Japanese, a dangerous precedent had been set effectively negating the purpose and legitimacy of the League. Though Pearson found the events troubling, he had continued to work diligently in Geneva with other members of the Canadian delegation to attempt to promote the League as a legitimate entity on the world stage. Unfortunately, the League's failure to react to aggression, and the subsequent failure to curb the expansionism moves of Adolf Hitler destroyed all legitimacy of the organization.

At the time the United Nations was staging a police action on the Korean Peninsula in response to the North Korean invasion of South Korea. Almost from the moment of his appointment, Pearson attempted to find some middle ground in the negotiations between the United Nations and the North Koreans. His actions in turn angered the United States who preferred a much harder line in terms of dealing with the North. The Truman Administration saw Pearson's diplomatic efforts as contrary to their agenda. Preferring instead an end game strategy with the maintained option of using atomic weapons against the North and their Chinese Allies, should it be deemed necessary. This willingness of the United States to resort to atomic weapons against Asian nations worried Pearson who feared the impact such a military strategy would have on future relations between the Asian and Western societies. Though the United States was the main military power confronting the North Koreans, she was not the only military power,

163

and as such did not have a complete mandate to speak for the other nations who had sent troops. In the case of Canada, 27,000 Canadian troops had been sent to the Peninsula. Of these, 1600 had been injured or killed. In addition, Canada had the third largest Navy and Air Force engaged against the North Koreans and Chinese, second only to the United States and Great Britain. What made Pearson and the Canadian situation even more unique was that Canada, militarily speaking, was the fourth or fifth most powerful nation on the planet. It was a status she had held since the final days of World War II and one she had quietly maintained following the demise and the destruction of German, Japanese, and Italian militaries. These factors, though viewed by Washington as trivial, meant something to Pearson and impacted greatly on his perceived responsibilities in terms of United Nations leadership and Canada's place in foreign affairs. By flexing Canadian military and diplomatic power, independent of America, Pearson had angered Washington creating a legacy of ill-will between Pearson and members of the Washington political elite. This bitterness would last two decades and be an underlying theme through the Vietnam War era, following Canada's refusal to involve herself officially in the military conflict. This political tension created a backdrop in future athletic competition between the two North American countries, escalating the already heated hockey rivalry all the while increasing the importance of winning in the games the two nations played.

1952 would also see the Soviet Ice Hockey Federation accepted as a member of the IIHF, with the expectation of their participation in the upcoming World Championship. The Soviet hockey team prepared for the 1953 tournament by attending the February 1953 Student Winter Games in Vienna. With wins against the strong Czechoslovakian and Polish teams, 8-1 and 15-0 respectively, the Soviets would cruise to a tournament championship.

The goaltender of the 1953 Soviet hockey team would be famed soccer legend, Lev Yashin. Known as *"The Black Panther"* or *"The Black Spider,"* Yashin is recognized as possibly the greatest soccer goalkeeper of the twentieth century, being named to FIFA's all-time team. In 1948, he joined the Moscow Dynamo soccer team and year later the Dynamo youth hockey team. He would be named to the Soviet National soccer team in the summer of 1953 resulting in his decision to quit hockey and concentrate full-time on soccer. Yashin would lead the Soviet Union to the gold medal in soccer at the Olympics in Melbourne in 1956 and to the 1960 European Championship. He would be voted the European Footballer of the Year in 1963, the only goalkeeper to ever win the award.

By the spring of 1953, the Soviet Union was prepared to go

international with their hockey, but an injury to Bobrov before the World Championships prompted top Soviet officials to abandon ideas of sending an entry to the Zurich tournament. Tarasov pleaded to send the team even without their star forward, but because of failure of the national soccer team to medal at the 1952 Olympics in Helsinki, Finland, Soviet officials were worried about Joseph Stalin's response to another possible poor result.

At the 1952 Olympics, the Russian National Soccer Team had been eliminated by the eventual silver medal winner Yugoslavia. A loss made worse by the fact that Yugoslavia had become the first Eastern European communist country to challenge Soviet control. In the late 1940's, Yugoslavian leader Marshall Josip Tito had consolidated his power and had continued to challenge the Soviet Union's attempts for complete and absolute control over the satellite state. By the time of the Olympics the two countries had been on the brink of war.

In a game in which the Yugoslavians had been leading 5-1, with less than 20 minutes remaining, the Soviets had rallied making a remarkable comeback and evening the score at 5-5 before ultimately losing. Stalin was so upset about the loss that the dictator would not permit the Russian press to report on the team's disappointing finish. Losing to Yugoslavia would bring the wrath of Stalin onto Soviet soccer officials resulting in the disbanding of the Central Soviet Red Army team.

In a culture that used sport, especially team sports, as a vehicle to promote their strength and superiority, uncertainty of how their team would compete without its top player caused communist official's to send only observers to the 1953 hockey championships, delaying the Soviet Union's entry by one year. The United States and Canada also did not send representative teams to the 1953 games. The Canadian Amateur Hockey Association President W. B. George explained why:

> *Every year we spend $10,000 to send a Canadian team over to Europe to play 40 exhibition games. All of these games are played to packed houses that only enrich European hockey coffers. In return we are subjected to constant, unnecessary abuse over our Canadian style of play.*

During this time two Eastern Bloc leaders would die only nine days apart of each other. First would be Stalin. Then the man who led a 1948 coup d'etat establishing Czechoslovakia's first Communist dictatorship, President Klement Gottwald would follow. As a result of Gottwald's death, midway through the 1953 World Championship, the Czechoslovakian team returned home as a token symbol of national

165

mourning leaving only three countries to finish the tournament. With less than half of the expected seven teams remaining, and the games biggest attendance draw absent, the championship would be a financial failure. In the end the Swedes would win their first World Championship with West Germany achieving their highest placement, taking the silver, and the bronze going to the host nation, Switzerland.

Overall, the championship would be a blow to the IIHF and its President, Bunny Ahearne. Ahearne needed Canadian participation in order for the games to be viewed not only as relevant but also to assure their financial success. Ahearne sent letters to the heads of the CAHA, reminding them that as a member nation of IIHF Canada had the responsibility to attend the World Championships as it tainted the whole championship if Canada was not present. To attend Canadian teams had to largely fund themselves if they were going to play internationally. Therefore, the decision of what team would be sent depended not only on their on-ice achievements but also on the club's financial ability to travel to Europe. The CAHA's inability to find a Senior A team willing to foot the bill forced the organization to turn to the Senior B division for a 1954 representative.

The Ontario league runner-up, the East York Lyndhurst Motors, would turn out to be the best available team. Though having only been formed in 1951, Lyndhurst had won their five-team Toronto area league their first two years of Senior B hockey. These weekend warriors' reached the all-Ontario Senior B finals in the spring of 1953 only to lose the last game to a team from Kingston. It was a strong enough finish to be recognized by the CAHA but nowhere near their first choice. Now named as Canada's delegate team, Lyndhurst was under media scrutiny when they lost an exhibition game to the Oshawa Truckmen, 7-5, and a league game to Leaside, 3-2. They followed-up these poor results with an embarrassing 7-7 tie against an industrial league team, the Avro Canucks. Lyndhurst would set out on 13-game European pre-tournament tour to a chorus of media ridicule and skepticism in the Canadian Press.

Viewed as an embarrassment upon their departure, the Canadian team went on to win 11 of the 13 matches against various top European competition. Just prior to the tournament Rudolph Kock, president of a Swedish hockey club, commented on Russia's chances of defeating Canada:

> *[Russians] appear to have mastered the sport and the time has passed when Canada could send a scrub team to Europe confident that it would be good enough to win.*

166

The Soviets March 1954 debut, in Stockholm, was a success as they defeated Czechoslovakia, The Federal Republic of Germany, Finland, Switzerland and Norway. Their only blemish was a 1-1 tie with a strong Swiss team on an outdoor rink where the earlier rain turned to snow stopping the game early due to excessive snow on the ice. One Russian would describe the conditions of the ice like *"trying to skate on porridge."*

The favored Canadians looked dominating outscoring their opponents 57-5 on their way to the finals. It would be the Lyndhurst team who educated the Soviet hockey players and coaches about the higher caliber of hockey played in the NHL compared to the amateur level. To the Soviets it was hard to imagine that this Canadian team, which scored twenty goals against the Finish nationals, was not some of Canada's best. To them it was disappointing that they could defeat the Canadians and be declared World Champions and still not be considered the best in the world. Even more disappointing to the Russians was the fact that not only were they not facing the best in Canada but also Lyndhurst was not even Canada's best Senior B team from the province of Ontario. For the Canadians, their toughest game would be a 5-2 victory over Czechoslovakia in which Lyndhurst was forced to depend heavily on the tournament's top goaltender, Don Lockhart. Before the gold medal game, CAHA President George accused the Swedish Press as running *"an anti-Canadian, pro Soviet propaganda campaign"* due to the Canadians rugged style of play. He openly expressed the possibility of pulling Canada out of future tournaments because of the Swedish Press' bias reporting and use of use of words like "swine" and "gangster" to describe the Canadian players.

In the final game, Canada only needed to tie the Soviets in order to win the championship. Right from the start the Canadians opened up with an aggressive, attack-first offensive style, a strategy that had been successful against the other European teams. "Dump-and-chase" was the Canadian style in which they would immediately throw the puck into the opponent's zone with the three forwards crushing every one and everything in sight. Unlike the other teams, the Soviet hockey players were more disciplined and didn't rush into a panic trying to defend their own net. With smooth transition hockey and a five-man offensive style, the Russians would score the first goal in the sixth minute of play. Lockhart would play his worst game of the tournament giving up two soft goals. The Canadian team could never get on track resulting in a 4-0 Russian first period advantage and ultimately a 7-2 victory for the Soviet squad. Bobrov would win the tournament's top forward honors. Goalie Don Lockhart attributed his poor play to bad nerves, caused by the pressures placed on the team before the game. He would remark:

> *The Russians are wonderful hockey players. Their skating, passing and stick handling are excellent. They deserve the victory they got. What we were up against was a political situation. We are not politicians. We are hockey players. But from the very beginning certain press circles whipped up animosity against us.*

The nearly 17,000 fans gathered in Royal Stadium were in shock. The Russian victory was considered one of the biggest upsets in the history of hockey. About forty Russian officials jumped onto the ice to congratulate the winners before Bunny Ahearne presented them with the championship trophy. In the eighteen World Championships and Olympic tournaments Canadian team has competed in since 1924, Canada had won fifteen times. Losing to the Americans in 1932 or the British team in 1936 was acceptable, but to lose to the Soviets was unforgivable. Such a loss was seen as disgracing Canada and its game. Later Canadian Coach Greg Currie would reflect:

> *The worst thing that ever happened to me was standing on the blue-line in pouring rain and watching that Russian flag go up. A lot of guys were crying. They felt they'd let Canada down.*

The Canadian physical style of play, defended by the CAHA president in Sweden just days earlier, was now coming under scrutiny back at home. Reporter Alf Cottrell of the *Vancouver Province* would write:

> *If the Canadian teams play in Europe the type of hockey that is being dished out in Canada today, it isn't real surprising that the Europeans disapprove. A lot of non-Europeans disapprove of it, according to my investigations. I have heard great professionals who played as late as 10 years ago snort in disgust when you mention modern Canadian hockey . . . If the Europeans can take the charging, the interference, and the hooking and the holding out of hockey, then they are doing hockey a service. Recently someone asked Neil Colville about this phase of the game. 'Whatever it is it isn't hockey' the former New York Ranger star said.*

168

Blame fell on the CAHA itself because of their decision to send such a weak team to represent Canada. *Montreal Star* reporter Andy O'Brien, acting on behalf of the Montreal Canadiens, talked to Ahearne about the possibility of Canadian professional NHL teams touring the Soviet Union. Smythe, Managing Director of the Toronto Maple Leafs, told the *Toronto Telegram* that a Leafs tour of Russia would be quite feasible and that he would be happy to personally lead the assault after the NHL playoffs. Smythe said:

> *Very much like to see Canada regain her lost prestige in world hockey . . . [The only condition] was suitable compensation which would include traveling expenses and a small remuneration for the players.*

New York Rangers Manager Frank Boucher was against the idea of Smythe leading the tour of the Soviet Union saying, "*If Canada would like to start a new war . . . I can think of no surer way than to send Conn Smythe to Moscow.*" Former President of the CAHA, Doug Grimston, summed up the shock of the unexpected loss:

> *It came as a rather unpleasant surprise . . . According to all available information, they have only been playing hockey for eight years. Until last December we had heard nothing of them. Suddenly they emerged as a potential threat for the world's amateur title. We are probably suffering from the same shock that England experienced in soccer when the Dynamos beat them.*

In reality the Soviet Union did not just develop the game in eight years as they claimed. They had been playing a form of the game throughout the country since the 1890's. The rise of team sports in Russia can be traced back to 1843, when British textile industrialists began to import machinery to the country in order to supply cotton to the textile mills of Lancashire England. The robust cotton trade between the two countries would bring an influx of British entrepreneurs and skilled labor into Russia and by the 1890's these transplanted Englishmen had created several new clubs the first of which being soccer, then later, hockey.

Seventeen years before Russian faith healer Rasputin met his demise under the ice of the Neva River in St. Petersburg, the first recorded Russian hockey game took place on the surface of the river's ice. Scottish cotton mill workers, who founded the *Nevsky Cricket, Football, Hockey and Tennis Club* in St. Petersburg, introduced hockey in 1898 when they played a team of Russian players from the *St. Petersburg Skating Club*. Among the participants was Russian World Champion figure skater Alexei Lebedev and speed-skating champion Aleksandr Panshin.

On the assumption that world revolution was in the not too distant future, Soviet leaders initially ignored *"bourgeoisie"* sport organizations refusing to affiliate with their international federations. By the 1920's "competition" and "sport" had become negative words in Russia and hockey clubs had all but disappeared.

With Lenin's death in 1924, his successor Joseph Stalin, established a clear policy and direction for the future of Soviet sport. Stalin, obsessed with turning the Soviet Union into a modern industrialized nation, recognized the advantages of promoting professional athletic elite to entertain and distract the newly urbanized workers. The Soviet Union would emphasize athletic greatness in order to use sports as a tool for propaganda in their pursuit of geopolitical dominance. As a result, the Communist Party called upon its citizens to take up the cause *"All World Records Must Be Taken By Soviet Athletes."* Soviet youth went around singing a tune that began, *"Anyone can become a hero when the motherland demands it."* With every defeat of the bourgeois sports records and their teams, the Soviet Union would serve notice to the world of the quality of their national athletic programs and thus the superiority of communist-socialism.

It was at this time that the international workers sports movement began to rise. Worker sports differed from its traditional counterparts becoming a populist movement that included members regardless of sex, race, or creed. It replaced capitalist with socialist values and emphasized less competitive physical activities, such as gymnastics, acrobatics, tumbling, pyramid forming, mass artistic displays, hiking, cycling, and swimming.

At its height worker sports united over four million people worldwide, but with its growth came the obsession with records, spectators, and victory causing it, more and more, to resemble the bourgeoisie sport it was to rival. In 1926, Germany and the Soviet Union entered into a sports agreement after an immensely successful tour by the Soviet National Soccer Team in which it played seven matches, including a 12 to 2 victory over a Cologne city team in front of 70,000 spectators. It was the mass turnout of spectators that convinced the *Worker Gymnastics and Sports Association* leaders to enter into an agreement. It would be through this agreement "Canadian style" ice hockey would be introduced to Russia.

Although some credit the Czechoslovakians with bringing the game of ice hockey to the Soviet Union, it was actually a workers team from Germany who would reintroduce modern ice hockey to the Soviet Union. In March of 1932, the Central House of the Red Army and the Moscow Selects hosted the Berlin trade union team Fichte in Moscow. At the time, Fichte was the largest workers sports club in Germany with approximately 10,000 registered members. Three exhibition games would be played in total, the first a 3-0 victory by the Red Army squad followed by a 6-0 and an 8-0 win by the Moscow Selects.

When they were leaving for home, the German Workers team left their hockey sticks and pucks for the Soviets. The equipment they had left was passed to the Moscow Institute of Physical Culture and used to teach students ice hockey, enabling the sport to be introduced into the school's official curriculum in 1939. Throughout the 1930's there had been attempts to develop ice hockey teams in Moscow by trying to have the Russian ball hockey organizations create separate Canadian style hockey teams. The games were similar enough that in 1933 the five Moscow ball hockey clubs would create permanent ice hockey teams, with the games counting towards their ball hockey championship. Due to a shortage of the proper sticks and equipment, the teams were not sustainable.

Taking a page from the Nazis, in the 1930's, the Soviets had effectively sought to use sports as a tool of propaganda. In the years following World War II, as the world entered into a Cold War, sports would become a political instrument used by both the Soviet Bloc and the Western Democracies. Sports would be used globally to instill the highest patriotism and to stir the emotions of the masses. Throughout history, emotional patriotism or nationalism has been used as a tool of arousing anger and hatred fostering an "US" versus "THEM" mentality. Wars for commercial or political advantage often are portrayed to the people of a nation as a war for some fine moral aim, calling for the highest patriotism and sacrifice. Nurturing these patriotic feelings through sport would become the centerpiece of Russian and Western domestic and foreign policy throughout the Cold War. World competitions, such as the Olympics, would become an arena of battle of political and cultural ideologies. By the 1950's sports on an international level had become a case of East versus West and Capitalism versus Communism. It was a war of propaganda where fields, stadiums, and arenas became the ideological battlefield for men's minds. The building of new sports venues in order to prepare Soviet athletes for competition would be made a top priority. Even though the Russians level of play was still behind the Canadian professional teams of the NHL, the victory in 1954 over Lyndhurst showed to the world that the Soviets were now a power in the area of ice hockey. *The New York Times* reported:

Representatives of all squads said the Soviet Union . . .
would probably remain a top force in ice hockey for as long
as the game survived and only Canada would be able to halt
their march - providing the Canadians sent only their best
amateur squad to future tournaments.

1954 would become a landmark year for Soviet sports. Not only did the Russians beat the Canadians at hockey, but they also defeated the British team, Arsenal, at soccer; the Norwegians at skating; and a crew of Soviet oarsmen carried away Britain's Grand Challenge Cup at the Henley regatta. Yuri A. Rastvorov, a former Soviet Secret Agent wrote in *Life Magazine,* in 1955:

Soviet teams do not "play" at their sports; they work at them
. . . I learned that no Soviet team is sent into foreign
competition unless it is practically certain of winning.

After the loss in 1954, the CAHA decided it would only send the Allan Cup winning teams to represent Canada. British Columbia's Penticton V's would be the surprising winners of the Senior A Championship, and the team tasked with going to West Germany to restore Canada's hockey prestige. The V's would be led the three Warwick brothers including Grant Warwick, the 1942 NHL rookie of the year with the New York Rangers, serving as the V's team captain. The CAHA was once again criticized in the press for sending another weak team to represent Canada. Montreal Canadiens Coach Dick Irvin proposed having *"each NHL team put in two players, and Penticton team can fill in the holes."* In the end, the V's would be sent intact. Unlike the Lyndhurst team that went to Europe in comparatively relative obscurity, the V's would find themselves under the watchful eyes of the Canadian nation.

In a pre-tournament exhibition game in Prague, the V's played the Czechoslovakian national team to a 3-3 draw by coming from behind to score the tying goal with fewer than three minutes to play. The game had been sold out weeks in advance in anticipation, as the V's would become the first Western World sports team of any kind to play in Czechoslovakia since the Communist take-over in 1948. In Scott Young's book *War on Ice* he would describe the opening moments of the game as emotional stating: *"as the Canadians walked through the crowd people touched their clothes and hugged them, with tears in their eyes."*

Such sentimentality towards the Canadians would quickly

dissipate however as the crowd of 15,000 witnessed an extremely rough game that featured 11 penalties and many more, which the officials ignored. Throughout the game there were frequent scuffles among the players as tempers flared. Although the Czechoslovakians had a more physical style than any other European team, due to the influence of their former Coach Buckna, they were not accustomed to the North American physical brand of hockey and objected to the body checking employed by the Penticton players. Some Czech players began to climb up on the backs of the Canadians in an attempt to kick and slash the Canadians with their skate blades. The last period was slowed down with several fights and skirmishes. At one point, the Czechoslovakian goal was overturned. Although the game ended with handshakes, the Czechoslovakian spectators showed their disapproval of the Canadian club with a relentless chorus of booing and whistling as Penticton skated off the ice. As they were skating off some of the V's players whistled back only to inciting the crowd further. Czechoslovakian President Antonin Zapotocky, who was in attendance at the game, described the Canadian play as *"wild-west ice hockey"* saying, *"The Canadians have started playing more like boxers in the ring than hockey players."* Not surprising, the *London Communist Daily Worker* deplored the Canadians for their play:

> *The name of Canadian ice hockey stinks in Czechoslovakia after last night's game in which the Penticton V's battered, slashed and punched their way to a 3-3 draw with the Czechoslovakian national side . . . the thousands of people who were stunned by the thuggery on ice in the end rightly booed them off the ice.*

Toronto Globe and Mail columnist Bobbie Rosenfeld profoundly summed up why the Europeans were starting to loathe the Canadian brand of hockey:

> *Certainly in the last 10 years hooking, holding, interference and high-sticking have become a part of the show. The customers grin and bear it. Coaches have to practice their players to hold and hook; otherwise they wouldn't have a chance. It must be remembered that the emigration of our coaches to Czechoslovakia, Germany, Austria and Poland took place before the war and just after it. And what did these coaches teach? Because of the era in which they had played they taught hockey minus hooking, holding and interference. Naturally there are misunderstandings now*

when our teams go over, despite the determination of Penticton V's to try to play by the book.

Hockey representatives from all over the world would attend the Canadian's first practice at the World Championships. What they saw was an extremely physical intra-squad scrimmage in which a fight broke out between Billy Warwick and George McAvoy. When asked by a reporter about the fight, player Jim Fairburn explained that the practices were more dangerous than the games jokingly stating: *"I've lost 23 teeth so far during practices."* The Europeans believed him.

The V's opening game would be against a highly touted American squad led by former University of Minnesota star forward John Mayasich. More than 600 Canadian soldiers and their wives from nearby military establishments would come out and cheer the V's on. To the amazement of the German crowd the members of the Canadian army yelled, *"Yankees go home, and learn to play hockey"* accompanied by the sound of a bugle. To the Germans, the rivalry between the two North American countries was unknown. They expected Americans and Canadians to be "like brothers" making the unexpected and outright hostility shown from the Canadian spectators unsettling. For Canadians, the post World War II era brought huge American foreign investment in Canada. Canadian national resources and their economy were becoming controlled by American business interests prompting *Time Magazine* to publish articles calling Canada the 49th State. Patriotic Canadians were afraid of being absorbed by the United States and displayed their resentment each time Canada played their North American neighbor.

The referees had allowed the two teams to play the rougher North American brand of game. In the end, the Canadians would fire 96 shots against the U.S. goalie Don Rigazio on their way to a 12-1 victory. Even in the loss, Rigazio would later be named top goaltender in the tournament. The one-sided defeat against one of the tournament's top teams sent a clear message that Canada would be the team to beat. Their speed was too much for the American squad, and afterward the American coach and former 1948-49 U.S. National Team member, Al Yourkewicz, would express that *"this is the best club I've ever seen play in a World Championship."*

In their next game against the Czechoslovakians, the V's would discover that the physical style of play demonstrated against the Americans would not be permitted against European teams. After a steady stream of penalties in the first period, V's player, Don Berry, was alleged to say to the team:

174

*We can't play like we played last night. We were playing the
U.S. so the Europeans didn't give a damn who won - that's
why they let us get away with everything.*

Throughout the tournament the aggressive play of the V's would
draw boos from the crowd. One reporter believed the translations
from German to English didn't help at all in calming the German
crowd as "high sticking" would be translated into "two minutes for
impermissible beating over the head with a stick," and "roughing"
would be translated into German as "two minutes each for jostling
without the puck." The toughest game of the tournament for the V's
would be their 5-3 victory over the Czechoslovakian team; a team the
Russians easily defeated 4-0.

Almost six months prior to the tournament, the Russians had
begun intensive training on an artificial ice arena in their occupied zone
of East Berlin. In a game against their satellite ally, the Czechs, 5,000
East Germans had showed up to witness the game displaying an
outward animosity towards the Russian team. This German hatred
had manifested from the rape, pillage and plundering of East Germany
and its citizenry by Red Army soldiers during World War II, and the
initial post-war occupational period. Historians have estimated that
Soviet soldiers raped as many as two million German women during
the initial military offensive into Germany, continuing well after their
surrender. Additionally, the Soviet army had looted enormous
quantities of precious jewelry and artwork along with forcible
expropriating German land and property. In post-war East Germany,
there was no greater villain than the Soviet Union and its people.

The game between the Soviet Union and Czechoslovakia showed
little camaraderie and, as soon as it was apparent the Russians would
defeat their Eastern Bloc rival, the match degenerated. The violence
climaxed with a kicking episode between Russia's Victor Shuvolov and
Czech defenseman Jan Lidral that prompted Soviet Team Captain,
Bobrov, to enter into the skirmish and begin punching the
Czechoslovakian player. In his book *Headline Hockey*, Canadian
reporter Andy O'Brien would write about a conversation with his
German guide:

*Now you know why it's important to us of West Berlin that
the Russians get stopped in everything they try ... and while,
to you from Canada, it may be only a bunch of hockey games
coming up, to us of West Berlin, surrounded by the
Communists, it will be a boost for morale every time they are
beaten. You people call it a Cold War ... but what better*

175

place is there to fight it than on ice.

Both the Canadians and the Russians would march through the tournament undefeated. Billed as a grudge match, the final game would create tremendous interest in Europe. The press box would have reporters from 20 different countries covering the game with famed *Hockey Night in Canada* broadcaster, Foster Hewitt, flying over to Germany to broadcast the match back to Canada. An overflow crowd of 9,500 came to watch the V's and the Soviet Union battle for the championship. With the bitterness of Soviet military occupation, the Canadians had become the German spectators' team of choice. The West Germans fans who had booed the Canadians throughout the tournament now cheered the V's with chant of *"Go-V's-Go."*

The Soviet team had been built around Bobrov and seemed to only have one set attack pattern. They played five man attacking style which was centered on head-manning the puck to the Soviet star in order to lead an attack. Throughout the play, the V's checked Bobrov heavily throwing the great Russian forward off his game until he became a non-factor. He would not register a single shot on goal. Forward Jim Middleton, a late addition from the Kelowna Packers, would later reflect on the Soviet's play: *"Great play makers but they really didn't know how to body check."* Tempers flared throughout resulting in Kevin Conway trading punches with a Russian near the end of the game. The V's would win 5-0. After the final buzzer sounded, the rink was rushed by hundreds of Canadian servicemen and women hugging and kissing the Penticton players. It would be ten minutes before Ahearne could award the V's the trophy.

No other Canadian international team has ever faced as much pressure to win. The loss was the first for the Russians in the two years they had participated in the World Championships and to this date, it is still the only shutout game that the Canadian Nationals have ever recorded against their Soviet counterparts. *The Toronto Globe and Mail* would describe the V's as *"the strongest team Canada has sent to a world championship since the prewar Trail Smoke eaters and the Varsity Grads."* Reporter Al Nickleson would describe it as more than just a game:

> *This wasn't merely a sports event. It was the free world against everything that smacks of the Iron Curtain . . . The publicity boys of the Kremlin turned that 1954 title into a propaganda medium. They fashioned it to suggest proof of Soviet supremacy in all things. Yesterday, Penticton V's exploded the hot-air myth of invincibility.*

176

During the tournament, members of the Russian Hockey Federation started talking about coordinating a tour of the Soviet Union involving both the Maple Leafs and Canadiens. Soviet officials estimated that at least 100,000 people would turn out in Moscow to view either of these storied teams. Yet again a tour would fall through, but unlike the previous year when the Soviets showed little interest in having a professional squad tour their country, this time it would be the Canadians who would be unwilling to send a team. The V's had restored Canadian dominance to the sport they called their own. Now, Canada had everything to lose by sending in their best and the Russians had everything to gain. The Soviets would meticulously study the film of their humbling 1955 defeat to the Penticton V's. Reshaping and refining their game, rehearsing their new twists and changes against top European professional and club teams as they prepared for the 1956 Olympic Games.

The following year, the Winter Olympics would be hosted in Cortina d'Ampezzo, Italy, and it would mark the first time the Soviet Union participated in the Winter Games. Overall, the Soviets would dominate, winning the total medal count with 16 medals in 25 events - five more medals than the runner-up Austrians. Included would be the impressive showing by Pavel Kolchin, who became the first non-Scandinavian to earn a medal in cross-country skiing, earning two bronzes while leading his Nordic Skiing 4 X 10km relay team to gold.

In hockey, the Allan Cup winning Kitchener-Waterloo Dutchmen would represent Canada. The tournament favorite Canadians would be stunned by the Americans, losing by a score of 4-1 and ending any Canadian hopes for gold medal. It would mark the first loss the Canadians had ever suffered to the United States in Olympic competition. In the book *Canada's Olympic Hockey Teams* reporter Thom Benson's opening words describing the astonishing loss for Canadian Broadcast Corporation (CBC) national radio:

> *Today, in this small mountain village, there was a funeral. The bells of the ancient church told the passing of a procession. The mourners chanted prayers as they trudged up the steep hills behind the coffin bearers. Those who were left were saying their farewells to a robust and lively friend.*
>
> *The cortege wound its way through narrow and twisted streets up past the Concordia Hotel. Inside that building, there was a similar ceremony where the inhabitants mourned the passing of an era. In the hotel was housed the*

Kitchener-Waterloo hockey team and all those other Canadians who aspired to Olympic heights in the field of amateur competition.

There was no joy there, no happy words, no jubilation, for last night Canadian amateur hockey suffered a blow to its prestige from which it may never recover. The Kitchener-Waterloo team was beaten fairly and squarely by a team which would never make the junior finals in Canada. If you think saying that is easy, then you are greatly mistaken.

Demoralized and disheartened, the Canadians would finish the tournament with an uninspiring 2-0 loss to the Soviets, having to settling for the bronze medal, their lowest finish in Olympic or World Hockey Championship history. The Americans would not be able to pull off another upset, losing instead to the Soviet Union by the score of 4-0 and settling for the silver medal.

The Cortina Olympics showed that no athletic event was a sacred cow for any long-time traditional power. Soviet athletes could not only compete but also win, whether it was against the Scandinavians in cross-country skiing or against the Canadians in hockey. They showed that their 1954 World Championship was not a fluke and that, indeed, their hockey system was adaptable. In this, they sent a notice to the hockey world that there would be no cookie-cutter blueprint for defeating the "Russian Bear," and that they would continue to be a medal favorite in world hockey play.

The CAHA, embarrassed by the Canadian performance in the Olympics, decided to create a Senior A All-Star Team for the 1957 World Hockey Championship to be held in Moscow. To prepare for what was expected to be an eventual showdown between themselves and the Canadians, the Soviets would travel across Canada playing a series of exhibition games against top Canadian amateur clubs in an attempt to condition and familiarize a new generation of young Soviet players to the harder-hitting Canadian style. Playing eight games against various Canadian amateur teams, the Russian would finish with a record of 5 wins, 2 losses, and a tie. However, before the start of the World Championships Cold War politics and tensions escalated.

After Stalin's death in 1953, the Soviet Union and Eastern Europe entered an era of "Destalinization." In February 1956, Nikita Khrushchev and the Soviet Communist Party publicly condemned and denounced Stalin's dictatorship while acknowledging the atrocities that had been committed during his reign of terror. For a time it appeared that the people in Eastern Europe might be freed from authoritarian

Soviet rule. In June 1956, Polish protesters had clashed with police in the Polish city of Poznan demanding reform, resulting in the death of approximately 75 demonstrators. The riot caused the Polish Government to implement moderate social and economic reforms. Fueled by the success in Poland, on October 23, 1956, students and workers took to the streets of Budapest, Hungary, demanding sixteen reforms, many of which had already been achieved in Poland.

Instead of receiving the promise of reforms, the Hungarian demonstrators were met with bullets. The shootings of demonstrators by soldiers in Budapest led to chaos, resulting in the Soviet appointment of Hungarian Communist reformist, Imre Nagy. Believing he was working within the bounds set by the Soviet officials, Nagy attempted to bring the situation under control by offering amnesty to the demonstrators and promising the abolishment of the one-party system. Following the refusal of the Soviet Union to remove their troops from the country, Nagy withdrew Hungary from the Warsaw Pact, declaring Hungarian neutrality in the hopes of getting United Nations and NATO support.

The events in Hungary would be overshadowed by another conflict. On July 26, 1956, Egyptian leader, Gamal Abdel Nasser nationalized the Suez Canal Company, taking control from the British. Britain, France, and Israel secretly met (known as "the tripartite collusion") for a response, and October 29, 1956, Israel attacked Egypt. Isolated internationally, Egypt turned to the Soviet Union. The Soviets, viewing the opportunity to gain access to a year-round warm weather port in the Mediterranean, supported the Nasser government sending in naval ships to the region. In turn, President Dwight Eisenhower responded by sending in American naval ships, creating a tense standoff. As a result, Hungary was left to fend for herself. On November 4, 1956, Khrushchev ordered hundreds of Soviet tanks into the Hungarian capital. From November 4 to November 11 there would be fighting in the streets of Budapest and the larger towns. An estimated 20-30,000 Hungarians would be killed, and Nagy would be taken back to Moscow where he was tried, executed, and later buried in an unmarked grave. By November 14, order had been restored. Soviet rule was re-established.

Canada's response to the international political developments would again have Pearson re-emerge as a thorn in the side of the United States as well as the Soviets. Following the Hungarian uprising Pearson had pushed to have a U.N. Mission established in Hungary. The Soviets vetoed the efforts. Not satisfied with sitting idle as Hungary was trampled under Soviet tanks, the Canadian Government would do what it could by allowing 25,000 Hungarians to seek asylum in Canada. Following the Egyptian nationalization of the Suez Crisis, and an ominous build-up of American and Soviet Naval forces in the Mediterranean, Pearson had lead the United Nations charge to establish a peacekeeper force that would take control of the Canal and replace British, French, and Israeli forces who had seized the Canal from Egypt. By offering to commit Canadian military forces to the operation, effectively giving the peacekeeping operation the necessary military muscle to fulfill its mandate and succeed, Canada had strengthened the United Nations and prevented the United States, Britain, France, and Israel from gaining post-conflict military control over the area. The Canadian move would mark the first time a Canadian military force was deployed for peacekeeping purposes. It would also mark a turning point in both Canadian Foreign Affairs as well as Military Doctrine. For the first time Canadians soldiers would be sent to a war zone in an effort to "force a peace" rather than "wage a war." The effort by Pearson would result in his being awarded the Nobel Peace Prize in 1957. The first and only time a Canadian has been so honored. It would also mark one of the few times in history that a western democracy would take a moral stand against traditional allies in favor of internationalism and world peace.

The Canadian decision to stand independent of the United States, Great Britain, France, and Israel and on the side of the United Nations would only add to a growing opinion in Washington political circles that Pearson could not be trusted as he was too much of an internationalist and visionary for U.S. tastes. Blinded by hatred towards Pearson and the Canadian stance, it would be years before Washington insiders would recognized the actions of Pearson and the Canadian government for what they were. In 1972, at the time of Pearson's death, the New York Times would write:

> *His skill as negotiator and mediator during and after World War II enabled Canada to play a world role out of proportion to its size and power . . . climaxed by his heroic part in defusing the Suez Crisis of 1956 that might have exploded into World War III.*

In response to the Hungarian invasion, America and Canada would both boycott the 1957 World Championships. Moscow had planned to use this event to showcase the new modern Russia with its impressive new Luzhniki Sports Palace, a series of athletic complexes, venues, and facilities covering an area of 160 hectares that had just been completed in 1956. The boycott would take the luster off the event. The World Championships would feature few teams.

Surprisingly, the Swedes would win the event in the face of limited competition.

As Cold War tensions heated up, the manifestation of heightened nationalistic feelings became a cause for concern among members of the International Olympic Committee (IOC). Worried that politics would tarnish the spirit of the competition, the IOC debated whether or not to remove team sports from further Olympic competition. In a circular letter to IOC members on August 26, 1957, IOC President Brundage wrote:

> *Referring to the item on the agenda for the Sofia meeting suggesting dropping team games from the Olympic program . . . I quote from a letter of our Dutch colleague, Peter Scharoo, who served on the Executive Board for many years:*

> *Exaggerated nationalism is one of the greatest dangers of our society. We must confess that this phenomenon is also manifested in the Olympic Movement . . . You will remember that during the years that I was a member of the Executive Committee, I urged again and again the necessity of eliminating all team sports. This will inevitably have the great advantage of preventing the promotion of national interests, because in team sports the competition the competition is obviously between countries and not between athletes.*

In the end, team sports remained in the Olympics.

Prior to the 1950's, a large part of the NHL's success had been its ability to capitalize on French and English tension and animosity and, to a smaller extent, on nationalistic feelings between the United States and Canada. By the mid-1950's social structures had begun to change within Canadian society. Having severed their close empire ties to England, Canadians were now aligning themselves politically, militarily, and economically with their southern neighbor, the United States. Critics said that English Canada was becoming an extension of the United States, as Canadians, especially the young, at times appeared more American than their American counterparts. Only Quebec, with its large French-speaking population, seemed determined to maintain its former cultural values and societal ways as the French Canadians struggled to differentiate themselves in the face of the American cultural onslaught. In 1938 F. R. Scott in *Canada Today* summed up the French Canadian culture within Canada when he wrote:

> *The French Canadian in a real sense is the truest Canadian.*
> *He has lived on the soil for three hundred years, and the*
> *family ties with another world have long been broken. To*
> *Canada alone does he feel attached, for England conquered*
> *him and France first deserted him and then traveled a*
> *political and spiritual road his clergy has taught him to*
> *abhor. He sees no hope coming from without; he knows he*
> *must build up his own resources.*

On March 17, 1955, the growing tensions that marked Canadian English-French society came to the forefront during a hockey incident involving Maurice Richard, star of the Montreal Canadiens, and the then President of the NHL, Clarence Campbell. It was the last week of the regular NHL season and by all accounts it appeared the Montreal Canadiens were on their way to a Stanley Cup championship. On March 13, however, this all changed when Richard, having received a severe cut on the forehead from the Boston Bruin player, Hal Laycoe, retaliated by attacking Laycoe with his stick. Subsequently, Richard turned his fists on a game official when the man tried to break up the fight. The next day Campbell suspended Richard for the remainder of the season, almost ensuring that the Canadiens would have no chance to win the Stanley Cup.

A day later Campbell decided to attend a game between the Canadiens and the Detroit Red Wings in Montreal. While sitting in the stands, Campbell was pelted with items thrown by Montreal fans. Later, he was assaulted by an enraged Montrealer, forcing Campbell and his wife to flee the arena for fear of their lives. The game was immediately cancelled and the Red Wings declared winners, as the violence spilled onto the streets of downtown Montreal.

In the hours that would follow, mobs of French Canadians would go on a rampage destroying countless shops and stores, targeting in particular, those owned by English Canadians. The situation was so tense that Richard went on the radio to appeal for calm. For decades the French Canadians had sat idle in the face of English repression. Now things were different. A new sense of cultural awareness was taking root in Quebec. No longer would French Canadians sit and watch while their institutions, culture, and heroes were defaced. A new day was dawning. Quebec society was awaking from its winter slumber.

Chapter Thirteen

War on Ice

The 1958 championships held in Oslo, Norway, would be Canada's chance to avenge their 1956 losses suffered in Italy. A changing-of-the-guard had happened on the Soviet team as Bobrov, along with other veterans, had been replaced by a new generation of young Russian hockey players. Representing Canada at the 1958 World Championships were the Allan Cup Champions, the Whitby Dunlops. The Dunlops, formally known as the Oshawa Truckmen, had been the Senior B team that had defeated the East York Lyndhurst Motors in a league match prior to Lyndhurst playing in the 1954 championship. Oshawa's years of petitioning to move up from the Senior B to the Senior A league had finally been accepted, and after their arena burned down the Truckmen were forced to move five miles down the road to the Whitby Arena, resulting in their name change.

Many of the Dunlop players had witnessed first hand the public lambasting that the Lyndhurst Motors team had been forced to endure after their defeat to the Soviets. No one wanted to experience the Dutchmens' fate of returning home from Europe accused of disparaging Canada's national pride and self-image. Pressure to win was mounting due to the on-going tensions between the West and the Soviet bloc.

With the October 4, 1957, Russian launch of the first artificial satellite, Sputnik I, the world had entered the Space Age. Combined with the high-profile public failures of America's attempt to put their own satellite in orbit, Project Vanguard, the Soviet Union had jumped ahead of United States in the Space Race. This was a time many began to feel the West was beginning to fall behind politically, militarily, technologically, and scientifically to the Soviets. From a psychological standpoint defeating the Soviet's wherever and whenever possible began to take on increasing importance. The World Hockey Championships would give the West its first opportunity since the Sputnik launch to defeat "the Communist horde" while providing Canadians the chance to re-establish themselves as the masters of winter's golden game.

In Oslo, both the Canadians and the Soviet teams stayed at the same hotel. When members from each team would encounter the other often the Soviets would come up and issue a bone-crushing handshake to the Canadians. The Dunlops were not prepared to let the Russians win at psychological warfare, so Assistant Coach Ed Redmond called a special strategic session to plan a counter-attack. Coach Wren Blair said it was quite a sight to see his Canadian players shaking and re-shaking one another's hands, while following Redmond's instruction:

> *Grip first and firm . . . no, it needn't be too hard but it's impossible for the Russians to apply a bone-crusher on a firm grip. In this way you will instill a feeling of futility in them.*

The championship would come down to the Canadians versus the Soviets. Future NHL coach and General Manager of the Boston Bruins, Harry Sinden, would captain Whitby. The Dunlops would march through the tournament defeating their opponents by a combined score of 78 to 3 with the most resounding score of a 24-0 blowout of Finland. On their way to the championship game, the Dunlops had avenged a Canadian 4-1 loss to the American team at the prior Olympics by routing the U.S. by a score of 12-1. The Russians had a harder time of it. In their game against the Czechoslovakians, they took an early 3-0 lead only to relinquish it when the Czechs became more aggressive at body-checking. Reporter Scott Young describes the game:

> *Russian bodies were flying all over the rink. [The Czechoslovakians] tied the score, 3-3. Russia went ahead 4-3. The Czechs scored a goal that was disallowed. It would have tied the score at 4-4. The Czechs raged at the referees. The Russian hockey boss, Pavel Korotkov, was yelling at his team to keep calm and get on with the game. Frantisek Schwach, a Czech player, skated up to Korotkov and cursed him loudly. The crowd pelted the Russians with snowballs. At 19:40 in the third, 20 seconds left, Miroslav Vlach scored the tying goal.*

Before the final, thousands of telegrams from all over Canada started pouring in. Blair would later state:

> *All day Saturday and Sunday we kept getting these telegrams. We got them by the bushel, from every premier, from the Prime Minister, every mayor, every head of every company, General Motors, Eaton's, Simpsons, friends of the players, people by the thousands . . . All the telegrams said the same thing, the same message. It was like: Bring Home the Bacon! Don't Let Canada Down! We Believe in You!*

There wasn't one that said, 'Win, lose or draw we still love you.' Our guys were saying, 'We lose, we're going out and jump in the North Sea!' It was all concentrated in one game.

The pressure to win before the game would affect the Canadian players. Caught in the grip of tremendous tension, several of the younger athletes broke down and cried in the dressing room prior to its start. Western propaganda often claimed that the Soviets had to win for fear of the consequences, but in truth even when they lost, the Soviet players were still seen as heroes by the Soviet public. The simple fact was, the Canadians had to win. If the Canadians lost, they would be the ones afraid to go home. The Dunlops came out tight falling behind 1-0 before rallying and tying up the game at one-a-piece, near the end of the second period. In the final period, each team would exchange goals remaining tied at 2-2 until the last three minutes of the game when Bobby Attersley scored for the Dunlops. The final score would be 4-2 and after the game team captain Sinden would say:

I think we could go back tomorrow and beat them by five goals. Now we've lost that awful tension and I think we could do a better job.

Later that year, in November 1958, Okanagan-Mainline Senior Amateur Hockey League Champion, Kelowna Packers, became the first western sports team to play in the Soviet Union. Captain Jim Middleton, who had played on the V's at the World Championship 1955, had led Kelowna to the 1958 Allan Cup final, losing in seven games to the eventually 1959 World Champion Bellevue McFarlands. About a month after their Allan Cup defeat, the Soviet Ice Hockey Federation contacted Canadian hockey officials requesting a high caliber team to come to Russia to introduce Canadian-style hockey to the Soviet public. The Packers would be the CAHA pick, resulting in Foster Hewitt's prediction that Kelowna would not win a game, and that their appearance would only be a propaganda victory for the Soviet's and another humiliation for Canadian hockey.

Upon their arrival in Russia, the Packers found their every move watched by the Soviet secret police. Team rooms were bugged and player conversations recorded. The first game would be against the Wings of the Soviet. With Kelowna holding a 3-2 lead to start the third period, armed Red Army troops entered the arena and surrounded the rink. It was an attempt to intimidate the Canadians. The tactics worked. It would be Kelowna's only loss of the five games played in the

Soviet Union, losing by a score of 4-3. Overall, Kelowna would win two, lose one, and tie two.

The U.S National Team would be invited to play in Poland, Czechoslovakia, and the Soviet Union later that same year. In the four days the Americans spent in Moscow, they were constantly reminded of the successful launch of Sputnik. The Soviets even included Sputnik centerpieces on the dinner tables where the Americans ate. The American team would lose both games to their hosts.

Since the end of World War I, American teams had developed a reputation in Europe as the dirtiest of any country, in terms of hockey. A Russian delegation member described the American game style as thus, *"They beat up their opponents, tripped them up and make fun of them whenever they score a goal."* In the 1952 Olympics, during a game against the Swiss, a fight broke out on the ice enraging the fans to the point that they began to throw orange skins, apple cores and snowballs at the U.S. players. After the game some members of the American team had to arrange a secret departure from the stadium for fear of being attacked by spectators. In 1958, the United States would be involved in another such incident after playing what had been reported as the roughest matches of the tournament against a feisty Norwegian team. After a 1-1 first period, the Americans started to pull away, and that's when the game began to degenerate. In the second period, Bill Christian of the U.S. and Norwegian forward Willy Walbye exchanged punches. From that point onwards both teams began body-checking each other at every possible opportunity, with the insuring free-for-alls threatening the games completion. Thirteen penalties would be called with four players being ejected from the game. Towards the end of the game, the irate crowd booed everything the Americans did. Assorted debris were thrown on the ice from the Norwegian fans with one spectator hurling a whisky bottle toward the American goalie Willard Ikola, who shoved the bottle into the back of his net as play continued. During the clean up, the referees called on the audience to desist. The Americans would defeat the home county's team by a score of 12-1, while enhancing their already tarnished reputation. Following the tournament, the Americans would seek a new hockey approach choosing war veteran, Jack Riley, to coach their national program.

Riley was a U.S. Naval Aviator from 1942-1946 who flew twelve combat missions in the Pacific theatre during World War II and eighteen more missions after the war. During the war, Riley was one of the pilots involved in the search and rescue effort of the battleship *USS Indianapolis* as she was returning to Guam. On July 30, 1945, two torpedoes from a Japanese submarine hit the *Indianapolis* on its way to Guam. Of the 1,196 onboard, 900 men made it off the sinking ship, most forced to jump into the water wearing only light clothing and "Mae West" life preserver jackets. It would be two days before a search for the survivors would begin, as the *Indianapolis* was under radio silence at the time of the sinking and no distress was sent. When the search was initiated, PBM seaplanes were dispatched and it would be one of the pilots in Riley's group who would find the survivors almost five days later. Most of the sailors had either died from shark attacks or exposure. Only 317 men survived.

Riley's closest brush with death would occur after the war, when he flew into Russian air space and was forced to evade two Soviet fighters firing upon him. A former 1948 Olympian and Head Coach of West Point Military Academy (1950-86), Riley would be the U.S. National Hockey Association's choice to coach the national team in the 1960 Olympics in Squaw Valley, California. He would run his team's training camp like a military boot camp. Later, U.S. captain and full-time firefighter Jack Kirrane, would recall:

> *On our fist practice at WestPoint, (Riley) skated us two hours, stop and starts. I was the last one off the ice, so I still had my skates on when he came in the locker room. Most guys were in the shower. He said, 'Where the hell do you think you are going? We still got another hour of practice.'*

Later, Kirrane said he and another player made the mistake of staying and watching Riley run the West Point practice. Riley, after seeing the two in the stands, told them to get dressed and join the squad. His demanding coaching style would payoff, as his team would enter the tournament in top physical condition.

In the two previous Olympics the United States had come away with the silver medal, placing runner-up to Canada and the Soviet Union. Even though the American program was able to place a respectable fourth in the previous years World Champions, they had experienced an embarrassing 18-1 defeat at the hands of the Soviet team. With only eight players on the roster with major international experience, many experts felt a fourth place U.S. finish would be a remarkable achievement.

Riley would adjust his team roster right up to the last minute, adding four players said to be *"a soldier, a television advertising salesman and two insurance salesmen."* Two months earlier, 24-year-old goalie Jack McCartan was an infantryman at Fort Carson, Colorado. McCartan had played in two games the 1959 World Championships, both had been losses. He had been dropped from the American team for being *"too erratic."* Mayasich, who was viewed as good enough to play in the NHL, had instead opted to become an adverting executive for a television company. His inclusion on the final roster would not be a surprise, as the entire team knew going into camp that he would be a late minute addition.

William "Bill" Cleary along with his brother Robert "Bob" Cleary had earlier passed up trying out for the U.S. Olympic squad because neither could afford not to work during the lengthy tryout period. Prior to being contacted by Coach Riley, the brothers had been running their own business selling insurance policies for the New England Mutual Life Insurance Company. Both brothers had been offensive standouts at Harvard University. In 1955, Bill Cleary led Harvard to its first National Collegiate Athletic Association (NCAA) Tournament appearance in ice hockey, scoring an astronomical 89 points in just 21 games - still the current day Harvard single-season scoring record. In all, there would be four former Harvard players on the American team, as the two Cleary brothers would be joined by backup goaltender Robert McVey and defenseman Robert Owen.

These roster changes created turmoil within the dressing room, as friends and teammates who had practiced and played all year long were cut from the squad at the 11th hour, in order to make room for the last minute additions. Ironically, one of the players to be cut was Herb Brooks, the future Head Coach of the 1980 U.S. Olympic Hockey Team.

With the new roster in place, the Americans started a one-month, 18-game exhibition tour in preparation for the tournament. In the preliminary round, the Americans looked impressive in victories over Czechoslovakia, Austria, Sweden, and Germany before their showdown with the gold medal favorites, the Canadians. The 1959 Allan Cup Champion Whitby Dunlops had declined the invitation to represent Canada in Squaw Valley. As a result, the CAHA would choose the Kitchener-Waterloo Dutchmen to represent Canada for the second consecutive Olympics. Over the last year, the Dutchmen had lost three of their top players to the NHL. Additional replacements were provided amongst which included Harry Sinden and Montreal Canadiens minor league prospect Bobby Rousseau, who later would become a star in the NHL. The Canadian team was considered the fastest of the tournament.

In their game against the Canadians, the American team would jump to an early 2-0 first period lead. From that point on, Canada would carry the play, peppering the U.S. goaltender with a total of forty shots on net, only managing to finally score with just over six minutes left in the game. The final score, 2-1 in favor of the United States. Afterwards, McCartan would describe the Canadian offensive onslaught: *"All I could see were streaks of green Canadian jerseys."* For the second consecutive Olympics the Americans had shocked the Canadians. Now the Americans would face the Soviets.

Months earlier, the Americans had watched Fidel Castro's Marxist revolution bring the Communist threat to within 90 miles of their border, escalating East-West tensions. Now, with the game broadcast live on CBS television, millions would tune in to watch the two Cold War super-powers battle it out on the ice. More than 10,000 spectators would pile into the 8,500-seat Blyth Arena. They witnessed the American team jump to a 1-0 lead, only to watch the Soviet team swarm the United States net, scoring the next two goals. The score could have been much worse if it was not for the spectacular play of McCartan. Coach Riley later said, *"McCartan kept us in the ball game. Without him, we would have gone down by ten goals."* American Bill Christian would score in the second and again in the third period, leading the U.S. to another huge upset victory and handing the Russians their first loss in Olympic history.

During the subsequent U.S. - Czechoslovakia gold medal game, and trailing 4-3 going into the third period against the Czechoslovakians, Soviet team captain Nikolai Sologubov rushed into the Americans locker room saying, *"Oxygen, Oxygen."* Advising U.S. team members to inhale oxygen to relieve their fatigue while also demonstrating that, at least in the sport of hockey, the animosity and rivalry between the Soviets and Czechoslovakians at times surpassed that of their Cold War enemy, the United States. Whether or not it made a difference was hard to say, but the United States would go on to score six goals in final period, winning the gold by a final of 9-4. In the end, Riley's roster changes paid off, as Bill Cleary would lead the Americans in scoring with six goals and six assists, while McCartan's performance would be regarded as one of the best in Olympic hockey history. The Westpoint coach's demanding physical regiment resulted in the United States outscoring their opposition in the third period by a combined score of 19-4.

Twenty-two years after capturing the world title for Canada, the Trail Smoke Eaters would once again represent Canada in the 1961 World Championships. In preparation, the Smokies would tour the Soviet Union, Czechoslovakia and Sweden. Their first game would begin in Stockholm against the Swedish National Team, considered by many to be the top team in Europe. In their European debut, Trail would be pounded 4-0, being outshot 56-27. The following day, the *Swedish Expressen* would publish a front-page cartoon of Smoke Eaters defenseman, Don Fletcher, wearing a halo and angel's wings, dubbing the Smoke Eaters team *"the least physical and poorest Canadian team to ever play in Europe."* In Canada, the shock of the one-sided loss caused panic. Coach Bobby Kromm called a team meeting the next day, telling the players if they lose the next game to Sweden, that replacement players would be sent from Canada to bolster the team. Years later player Normie Lenardon would say, *"We decided, let's go out and beat the hell out of them."*

In game two, one of the Swedish top players, Nils Nilsson, while skating over the Canadian blue-line, was hit by defenseman Darryl Sly. Sly, who did not wear any shoulder pads, laid his shoulder into Nilsson breaking his jaw with a clean hit. No penalty was called on the play. A few minutes later, another one of their star players, Lars Lundvall, was given a hip check by Fletcher tearing Lundvall's knee ligaments. In the second period, a fight between Sly and Tumba Johansson broke out. During the altercation one police officer reached over the boards and grabbed Sly. When another officer tried to grab Johansson, the big Swedish player fought back causing the Swedish fans to go into an uproar. The Swedish Coach, Arne Stromberg, began yelling, *"Butchers, gangsters, murders."* The crowd pelted the Smoke Eaters with snowballs, lighters, candy, and oranges. In the third, Johansson, skating with his head down, would be checked at mid-ice. He would leave the game on a stretcher. The Canadians would win the game 3-1. The next day headlines in Sweden read, *"Canada Sabotages Sweden's National Team,"* with a front-page picture of Nilsson and Lundvall in hospital beds. Both were injured badly enough that they were unable to play in the World Championships.

The 1961 championships, held in Geneva, Switzerland, would be the last time the games were played in an open-air arena. Twenty teams in three pools participated with South Africa making their international debut. Both East and West Germany would qualify for pool-A (the medal round) resulting in a forfeit, as West Germany had a policy of not playing their Eastern counterpart. Czechoslovakia would upset the Russians 6-4, resulting in the Soviets eventual third place finish. The Smoke Eaters would tie the Czechs 1-1 forcing the Canadians to defeat the Russians by two goals in the final game in order to capture the gold, via total goal differential over the Czechoslovakians. Canada would defeat the Russians 5-1. It would be the last time a team of Canadian amateurs would win the World Championships until 1994.

The Smoke Eaters physical domination of the Russian team showed Tarasov that he needed to have his team physically prepared for the roughness of hockey now found in world tournaments. To accomplish this, throughout 1960's the Russians would continue to send various Soviet hockey teams on tours across Canada. On average, the

Soviets would play ten games against regional semi-pro Canadian squads during these tours. It would be during these visits to Canada where Tarasov had the opportunity to evaluate the players who could tolerate the rough brand of Canadian hockey or, as he would describe it, could tolerate a *"cruel"* brand of hockey that wasn't seen in Europe. Later, Tarasov would write:

> *The powerful, passionate, and at times brutal contests over there in Canada hardened our fellows . . . Canadian players of all classes were always known for a sort of playing terrorism . . . But not all the members on our team had the self-possession and determination to endure an opponent's brutality, and be able to demonstrate their skills to the best of their ability.*

Former Coach of the Philadelphia Flyers Fred Shero, whose team in the 1970's was nicknamed the *"Broad Street Bullies,"* had gone to the Soviet Union in 1961 to meet Tarasov and study the Russian training techniques. He was the first NHL coach to borrow from the Soviet style for the purposes of professional hockey. Ironically, it would be Shero's teams of the 1970's who would play the brand of hockey that best exemplifies the roughness Tarasov described. Shero would write in his 1975 book, *The Man behind the System:*

> *One must realize that hockey is full of intimidations and often these attempts to terrorize do result in violence. If the opposition allows itself to be terrorized, for instance, it will lose the offensive edge and, finally, the game. Many a goal has been scored dumping the star player.*

In terms of their analysis of Canadian hockey, one factor in the equation Tarasov and his coaches could not quite understand nor discover from Percival was the reasons behind, as well as the origin of, the on-ice hostility and violence displayed by Canadians towards their opponents. Tarasov was not a student of Canadian military history, so these attributes were both troubling as well as puzzling. Canadians approached hockey games not as simple sports contests but more like mini-battles in a drawn out war. It was this controlled warfare concept that was at the heart of Canadian hockey and its ruthlessness. It was this heritage of pain and violence that had been carefully shaped and fostered in the minds and souls of Canadian youngsters, from the first day they picked up a stick and learned to skate to the day they died. It was these qualities that made the Canadians stand out from other hockey players. The Canadian psychiatrist Dr. G. H. Stevens once wrote:

A fight of any kind has a hypnotic influence on most men. We men like war. We like the excitement of it, its thrill and glamour, its freedom from restraint. We like its opportunities for socially approved violence. We like its economic security and its relief from the monotony of civilian toil. We like its reward for bravery, its opportunities for travel, its companionship of men in a man's world, its intoxicating novelty. And we like to take chances with death.

Had Tarasov studied Canadian history and read Stevens' work he would have understood the mindset and violent nature of Canadian hockey.

In many ways, hockey offered Canadian boys and men the opportunity to wage war. Not since the time of the ancient Spartans had a warrior cult as complex as Canadian hockey existed. Not since the Battle of Thermopylae in c.480 BC, between the outnumbered forces of Leonidas and the Persians, had such a heroic concept of "the few against the many" been witnessed or played out. Canadian hockey was ancient warfare reenacted. Canadian hockey players were the modern personification of the Spartan warriors sent into battle against great odds. Following the battle of Thermopylae, the Greeks erected a monument to their fallen. It read simply: *"Go tell the Spartans, passerby that here obedient to their laws we lie."* No simpler words carry as much meaning and heroism as these. No words are as timeless. In a true sense, no words reflected the value and expectations placed upon modern Canadian hockey as these. When Canadian teams battled internationally they were expected to win at all costs. Failure was worse than death. Death would be respected. Defeat would not.

World politics would once again impact world hockey. Tensions escalated from a disastrous meeting in June 1961 in Vienna between U.S. President John F. Kennedy and Soviet President Nikita Khrushchev. The deterioration of relations between the two powers would result in East German soldiers building temporary fortifications in August of that year, in an effort to stop the flow of East Berliners from crossing into the Western part of the city. Eventually, these fortifications would evolve into the forty-seven kilometer long Berlin Wall. With the 1962 World Hockey Championships held in Colorado Springs, Colorado, the Americans response to the construction of the Berlin Wall was to refuse the East German team entry into the tournament. In a move of supposed solidarity, the Soviet Union and

Czechoslovakia boycotted the tournament. In truth, the Russians response was more a retaliation for the U.S. boycott of the 1957 championship in Moscow than a gesture to their satellite ally.

Led by 18 year-old sensation Ulf Sterner, Sweden upset the favored Canadian team en route to winning their third World Championship. Sterner would be later drafted by the New York Rangers in 1964, becoming first European to play in NHL. Fear that European player entry into professional hockey would result in jobs being taking from Canadians, Sterner became a target of racism and extreme physical play. Sterner would only play in four professional games in 1965 before deciding to return to Europe to finish his career.

During this period, tensions between Canada and United States also grew as former Oxford hockey star, Lester Pearson was elected Prime Minister of Canada. Pearson's greatest critic in Washington was none other than President Lyndon Johnson. Though the two men had assumed the Presidency and Prime Ministership in the same year, their visions of the world were quite different. This difference of perspective could be seen in a statement Pearson made to the Canadian Club in Ottawa in February 1965. On the issue of U.S. and Canadian foreign policy he remarked:

> *Our position is one of respectable importance, while we are not big enough to alarm anybody or dominate anybody's way of life. We have American plumbing without American power.*

In a previous speech years earlier, he had remarked that as the two countries moved closer together in terms of cultural and economic transactions, differences would emerge. Said Pearson, *"there will be difficulties and frictions."* Later he would comment, *"it would also help if the United States took more notice of what we do, and, indeed, occasionally of what we say."* These sentiments may have helped Pearson win friends abroad and among Canadian nationalists, but they were met with indifference and surprise in American political circles where the concept of Canadians being just like Americans had long been believed and promoted. The idea that Canadians were different, or viewed themselves as such, was akin to a gray elephant promoting itself as blue when in fact, all-in-the-know knew otherwise. Canadians could proclaim themselves to be whatever they wished, but when it came to international affairs, especially when dealing with the Soviets, Canadians were expected to display their allegiance to America.

On one occasion, during a 1964 discussion with U.S. Secretary of State Dean Rusk, Pearson, while commenting on an infamous cross-border murder case, sarcastically remarked:

> *That's the way we Canadians feel about you Americans.*
> *You can decapitate us and you can dismember us, just so*
> *long as you don't interfere with us.*

The comment did not go unnoticed. President Johnson had long been known for his remark: *"I never trust a man unless I've got his pecker in my pocket."* When it came to Pearson, the fact that the Texan's pockets were empty did not sit well in the White House. Years earlier, during the height of the Suez Crisis, Pearson had commented, *"It is bad to be a chore boy of the United States."* Time had not changed his perspective. Just as he had done during his hockey days at Oxford, Pearson had entered the political arena determined to play his own style of game. Pearson was insistent on having Canada maintain a separate independence from that of the United States. This decision would cost him friends in Washington. *Herr Zig Zag* was on the offensive. Canada was about to be changed politically forever.

On February 15, 1965, Pearson's Government inaugurated a new Canadian flag. The Red Maple Leaf replaced the Red Ensign and Union Jack, the two flags that had been the official flags of the country since 1867. The Maple Leaf had been the design concept of the historian George Stanley, a former Canadian Rhodes Scholar and ice hockey star at Oxford University in the 1930's. In the months leading up to the inauguration, Stanley had received death threats from many Canadian military veterans angry at the decision to replace the Union Jack and Ensign with a new "unbloodied" flag. Many veterans argued that Canadians had died for those flags and replacing the flags was akin to treason. What escaped the critics, and most people since, is the true symbolisms of the Red Maple Leaf. Far from being a passive image of a mid-level nation, the Canadian flag is one of the most militaristic symbols ever created.

George Stanley had served with the Canadian military during WWII. At the time of his design submission he was teaching military history at Canada's Royal Military College. Among his greatest endeavors was his on-going attempt to document the stories of Canadian survivors of the Dieppe Raid. He had written numerous books on Canadian history focusing on Canadian-American military conflicts including the War of 1812. Stanley understood the importance of *"military factors in Canadian history."*

Two blood-red pillars bordered the new flag. The pillars represented the historic human sacrifices made by the French and English peoples who founded Canada. The white background

194

represented the land blanketed in snow. The red maple leaf, the symbol worn by Canadian troops in WWI and WWII, represented the military sacrifice of Canadians. Interpreted in a purely militaristic context the flag's meaning is stark. *'From blood to earth to blood to earth to blood.'* It stands as a solemn reminder of the price paid and a statement to all Canadians, and their enemies, of the cost Canadians have paid in the past and are prepared to pay in the future for their freedoms. Stanley understood that Canada was a country created through personal sacrifices and wars. Historically speaking, few nations have been as militaristic as has been Canada. Canada is a proverbial "wolf in sheep's clothing" a characteristic which has allowed her people the ability to remain independent of the United States and victorious in every war for which she has fought.

There are other concepts to the Canadian flag worthy of mentioning. The flag's design is borrowed from a 1915 French Canadian postcard designed to instill Quebec nationalism and support for the Allied WWI war effort. The original design was a pillared flag of the Republic of France with a three-headed maple leaf at its center with the words *"Je me Souvien"* (I remember) emblazoned across the top of its white center. It is more than ironic that "Je me Souvien" is today the catch phrase of Quebec Separatists. Originally the term was designed to recall France's humiliating defeat in the 1870 Franco-Prussian War and not the French Canadian defeat on the Plains of Abraham. Today French Canadians proudly drive around their communities with the expression emblazoned on the backs of their car license plates making them the only people on the planet still visibly espousing anger at the Prussian annexation of Alsace-Lorraine. More ironic is the fact that the Canadian flag, as mentioned previously, is more a symbol of Quebec than the Fleurs-de-lis, the present day symbol of the Province. The Fleur-de-lis has historically represented French Aristocracy and the Catholic Religion, both historic suppressors of French Canadian nationalism.

In addition, there is one more historic irony of the Canadian flag. Created by a hockey warrior, the flag is a reborn symbol of the Red Branch Warriors of ancient Ulster. A symbol of early hockey and a heroic age of sport. A symbol of ancient independence, bravery and legend. Symbols that fit well within the framework of Canadian history and hockey.

It was at this time that Canada moved away from having Senior A club teams represent the country in world amateur tournaments. Instead, Canada had formed a National Team program comprised of top university students and Senior A players who playd together in preparation for all the major international tournaments.

The concept was the brain-child of Father David Bauer, a Catholic Priest. Bauer proposed to the Canadian Amateur Hockey Association (CAHA) the creation of a team of players from all over Canada, which was to have a unifying effect for a country that, since its inception, has been torn between French-English, east-west lines. He believed, not only could a full-time national team better represent Canada in world tournaments, but a national team would also allow an opportunity to players to attend university. Many a former Canadian professional hockey player, after his playing days were over, found himself living in poverty or even homeless. Bauer's plan was to give Canadian hockey players not only an alternative to turning professional, but also a future when their playing days were over. During the 1960's, less than 25 percent of the NHL players had obtained a high school graduation. In comparison, 75 percent of all professional football players and over 60 percent of all professional basketball players were college graduates. Phil Esposito would write in his book *Hockey is My Life*:

> *I made the NHL in 1963. I cut school short like practically everyone else playing hockey. When I came up, 75 percent of the NHL players hadn't graduated form high school. What the heck did we know about contracts? Nothing. What did we know about negotiating with a general manager who's been around 20 years and has only one thought in mind: getting this kid as cheap as possible? And another thing - we were frightened. When you're a high school dropout and all you know is playing hockey - well, brother, you sign.*

To the NHL, the time spent pursuing a university degree impeded on a Canadian player's development. In addition, a university graduate, as was the case with many American hockey players, meant that the player had private sector options that could be used as a bargaining tool in contract negotiations. This was frowned upon by club owners since, simply put, the less educated a player the easier to control. In other words, the last thing the NHL needed was an intelligent, educated, Canadian hockey player. Intelligence meant empowerment. Empowerment meant the ability to understand one's rights and options. Years later National Hockey League Players Association (NHLPA) President and player agent Alan Eagleson would say:

> *Most teams are downright impatient to whisk their boys out to the classroom and onto the rinks. To them a university*

education is extra baggage.

To understand the complexities of Canadian Society and limited options available to Canadian hockey players and others like them, it is important to place this period within an historic context. We know today, that a Canadian boy growing up in Canada during the decades of the 1950's and 1960's had a far greater chance of wearing a U.S. military uniform than ever wearing a professional hockey jersey. A Canadian boy was ten times more likely to land in Vietnam than in the NHL. A Canadian boy had just as likely a chance of having his name inscribed on the Vietnam Veteran's Memorial in Washington DC than on the Stanley Cup or on a plaque at the Hockey Hall of Fame in Toronto, Ontario. At a time when an estimated 60,000 Americans fled north to Canada to avoid military conscription and the Vietnam War, an estimated 30,000 - 40,000 Canadians went south to serve in the United States military. It is one of the great "secrets" of Canadian history that even though Canadian troops did not officially fight in Vietnam, many Canadians did. Today, the Vietnam Memorial records the names of 110 Canadians who died in Vietnam or are listed as POW/MIA.

In August 1963, Father Bauer's new Canadian National Team, nicknamed "the Nats", began practicing and touring in preparation for the 1964 Olympics. Bauer preached to the players that the team should represent Canada with class and integrity stating: *"to play to win, but not at any price."* Initially based in Vancouver, British Columbia, the Nats players enrolled at University of British Columbia. Later, the team would become headquartered in Winnipeg. Even though the Nats could not offer financial inducements they could offer education with the government-paid tuition, worldwide travel, and the lure of representing Canada in the Olympics. During the 1960's, Father Bauer would be successful in attracting prominent players like Fran Huck, despite Huck having received an excellent financial offer from the Montreal Canadiens. In addition, Danny O'Shea, who scored 132 points in only 48 games with Oshawa Generals junior hockey team, also joined after turning down several offers from the Minnesota North Stars. Cornell University All-American Ken Dryden also joined the Nats, after rejecting offers from the Montreal Canadiens, due to the fact that the Bauer program allowed him an opportunity to attend law school. The Canadian Nationals most notable player would be Toronto Maple Leafs All-Star defenseman, Carl Brewer, who left the NHL to continue working on his post-secondary education.

At the 1964 Olympics in Innsbruck, Austria, Bauer's team would have former 1961 Trail Smoke Eater and World Champion goaltender

Seth Martin in the nets. Martin would be named the Olympics' top goaltender, but it would not be enough to stop the Soviet Union from winning their second Olympic gold medal. Canada, Czechoslovakia, and Sweden all would tie with a record 5-2. Canada, believing they had won the bronze based on better goal differential than Sweden, was shocked 10 minutes before the medal presentations when IIHF President Ahearne changed the agreed tie breaking formula, instead awarding Sweden the bronze medal. Canada's bronze was a casualty of Ahearne's dislike of Canadian hockey officials and a political blow to Bauer's program. Ahearne's decision would make the already unpopular president the most hated man in Canadian hockey circles.

The Soviet's continued victories over Canadian hockey teams were due to their excellent physical conditioning and ability to skate forcefully with endurance. In 1964, Percival stated:

Today, Russian hockey players are skating an average of four miles an hour faster than NHL players and keeping up the faster pace twice as long or more. The Russian players are not only in far better shape than NHL players, but they are better coached in theory and technique of the game.

At a reception in the Kremlin for the 1964 Soviet Winter Olympic champions, Coaches Chernishov and Tarasov, along with Yuri Gagarin the Russians first cosmonaut, pleaded with Khrushchev to give the okay to exhibition matches between the Soviets and the North American professionals. Khrushchev deferred to Leonid Brezhnev, the second highest-ranking communist official at the time. Brezhnev reluctantly permitted Russian hockey officials to approach the NHL, only with final approval of any possible matches coming from the highest levels of the government. Andrei Starovoitov, a founding member of the Soviet Union's post World War II ice hockey program and General Secretary of its hockey federation, had written the Montreal Canadiens about setting up an exhibition match but never received a response. The NHL teams agreed not to make individual deals with the Russians and as a result no game would materialize, largely due to Clarence Campbell's political views.

Instead the Russian National Team would tour Canada in November 1965, playing several amateur teams including the Montreal Junior Canadiens. Played in Montreal, the Junior Canadiens included future NHL hall-of-famers, Jacques Lemaire and Serge Savard and future NHL all-star, Carol Vadnais. Coach Scotty Bowman had persuaded legendary hockey goaltending great Jacque Plante to come out of retirement and to play in the exhibition game. Plante was a seven time Vezina Trophy winner for best goalie in the NHL and the leagues Most Valuable Player in 1962. He may be best known today for being the first professional goalie to regularly wear a protective facemask. At the end of the 1964-65 season, Plante had retired but was granted clearance from the New York Rangers, who still held his hockey rights, to play in the exhibition game. Even though Plante was grossly unready for such a test against a team he had never seen play, he was able to turn in what was hailed as one of the greatest exhibitions of goalkeeping ever seen in Montreal. Plante stopped five Russian breakaways, allowing only one goal in 26 shots, as the Junior Canadiens scored with 29 seconds left in the game, winning the game 2-1. At the end of the game his teammates hoisted him onto their shoulders and skated around the ice to a rambunctious standing ovation. His play would have a profound impact on Soviet hockey, as Plante's style and technique would become the blueprint that future Russian hockey goaltenders would be patterned after.

Second-class citizens in their own land, the French Canadians had watched silently throughout the 1950's and 1960's as former colonial regions throughout the world achieved independence. Well aware that the interests who controlled Quebec (mostly English-Canadians and American business and corporate concerns) would not allow Quebec the opportunity to throw off its colonial shackles. While English Canada was seemingly being conquered culturally by American television, Quebecers were being liberated. The greatest weapon at the disposal of Quebecers was the television. It allowed them to see what was happening worlds away via the quiet confines of their isolated homes. No longer did they have to rely solely on the pulpit sermons of the parish priest for the latest news. No longer did he or she have to take as truth the word of outside politicians who preached whatever they felt Quebecers should hear. By the mid-1960's, a great revolution was underway throughout the province. Quebecers would no longer accept the notion of feeling second-class.

In October 1964 the tensions between the French and English cultures of Canada became self-evident during the visit of Queen Elizabeth to Quebec City. Few crowds met her motorcade. Traveling journalists could sense the coolness in the air and the indignation being directed towards the royal. What the journalists failed to understand was that the Queen's visit to the city served as yet another reminder to the French Canadians of their servitude status. The visit took an even uglier tone when demonstrators marching to show their displeasure with the visit were met by club-wielding police. The event would go down in Canadian history as *"The Saturday of the Truncheons."*

It would be Pearson's Liberal government that would attempt to protect the rights of Quebeckers by establishing a Royal Commission on Bilingualism and Biculturalism, effectively ensuring the survival of the French language and culture in Canada. Even with the reforms, by the late 1960's the political tension in Canada among the French and English societies was reaching a boiling point. Culminating in a series of Quebec political attempts to separate from Canada, a process that continues to this day. Though the two groups shared little in terms of unifying commonality, one of the few things they shared however was a genuine love for hockey. It was a great unifier and an even greater symbol for Canadians. Hockey gave Canadians a sense of identity. It gave Quebeckers in particular a sense of regional importance and pride. With Canada losing throughout the 1960's in international hockey, Canadian supremacy had come into question.

Montreal Junior Canadiens defenseman, Savard attended the Nats training camp in Montreal and was on his way to Winnipeg to join Bauer's team when Canadiens General Manager, Sam Pollock, intercepted him in the airport with the contract he had been asking for. In 1966, the best young prospect in hockey was the best hockey player in the world. Only 18 years of age, Bobby Orr was a hockey phenomenon. In his first negotiations with Boston, his agent Alan Eagleson used the possibility of him reporting to Bauer's Nationals as an option. The result was more than four times the original *"best offer"* Boston had proposed to Orr. Father Bauer had become more than just a hindrance to the NHL; his program was costing them financially.

That year, in 1966, a Russian B team would start a ten-game Canadian tour. Comprised of some of Russia's finest top young prospects, including up-and-coming Soviet star left winger Alexander Yakushev, the Soviets would begin their Canadian schedule against the Newfoundland Provincial Champion, Corner Brook Royals. Led by the province's legendary Player-Coach Frank "Danky" Dorrington, the Royals had been one of the top teams in Newfoundland for several years, previous winners of Herder Memorial Trophy as the top Senior A team in Newfoundland, in 1962 and 1964. In a game with little body-checking and only one penalty, the Soviets would have open ice to skate and execute, resulting in the 28-0 thumping of the provincial champions Royals, outshooting the Newfoundlanders by a 74-18 margin.

After seven more wins against various Senior A teams throughout the country, the Soviet's would suffer there only loss of the tour in their final game against Bauer's National Team in Vancouver, BC. After a falling out with the Toronto Maple Leafs, 27-year-old NHL all-star defenseman, Carl Brewer, had become a reinstated amateur making his national team debut against the Russians. It would be the Soviets' hardest fought game of the tour, and in stark contrast to their first game against the Corner Brook Royals. The game, which was slowed to a near standstill, featured several fights with the press describing the Canadian squad as being guilty of *"many needless, non-tactical body checks aimed solely to physically intimidate and punish their opposition."* In international tournament competition, the Canadians' aggressive NHL style of play would have resulted in a continuous chorus line of players being sent to the penalty box. But in Vancouver, the referees turned a blind eye to the international rules that prohibited neutral zone body-checking, giving the Nats the green light to proceed with a physical ambush without impunity. What ensued was a chippy game with both teams displaying an eagerness for unnecessary roughness. The Russians' response to the intentional physical intimidation was to retaliate with their sticks. The result was a series of high-sticking and interference penalties charged to the Soviet team. Even though many obvious infractions were overlooked, the game still finished with a total of eighteen penalties, ten of which were committed by the Russians. The Canadians would score five power play goals, defeating the Soviets 7-3.

The next day, the newspaper headlines in the *Vancouver Province* would read *"Canada Dumps Russians - all over the ice."* Re-affirmation and indication to Canadians that physical hockey would be the only way to defeat the visitors. Faced with physical, professional style hockey, it was believed the Soviets would fold like a house of cards. Leaders of Canadian international ice hockey would begin to lobby for a change to the international rules legitimizing body-checking throughout the entire rink, with its adoption finally culminating in 1968. Tarasov wrote:

> *This innovation was mainly directed against us. Hockey became embittered. By means of powerful pressure the Canadian coaches wanted to deprive us of an easy performance . . . We had to find an efficient decision. One of such seemed easy: to teach hockey players to tolerate the cruelty of the Canadians.*

Throughout the 1960's, the Soviet Union dominated the international hockey scene. Although they continued to defeat Canada in every tournament throughout the 1960's, according to Tarasov:

> *Canadian teams tried to find some accidental reason each time they were defeated [as a result] they were not enriching or changing their hockey.*

201

An astute observer, Tarasov closely monitored the training techniques of other countries writing that during one of his tours to Canada, he asked a Canadian official, *"How many miles does Bobby Hull skate in a game?"* Not only did the official have no answer, until Tarasov asked, no one had considered the question. Tarasov's reply, *"If you don't know the answer to that, then you can't be serious about the game."*

Twenty years after Percival's study of amateur and professional hockey was ridiculed in Canada for, in part, logging how many miles a player skates, the European hockey community had seen the work as a modern hockey bible. Tarasov may have built the house that was Russian hockey but the architect of the structure was Percival. Modern Russian hockey was, quite simply, nothing more than forgotten Canadian methodology. Tarasov would send Percival a copy of his book, *Road to Olympus,* in it, he wrote:

> *Your wonderful book which introduced us to the mysteries of Canadian hockey. I have read it like a schoolboy. Thank you for a hockey science, which is significant to world hockey. I wish you all the best in your professional endeavors, confidence in your decisions and good health. Your Canadian hockey is powerful, especially your professional hockey. Recently the young Soviet hockey school has also proven that it needs no recommendation. My friend let us compete and communicate professionally. Nothing can be lost in such an exchange. However, I personally believe that on ice we will even defeat the professionals. Regardless, it will be the greatest victory for world hockey and friendship.*

Yours with respect, Anatoli Tarasov, December 27, 1969

As loses continued to mount to the Soviet Union, Canadians turned to the rhetoric of paper victories stating the likes of "the scores would be much different if only we could use professionals." The public began increasingly calling to have the NHL's best play the Soviets in a once-and-for-all showdown.

From the time of the Bolshevik Revolution of 1917 to the late 1960's, the Soviet Union had increased its sports participation from 50,000 to 50,000,000 people becoming a leading athletic world power. Ice hockey in the Soviet Union would rise in popularity second only to soccer. Throughout Russia, over 300,000 boys were playing in registered hockey leagues and millions more playing what they call "city courtyard hockey". This compared to the 230,000 in Canada, 140,000 in Sweden, 77,000 in Czechoslovakia, and 48,000 in the United States. Youth coaches were granted time off work to train and participate in the latest techniques. By the mid-1960's, the Soviet Union was investing over two billion U.S. dollars a year to build "The Big Red Machine" of sport. Even the Soviet fans were becoming bored with their dominance of the international scene. Now was the logical time for their hockey program to play the Canadian professionals.

In a Stockholm hotel room in 1968, Tarasov had asked Lester Patrick about the possibility of his national team playing the New York Rangers. Patrick's response: *First, no one would want to see the game. Second, we would beat you 15-0.*" That same year Starovoitov approached *Toronto Globe and Mail* reporter Scott Young to propose financial terms to the Toronto Maple Leafs for an exhibition match. While the Soviet Nationals were on a North American tour, the Leafs, seeing a chance for a financial windfall, would invite the Russians for a three-game series to be held in 1969. The Soviet team agreed, but due to political reasons the games would not materialize. According to Tarasov:

> *We asked the leader of our delegation to contact Moscow immediately . . . He was a career official, being afraid of all sorts of things. He did not make any calls to Moscow at all. Lying to us, he said that the managers in Moscow "were against" the idea that they were expecting us to come home and that there was a schedule that could not be broken.*

Even with Bauer's success in obtaining quality players, the lure of the NHL had cost the Nats the talent needed to stop Soviet dominance of international hockey. In order to keep players from taking lucrative professional contracts, while also injecting more money into the program, the Canadian delegation would make a proposal to the IIHF whereby a six-team World League would be established with one team from the Soviet Union, Czechoslovakia, Sweden, U.S. and two from Canada. The reason for two Canadian teams was the 1967 creation of a second Canadian National team headquartered in Ottawa. Considerations for as many as four national teams were being made in order to give more players an alternative to turning professional. In the proposal, the World League would include a twenty to thirty game schedule that would be worked around the World Championships and the Olympics. This way Canadian professionals could participate, make a living in hockey, all without having to give up amateur status. The various European countries could not agree on the specifics and the idea was ultimately rejected.

In 1967 the number of NHL teams doubled from its original six-team format to twelve teams. To fill these new teams, the NHL would look to non-traditional avenues. This meant that the players once considered to have *"extra baggage,"* because of post secondary education, now were sought after commodities. The NHL could not afford to lose up to four teams worth of players to Bauer's Canadian national hockey program and, in addition, a professional European hockey league with ties to the NHL was an idea league President Campbell had considered developing. Campbell said:

> *I have predicted many times . . . that the Stanley Cup will eventually be a challenge series between the NHL champion and some European, possibly a Soviet, representative.*

The most serious discussions would come in 1972 when members of the Detroit Red Wings management, along with future league commissioner John Ziegler, went to Europe to discuss the possibility of a professional European league with teams in England, Sweden, West Germany, Austria, and Switzerland.

With a 5-0 loss to the USSR at the 1968 Olympics, Father Bauer's hopes for reestablishing Canada's international hockey supremacy were dashed, having to settle for the bronze. A few months later, Prime Minister Pierre Trudeau commissioned a three-member Task Force on "Sport" to investigate Canada's continued amateur hockey failures. The results would be a profound change in Canadian hockey. The Task Force recommended that a non-profit corporation be established for the purpose of managing and financing all levels of amateur hockey. In February 1969, Hockey Canada was established. It would include various amateur organizations including the two Canadian NHL teams, the Leafs and Canadiens. Under Hockey Canada, NHL interests would steer the future direction of Canadian amateur hockey and immediately they began to lobby for the use of professionals in world international hockey.

Sweden would lead the charge against allowing NHL professionals playing IIHF World Championship competition. Their concern was that the International Olympic Committee would not allow the Canadian professional to participate in the Olympics, while also disqualifying other team's players who faced the Canadians in the IIHF's tournaments. Therefore, would the European teams then have to create an "A" team to face the Canadian professionals and a "B" team, made up of individuals who only would play in the Olympics? Even without the NHL professionals, Canada was always a threat for a goal medal, whereas, the European countries did not have the depth of talent that the Canadians had to have a second team viably challenge for an international championship.

As it stood, full and open professional inclusion in world competitions would not be approved. Canadian officials compromised and proposed that the Canadian National Team be allowed nine professionals, none of them to be active players in the NHL, and that these players be allowed to participate in future world tournaments including the Olympics. The opposing European nations were not convinced that such a move would still not endanger their own players' Olympic eligibilities. The deciding vote would be from Ahearne. Ahearne agreed to the Canadian motion casting the tie-breaking vote, ruling that in the 1970 tournament, scheduled for March in Montreal and Winnipeg, that Canada could use nine non-NHL pros. It would be a one-year trial run, giving the IIHF the needed time to get clarification on the Olympic eligibility issue.

In December 1969, after the Isvestia tournament in Moscow, where Canada placed second with the assistance of five newly added professionals, International Olympic Committee President Brundage wrote Ahearne stating that for the IIHF to open its World Championship in such a manner would jeopardize Olympic eligibility. He wrote:

> *Opening up the world championships as well as other tournaments, to professional players, will no doubt affect the Olympic eligibility of all participating teams. While the IOC hadn't passed officially on this specific situation, you should know that all teams participating in the soccer World Cup, in which professionals are permitted, are ineligible for Olympic competition. It can be expected that a similar decision will be reached in the case of ice hockey.*

Canada's Olympic Association refuted Brundage's position, responding in kind that this decision was not supported by official Olympic rules. While Ahearne called for another vote on the issue, Hockey Canada announced if the decision went against them that the upcoming world tournament would be canceled. An ultimatum was sent to the other IIHF participants: *"We will get our way or we will quit international play."* The vote went against Canada. Canada's first ever world hockey tournament as the host country was canceled. Two years of preparation was lost with the net result costing the Canadian government $400,000. This surprised some of the European nations which felt, when push came to shove, Canada would not actually pull out.

Ahearne's refusal to back the original decision and fight the IOC was seen by Canadian officials as Ahearne being *"an errand-boy for the Swedes and Russians."* Ahearne responded to Canada's withdrawal by calling the Canadian delegation *"crybabies,"* while also declaring that international hockey could get along without them. In reality the IIHF lost its biggest draw. Instead, the 1970 games would move to Stockholm, Sweden, the site of the 1969 World Championships. Total attendance would be down 40 percent from the previous year, exactly the percentage the Canadian Nationals games drew. Not only was Ahearne being criticized by the Canadians, he was also under fire from his most powerful European members. The Swedish Press called for Ahearne's head for mishandling the whole affair and allowing Canada to leave.

Ironically, Lloyd Percival would be affected by this decision. The man who first offered his assistance in 1936, only to be rejected by the Canadian Olympic Association, was finally being seen by governmental agencies as someone who could help, not only Olympic hockey, but also the entire Canadian Olympic program. In 1970, Percival was asked by Hockey Canada to be a consultant and to draft a training program.

> *I did as suggested and drafted a total plan. They accepted and we started it and did well in Canada. Remember, I've been saying we don't need pros. We can beat the Russians with amateurs if we prepare the right way. Then Canada withdrew from international hockey when we were on phase two. That was the greatest single disappointment in my life.*

Under the Percival training program the Canadian National team's results had begun to improve. They had beaten several pro teams and, in their last game together in Ottawa the night the pullout was announced, they beat the touring Czechoslovakian national team 2-1. This would end the Father Bauer era of hockey. It would not be until after the 1972 series between Canadian professional and the Soviet National Team that Bauer's accomplishment would be fully realized. After the Nationals were disbanded, Bauer began working with the Japanese National Team turning their program into a top contender in the World "B" hockey. With Bauer's assistance, Japan would have their best results since 1962, just missing group "A" qualifying with three consecutive second place finishes.

In less than two years Hockey Canada, led only by NHL interests, had moved Canadian hockey away from Bauer's ideals to a crusade for professional players in world competitions. The national team would be dismantled with many of the players signing with NHL clubs. The bitterness of some longtime national team players was reflected in Roger Bourbonnais' statement years later:

> *The whole deal was based not on what was good for the country, or for sport or young hockey players at all, but strictly on money.*

In the end, Canada put a ban on sending Canadian teams of any age group to Europe, but at the same time they continued to attend IIHF meetings, keeping their lines of communications open. Canada would not participate from 1970-76 in IIHF sanctioned competitions, missing both the 1972 and 1976 Olympics and seven world tournaments. Any future competition would now be negotiated directly through the NHL or indirectly through the NHL, via Hockey Canada. Canadian hockey was no longer an amateur sport. It was now a corporate controlled business controlled, in large part, by American NHL interests.

Neither politics, nor sports, operates in a vacuum. The changed political climate of the 1960's would continue to impact and shape international hockey. International tensions between countries would boil over onto the ice. During the sweeping social tide of the 1960's, Czechoslovakian political leadership attempted to reform their Communist system. Between January and August of 1968, Alexander Dubcek's Czechoslovakian government would introduce domestic reforms ending press censorship while also trying to move the country to a more progressive economy. It would be dubbed *"Socialism with a Human Face."* Liberal reforms in Communist Eastern Europe were regarded as poisons that could seep across frontiers, stirring up trouble inside the Soviet Union, and ultimately result in bringing down the empire. Just before midnight on the night of August 20, 1968, the Soviet Union and its Warsaw Pact allies from East Germany, Poland, Bulgaria, and Hungary invaded Czechoslovakia. The Soviet-led maneuver was aimed at thwarting Dubcek's democratic reforms. During the ordeal, a half-dozen people were killed and thirty-five were injured. After being arrested and taken back to Moscow, Dubcek was returned to Prague on August 27. Even with the country being occupied by 600,000 foreign troops, the reforms introduced would not be undone until April of 1969, when the Soviets would finally drive Dubcek from office and replace him with the more conservative Gustav Husak. All reforms that had been achieved were lost, and in the end Czechoslovakia remained "officially" one of the Soviet Union's most loyal allies. The less-than-camaraderie tank tracks left on the streets of

Prague would eventually disappear and with them so would the Czechoslovakian people's sense of optimism. The void left would be filled with animosity towards their Soviet ally.

Following the invasion, hockey games between the two countries would intensify becoming battles of nationalistic pride. At the Stockholm games in March 1969, the Russians won their seventh consecutive World Championship, despite two losses to the Czechs. After the second victory, tens of thousands jammed Wenceslas Square in Prague in an anti-Soviet demonstration. The office of the Soviet airline Aeroflot was ransacked. Warsaw Pact troops stationed in the country were placed on alert and Soviet officials warned the Czechoslovakian government to restore order. The two games revealed all the ill-will engendered by the Soviet invasion of Czechoslovakia.

Overtime

Chapter Fourteen

Eternity

Television was a catalyst in spurring the popularity and success of the NHL throughout North America. A poll in 1972 showed 24 percent of the U.S. sports fans said they followed hockey - a seven percent increase over 1971 figures. The NHL, which expanded from six to twelve teams in 1967 and had added two new teams to Vancouver and Buffalo in 1970, didn't want to accelerate the expansion program due to a lack of hockey talent to draw on. Although the number of players in the league had more than doubled, only a few were non-Canadians. With demand for hockey on the rise, Dennis Murphy and Gary Davidson, co-founders of the American Basketball Association in 1967, met to start a new hockey league that would rival the NHL. Whereas the NHL was selling franchises for six million, to buy one of the initial World Hockey Association (WHA) franchises would only cost $25,000 with a $100,000 performance bond. In January 1972, the twelve-team startup league was unveiled. The WHA would operate in seven cities that formerly never had big-league hockey and five cities with existing NHL teams. The league located in New York City, Winnipeg, Chicago, Edmonton, Los Angeles, Quebec City, Philadelphia, St. Paul, Ottawa, Boston, Houston, and Cleveland would begin to raid the NHL for top players. With the new league in areas the NHL had been courting and considering for future expansion, it would now become a race for the remaining new markets. The NHL would announce the addition of Atlanta and Long Island to start in the fall of 1972 and also revealed plans to increase its membership to eighteen teams in 1974-1975, with the addition of Kansas City and Washington, D.C.

This meant that overall, fourteen new professional hockey teams would begin playing in North America in the fall of 1972, doubling the total that played in 1971. Now professional teams in both leagues would be forced to look for talent from non-traditional sources in order to ice a competitive hockey product.

On February 12-13, 1972 in Anaheim, California, the WHA would conduct their first draft. In two days the teams drafted 1,081 players, nearly four times the amount needed to man the teams. Some of the more interesting picks included Wendell Anderson, the 35-year-old governor of Minnesota and former 1956 U.S. Olympic player, drafted by the Minnesota Fighting Saints. Edmonton drafted the great Swedish National Team goaltender Leif Holmqvist. Holmqvist, a veteran of international play since 1962, had been named the 1969 top goalkeeper at the World Championships and had led Sweden to three second place finishes at the Worlds between 1967-70. The WHA draft would mark the first time a professional hockey team had ever drafted a Russian, the five-time World Championship and all-star defenseman Alex Ragulin. Owner Bill Hunter commented on picking the Russian star: *"We took Ragulin because he's a great player, and you have to be prepared for the possibility that one day that entire team might defect."*

The new WHA league continued to go largely ignored until June 27, 1972. After fifteen years of playing with the NHL's Chicago Black Hawks Bobby Hull, the first hockey player to ever appear on the cover of *Time Magazine,* would sign a $2.75 million deal as a player-coach. The contract included a one million up front bonus that all the franchises in the WHA would contribute to. Professional hockey's most popular player instantly gave the league credibility and the NHL's second-rate perception towards the new startup league would turn to fear. Hull was expected to sell the league. Ben Hatskin, the Winnipeg owner, would say:

> *I had seen what Sonny Werbin had done just by giving Joe Namath that $400,000 contract to sign with the New York Jets. That's what made the American Football League and eventually made it a partner with the National League. I think that we can accomplish the same thing for the WHA by giving Hull this deal, which I believe to be the biggest ever for any athlete.*

One-by-one, top NHL players defected to the WHA. NHL teams slow to react to their new competitor's challenge would soon have their rosters raided. Maple Leafs goaltender Bernie Parent, who was slated to be their fall starter, agreed to play in the WHA at more than three times the salary that the Leafs were offering. The Stanley Cup Champion Boston Bruins would be the most affected losing three key players: goaltender Gerry Cheevers, defenseman Ted Green, and forward Derek Sanderson. All would sign big contracts with the rival league, with Sanderson agreeing to a 2.6 million dollar deal with the Philadelphia Blazers. The NHL owners, who originally agreed to avoid any bidding wars with the WHA, were now being forced to raise salaries in order to keep their players. Due to competitive bidding from the Philadelphia Blazers, junior hockey star Billy Harris became the highest paid rookie in NHL league history inking a three-year contract with the expansion New York Islanders for $300,000, approximately four times the salary a star rookie traditionally received. Overall, player's salaries escalated, increasing on average, over thirty percent in a year. Prior to 1972, about twenty-five percent of a team's gross receipts had been paid out in wages; now player salaries would increase to 40-45 percent of a team's total revenue. Alan Eagleson, legal representative and agent for over 150 professional players, would say:

> *Conservatively, the WHA in conjunction with the regular inflation has made a difference of $5 million and maybe more in NHL player salaries for the upcoming season.*

Many NHL executives believed that escalating salaries would be the demise of the new league. NHL President Campbell remarked:

> *My personal opinion is that the WHA won't last a year. But we can't afford to proceed on that assumption. The position I'm taking with our people is that you have to take the cautious course and fight a good fight.*

1972 would also mark the first time that the Olympic tournament champion would not be the IIHF World Champion. The IIHF decided to separate the two tournaments opening the door for professionals to compete in World Championships without affecting competing players' Olympic eligibility. It would be the first step towards trying to bring Canada back into international hockey. Even so, Canada would still continue to boycott international hockey, allowing for the United States to fill their spot at the Sapporo Olympics, in Japan.

Two future WHA stars, Robbie Ftorek and Mark Howe, son of the great Gordie Howe, would lead the American hockey team into Olympic competition. The six-nation tournament would feature teams from the Soviet Union, Czechoslovakia, Sweden, Finland, and Poland. Once again the Russian bear would capture the gold medal but the surprise of the tournament would be the U.S. team. After dropping their opening game 5-1 to the Swedes, they would rebound in their second game as American goaltender, and future WHA player, Mike "Lefty" Curran would be superb, making 51 saves in a 5-1 U.S. victory over Czechoslovakia. After losing their next game to the Soviets, the young American team would finish the tournament by defeating Finland and Poland winning the silver medal by virtue of a better goal differential than Czechoslovakia and Sweden. American Olympic success would not carry over into World Championship play and over the next few years the United States would struggle to stay qualified in Pool A, dropping back and forth between the top seeds and Pool B qualification - "the battle for 7th place."

Later that same year, at the World Championship in Prague, Czechoslovakia, the Soviets would replace their long time national team coaches including Tarasov. Tarasov would eventually be introduced into the International and the NHL Hockey Halls of Fame falsely credited with the *"invention"* of the Soviet system. Replacing Tarasov would be former Russian star Bobrov, whose first international tournament would be the 1972 championships.

Winners of the bronze medal in Sapporo, Japan, the Czechoslovakians would defeat the Soviets snapping the Soviet Union's nine-year string of World Championships and spoiling Bobrov's debut. It would be Czechoslovakia's first World Championship win since 1949. In the ten games the two hockey rivals played since 1968, the Czechs had won five, lost three and tied two. In the wake of the 1968 invasion of Czechoslovakia, the Soviet-Czech rivalry had become one of the most intense and heated in sport.

It would be in Prague where Hockey Canada's representative, Alan Eagleson, would make the final arrangements for Canada to re-enter the international competition. Canada and the Soviet Union would agree to play an eight-game series with the first four in Canada and the last four in Moscow. At the halfway point of the tournament, Canada would play two games in Stockholm against the Swedish National Team, finishing with one game in Prague against the new World Champion, after the eight-game series concluded with Russia. In total, 11 games would be played against the top three teams in international play.

The Canadian team would be made up of the top 36 NHL players. Players who signed with the new rival WHA would not be allowed to participate for Team Canada. Goalie Gerry Cheevers, who had set a record by going unbeaten in 32 consecutive games for Boston the previous season, NHL all-star forward Derek Sanderson, defenseman J.C. Tremblay, and forward Bobby Hull would all have to watch from the sidelines. Initially, Coach Harry Sinden had expected to be able to use WHA players but NHL President Campbell would not allow any player outside the NHL to participate. When asked why not let Bobby Hull play? Campbell responded:

Why should we supply a showcase for our opposition's best feature? This is an economic battle, and we are being wounded very seriously.

The decision to exclude Hull sent shockwaves across Canada. Canadian Prime Minister Trudeau would send a letter asking for

Campbell to reconsider, but to no avail. Team Canada would also not have the services of hockey's best player, Bobby Orr. Although he would be added to the roster, Orr would not be able to recover from knee surgery fast enough to participate. Even without the two best players in hockey, Orr and Hull, or the WHA defectors, Percival would describe the team as: *"The greatest collection of hockey players we've ever had in one place. Potentially, it's the greatest team ever."*

After being defeated at the World Championships, followers of international hockey believed the Russian team was in decline. Yet, even though the Russians were not the international hockey's reigning champs, the series would still be billed as the showdown that would finally determine hockey supremacy. Maple Leafs defenseman, Brian Glennie summed up the situation by stating:

> *The Europeans always thought it was sour grapes on our part when we told them our best players weren't eligible. Now we'll see.*

Hockey experts were almost unanimous in their analysis of the series, stating Canada would win six or more of the eight games. *Sports Illustrated* predicted Canada would win seven games and respected *Toronto Globe and Mail* columnist Dick Beddoes foresaw an eight game series sweep. Each prediction only fueled expectations to the point that nothing short of near perfection would do. Tournament organizer Eagleson proclaimed:

> *We got to win eight games. Anything less than an unblemished sweep of the Russians would bring shame down on the heads of the players and the national pride.*

The Canadian scouts sent to watch the Soviets only seemed to reaffirm the impending slaughter. John McLellan, Head Coach of the Maple Leafs and Leafs' head scout Bob Davidson both came back from Moscow with the impression the Soviet Union had a good squad but that it would still be possible for an eight game Canadian sweep of the series. Their only concern was that the Canadian players might take the Russians too lightly and become overconfident and under prepared, resulting in the team not being physically conditioned for the start of the series. To them, only one player on the Soviet squad was a standout, Alexander Yakashev. In addition, the scouts reported that the Russians were pinning their hopes on the shoulders of their goalie Vladislav Tretiak. McLellan would remark:

We saw Tretiak, their No.1 goalie, and he didn't look particularly good. He let in eight goals, some high over his shoulders and a couple between his legs.

Later, it would be told that the night they saw Tretiak play was on the eve of his wedding day. *"My mind was away from the hockey game,"* the Soviet goalie later explained.

With so-called hockey experts seemingly all in agreement, any contrasting viewpoint was considered unpatriotic or viewed merely as someone looking to get their name in print by going against the conventional grain. One dissenting opinion would be former Maple Leafs and Sweden National Team Coach, Billy Harris. Harris had led the Swedish team to a 3-3 tie against the Soviets at 1972 Olympics in Japan and had returned to North American hockey becoming the new coach of the Ottawa Nationals of the WHA. He warned that the Soviets would be considerably better than anyone expects, and predicted it would be the Russians who would win the series, largely on the strength of Tretiak's goaltending. Stating the opposite of what Team Canada's scouts had observed, Harris's prediction would be viewed as nothing more than someone exclaiming that "the sky is falling," - hockey's Chicken Little.

While many of the Canadian players spent their off-season running businesses before reporting to training camp on August 13, the Soviet players began working out six hours a day playing basketball, soccer, and other off-ice sports. The Soviet athletes had started preparing for the series at the beginning of July, following an accelerated physical training program that would have them in peak condition by the September 2 opening game. At the time, the North American hockey establishment still espoused archaic beliefs about hockey conditioning. This attitude was prevalent in the statement of veteran Team Canada defenseman Rod Seiling who said:

I don't think conditioning will be a factor at all. The Russians may be more conditioned overall because they run (and) play soccer. But who's to say their way is the best? Once you reach a point in your conditioning, as a hockey player, I don't think you can improve on it.

Under enormous expectations, Coach Harry Sinden would run a tougher, more aggressive, training camp than was typically done by NHL teams. The players appeared to respond, showing they were taking the upcoming games seriously. Defenseman Gary Bergman said the team wasn't taking the Soviets lightly, remarking:

When they first entered world competition and the Olympics they did it to learn to improve their game. They expect to learn from us. But they've come such a long way and iced such a solid team that the main problem for us is underestimating them.

Training camp would be held in Toronto with the coaches deciding to divide the team and play several intra-squad games, instead of scheduling outside exhibition games. Tickets to the games were sold to the public and hailed as the equivalent to an NHL all-star game. To the disdain of Smythe, it would be during these intra-squad games that goals, assists, and penalties would be announced in English and French over the Maple Leafs Garden's public-address system - the first such time French had been heard over the public address system in English Canada's hockey shrine. Sinden, who had captained the Whitby Dunlops to victory over the Soviets at the 1958 World Championships, cautioned his players about falling victim to being too emotionally high when they stepped out onto the ice for the first game in Montreal. Warning the players, not to *"forget to put the puck in the net,"* like his Dunlop team had done 14 years earlier.

An hour before the first game in Montreal, former goaltender Jacques Plante was asked by the Soviet coaches to go into their dressing room to talk to the 20-year old Tretiak. Plante also had previously predicted an eight game Canadian sweep saying:

I know how the Russians feel. It's like when I played for the St. Louis Blues and we would meet the Montreal Canadiens for the Stanley Cup. We use to say that it would be nice if we could tie a game and force it into overtime. We never expected to win.

The two goaltenders met three years earlier, when the 17 year-old Tretiak was visiting Canada with his national junior team. Plante had worked with him on his technique and was worried how the young goalie would manage against the premier players of the world. Later, Tretiak would say Plante's advice would help him in the opening game:

He showed me on a [chalk] board how the Canadian players shot the puck. He talked about Cournoyer, Mahovlich, Esposito. I think he felt a little sorry for me. He didn't think I'd do well.

216

Each team would dress 19 players per game. For the first game, Sinden and Assistant-Coach John Ferguson picked an offensive lineup that they felt would overwhelm the Soviets. Going strength-against-strength, the Canadian coaches reasoned an *"improvisational offense"* would throw the Soviets, *"a patterned-passing offensive,"* off their game while, at the same time, expose the weak Soviet goaltending.

Although the first game would be televised at 3 a.m. Moscow time, over 100 million Russians would tune in only to see the Canadians jump to a 1-0 lead barely 30 seconds into the game. Six minutes later, the Canadians would score again taking an early 2-0 lead. Everything was going as the Canadians had predicted. As the game drew on, the better-conditioned Soviet squad found their rhythm, slowly taking control of the game and tying the score at 2-2 after the first period. In the second, the Soviets would again score two more times giving them a 4-2 lead heading into the final period. Bobby Clarke's goal at 8:22 into the third period would spark a short lived Team Canada rally but, in the end, the Russians would weather the storm and respond with three unanswered goals in the last seven minutes to finish off the fatigued Canadian squad. The 7-3 final score would be a bitter pill for Canadians to swallow. The North American hockey world was in shock! The loss would make headlines across Canada; the *Toronto Globe and Mail* would proclaim *"Canada Mourns Hockey Myth."* Even in Moscow, the Russian victory came as a surprise. The Soviet news agency *Tass* reported that the game had destroyed the Canadian professionals' myth of invincibility stating:

> *The defeat showed that Canadians, accustomed to competing in 'self-isolation', play an 'archaic' brand of hockey.*

Columnist Dick Beddoes wrote that the Soviets were not here to learn from Canada's best but here to defeat them:

> *We should have learned from Soviet tactics in other sports that they would not be here against most of our best if they were going to be muscled into embarrassing submission.*

After the defeat, Campbell would publicly criticize Sinden on his game-one player selections, upsetting many of the Canadian players. Several roster changes would be made for the second game with the most dramatic being the benching of the New York Rangers forward line of Jean Ratelle, Rod Gilbert and Vic Hadfield, the highest scoring line in the NHL and the second highest scoring line in the history of professional hockey. Sinden criticized them for not skating and a lack of effort while Gilbert attributed the line's poor performance to nerves, claiming he had never seen the line play so poorly. Critics blamed the team's failure on conditioning, but after watching game films Sinden mainly attributed their loss to lack of fore-checking:

> They outplayed us in every aspect of the game, from goaltending to shooting, skating and passing. And yes, they showed they are in better condition than we are. I was stunned how well they played at times. You play just about as well as the other team permits you, and they didn't allow us to play very well . . . This game burst a few balloons in our team's thinking. There isn't any doubt that we were outplayed and out checked. It was a good game and we don't have much to be ashamed about, but it proved to our guys that the Russians can't be taken lightly.

In addition to fore-checking problems, there were incidents of helmetless Canadians being hit on the head with Soviet hockey sticks. A bigger, harder-checking Canadian line-up would play the next game as forwards Jean-Paul Parise, Wayne Cashman, and Stan Mikita along with defensemen Serge Savard, Pat Stapleton, and Bill White, would be inserted into the starting line-up. Each of the new additions would contribute, as Team Canada would even up the series at one game a piece with a 4-1 victory, played in Toronto. The aggressive play of the home team, particularly Cashman, would dominate the discussion the next day as Pat Stapleton described Cashman as playing *"like he meant to kill."* The Russian's, on the other hand, cried foul as seen in Soviet Coach Bobrov reaction when questioned about the play of Cashman:

> We believe in rough play when it means bodychecking, roughness within the framework of the rules. But our spectators do not like that kind of roughness you saw in Toronto. If that had been in Europe [Cashman] would have spent the entire game in the penalty box.

The Soviet News Agency *Tass* would report that it was the two U.S. referees who were mostly to blame for the Soviet Union's 4-1 loss declaring: *"the U.S. referees often ignored violations-of-rules by the Canadians."* In an interview with *Tass*, Cashman, the center of all the controversy, responded to questions about his aggressive play saying: *"I enjoy both giving and receiving pain."* In Canada, some in the media criticized the manner in which Team Canada won, but Assistant-Coach Ferguson would insist that the Soviets were no angles themselves stating:

> *The Russians must have taken home some old Gordie Howe films. They have abandoned any obvious fouls such as slashing, high-sticking, and charging. They concentrate on finesse-spearing, stabbing, cross-checking, butt-ending, and elbows.*

Played in Winnipeg, game three would be just as rough but less vicious than the one in Toronto as the referee cracked down on excessive physical play. The game would wind up in a 4-4 draw as the Soviets, again, would show their superior conditioning by staging a late come-back with two goals in the last five minutes of the game, salvaging the tie. Goaltender Tretiak would again be the story of the game as Canadian backup goaltender, Eddie Johnson, would compare Tretiak's play to that of Plante, saying:

> *You can see Jacques Plante's influence very clearly. Tretiak sat and talked with Jacques in Montreal and Toronto, and he had met him before. More than that, though, you know the Russians follow his theories. Tarasov always said that Plante taught them what there is to goaltending.*

Sinden's praise of the Soviets would go even go further, as he touted his opponents individual talent, proclaiming:

> *I don't see one Russian who couldn't make the NHL. The myth of hockey belonging to one country or one continent is dead.*

Game four in Vancouver would see the Soviet Union dominate from start to finish, winning handily by a misleadingly close score of 5-3. The game illustrated the NHL player's weaknesses: insufficient training, lack of team play, and an over-dependence on lucky breaks and physical intimidation. For many, it seemed to confirm that these weaknesses are endemic in the system built to serve the NHL. Throughout the game, but especially during the commercial breaks, the Vancouver fans booed Team Canada unmercifully. Afterwards, an emotionally charged Phil Esposito would agree to be interviewed on Canadian national television. Esposito used it as an opportunity to voice his displeasure with the Canadian fans expressing the long held feelings of many Canadian hockey players who had received a similar wrath from the Canadian public, in the years since Canada's first loss to the Soviets in 1954:

> *I am disappointed that some Canadians are against us. Most of us make our living in the States, but we love Canada. That's why we're playing against Russia. But the ridicule we're getting form some Canadian fans is below my dignity . . . We gave it all we had, why can't people just take some satisfaction from that and simply recognize the fact that the Russians are good?*

The Russians would head home for the final four games leading the series by a count of 2 wins versus 1 loss and a 1 tie, prompting Smythe to criticize Team Canada executives for the team's poor performance in the first four games:

> *First we all made the mistake of underestimating the Russians, including myself. Second, you can't send a boy to do a man's job. I'm referring to the management, not the players, of Team Canada. Name me one of the fellows running Team Canada that has had anything to do with putting a championship team together.*

In a column written by Coach Bobrov, he warned his team against being overconfident going into the final games of the series:

> *Upon my return to Moscow I had occasion to hear that the Canadian professional were a disappointment; they are not so strong. I disagree with this, of course. The Canadians are not gods as many of our fans believed. But they are undoubtedly first-class players. True, at the beginning of September the professionals were still insufficiently prepared. But in Moscow they are going to show everything they are capable of.*

The Canadian team would first travel to Sweden where they would play a two-game series intended to prepare them for larger international ice surface (2600 square feet bigger than a regulation NHL rink) while also allowing the players to become familiar with European officiating. For the Canadians it was also intended as a bit of a holiday and a chance for some of the reserves to play. For the Swedes the two games were to be the highlight of the 50th anniversary celebration of hockey in Sweden. Unfortunately, for them there wouldn't be much to celebrate, as the first game in Stockholm would be

220

a vicious affair that would end in a 4-1 Team Canada victory. The Swedish Press would criticize the Canadian team for the manner in which they won, nicknaming them *"Team Ugly."* After the game someone would call in a bomb threat to the hotel where the Canadians were staying, but after a few hours wait it was found to be a hoax.

The next game would pick up where the last one left off. The match would have several nasty incidents with the worst being when Cashman attempted to body-check Sweden's star forward, Ulf Sterner, against the boards. Sterner reacted by bringing his stick up. The result was cutting Cashman's tongue so badly that it swelled up to the point where he had to have medical assistance so he didn't suffocate. Cashman, who could only grunt at the time, motioned that Sterner had deliberately sliced him and he had to be restrained from trying to get back on the ice to get at Sterner. Sterner would later claim the incident was accidental. After seeing Cashman's mouth, Sinden would say: *"I nearly vomited on the spot. His tongue was just dangling . . . I couldn't believe there wasn't a penalty."*

Sweden was up 4-3, with a little over five minutes remaining in the game, when Hadfield was run into the boards from behind. Hadfield would retaliate by crosschecking Lars-Erik Sjoberg in the nose. Sjoberg would fall on to the ice causing the fans to scream for the Canadian forward's head. Bleeding, Sjoberg would skate around the rink displaying the blood and working the Swedish fans into frenzy. Later, Hadfield claimed he had retaliated after receiving the butt end of Sjoberg's stick, striking the helmetless Canadian in the head. Hadfield would receive a major penalty for the crosscheck and in the dying seconds, with Team Canada shorthanded, Esposito would score a dramatic tying goal. The game would end as a 4-4 draw. Afterwards the Swedish newspapers lashed out against the NHL stars branding the team as *"criminals and animals."* The Swedish media reactions included:

This is not sports - either here or in Canada, its assault.

Scandal is the right word for the behavior of Team Canada. If Hadfield had attacked Sjoberg like he did somewhere other than on an ice hockey rink, he would have been convicted. And if not jailed, at least fined by a court.

The Canadians would be equally critical of Sweden's play, as Esposito, would describe them as being dirty players:

I've never seen any one team do so much spearing. And they

*kick you, when you're in front of the net. Spearing, kicking
and then they run away . . . The Russians are gentlemen
compared to these guys.*

After the two game showdown, Swedish Coach Kjell Svensson
said he wasn't impressed with the Canadians and that he had lost
respect for their team. He also made the prediction that the Soviet
Union would win all of the final four games of their series, played in
Moscow. The games in Stockholm did reveal one shortcoming in Team
Canada's play - they were not prepared for the differences between
NHL and international officiating. In the two games, Canadian
penalties outnumbered the Swedes by a margin of 19-6. It was in these
games that they would first become introduced to refereeing style of
Franz Baader and Josef Kompalla. The two West Germans would
officiate two of the final four games in Moscow, plus they had already
been scheduled to work the game in Prague. Both men would
eventually become household names in Canada.

Sighting the lack of playing time, Vic Hadfield, Rick Martin,
Jocelyn Guevremont, and Gilbert Perreault decided not to continue on
to Moscow, instead returning to their club team's to participate in their
respective NHL training camps. Many members of Team Canada
viewed the departure as abandoning the team at its lowest moment.
The adversity would help unite the team.

In Moscow, the Canadians would face a larger and even more
experienced Russian roster of 35 players, eight more than had traveled
to Canada. The Soviet team now would include two veteran stars,
Anatoli Firsov and Vitaliy Davydov. Roughly three thousand
Canadians flew to Moscow to cheer on the team with a 2,700-seat
section, of the 15,000-seat Luzhniki Sports Palace, set aside. Through
the rest of the series the cheering Canadian fans would drown out the
comparatively milder-mannered Russians.

Game five would have the Canadians get out to a two period,
3-0, lead only to run out of gas in the third, losing the game by a score
of 5-4. The Russians, who were outplayed for two-thirds of the game,
stole the game and now were in full command of the series. Sinden
would later comment on his team's third period letdown:

*We beat ourselves with obvious individual mistakes.
Fundamental errors like giving up the puck in your end
when you controlled It . . . They're ingenious the way they
take a man who doesn't have the puck. It's like screening in
basketball and international referees never call it for a
penalty. In the NHL, they'd be shorthanded all night.*

222

Interference is one of their better plays, and we've told our guys to copy it.

Bunny Ahearne, who had been accused for years for being anti-Canadian, would make his first comments of the series, which now was 3 wins, 1 loss, and 1 tie in favor of the Soviet Union: *"It's just what I've been telling you Canadians for 10 years . . . but you never listen. To lose a game after leading 3-0, my goodness."* Ahearne would call out to Sinden after the game: *"I've heard talk about a bush league. I wonder who has the bush league now."* The Soviets would now only need to tie one of the last three remaining games in order to guarantee a tie in the series, one more win and they could claim to being the best.

The sixth game would be a hard-fought battle where officiating would come into play. Despite receiving 29 minutes in penalties versus only four minutes for the Russians, the Canadians would battle to a 3-2 win. Canadian players and officials would harshly criticize the German referees, Kompalla and Baader, working their first game of the series. When asked about the officiating, Sinden used the opportunity to get a barb back at Ahearne:

> *Entirely incompetent. Two of the worst officials I've ever seen referee a game. They're the product of international amateur hockey under Bunny Ahearne. [The players were so upset] it was almost impossible to calm the players down between the second and third period.*

Unlike North American officials, European referees worked only part time. Kompalla, who referees about 75 games a year, would be surprisingly candid when questioned about his qualifications and his observations of Team Canada, giving his own explanation as to why the once heavily favored Canadians were losing the series:

> *They make a lot of noise about one face-off, whether it should be a few feet away. They're very childish. They come and swear at us and call us blinkety-blank German referees who don't know anything . . . The Canadian team is no team at all. They've spent four weeks together . . . The Russians have been getting together for four years. The Canadian players are hot shots, but Phil Esposito cannot play 60 minutes. The Canadians need 10 to 15 games to be in top condition. I do think they could win if they were in top-condition.*

Do you now how much I get at home in Germany for a First Division game? Fifteen dollars. Imagine how much the NHL referees make. For me, this refereeing is just a hobby. My job is as a manager of a discothèque. We're open from 5 p.m. to 3 a.m. I show people to their tables, you know?

Prompting Paul Henderson to later add:

I don't get too excited too often, but I swear I can't make it through another game without punching Kompalla. You say he makes $15 a game refereeing in Germany? He's overpaid.

The next game would become the most physical of the series as it including the series' first fight. In the third period, Bergman and Soviet forward, Boris Mikhailov, would begin kicking each other, Bergman remarked:

I was amazed. In my whole life I've never been kicked in a hockey game, until now. I looked down and there he is kicking at me. He got me one good one, good enough that it left a welt on my shin, right through my shin pad.

Canada would go on to win game seven by a score of 4-3, tying the series at 3-3-1 with one final game remaining.

Throughout the series each team had alternated selecting the officials and, for game eight, the Soviets would choose the controversial dual of Kompella and Baader. Earlier in the week the Canadian delegation believed they had an agreement in place with the Russians whereas, the pair of German referees would not officiate in the final game. The agreement was such that if Bergman ceased swearing at Coach Bobrov that alternative officiating would be chosen for the final game. In the series, Bergman had taken to skating past the Soviet bench upon where he would threaten and taunt their famous coach. The Soviets had agreed to the compromise but at the last minute, they backed out of the agreement deciding instead to choose the two officials for the game, a move almost resulting in Canada pulling out of the series.

Finally after several tense moments, the Canadians agreed to play the final game. In Canada more than 16 million viewers would tune into the game - double the figure that watched the previous season's Stanley Cup playoffs and four million more than watched the first moon landing. Business virtually came to a standstill. School

224

children were either sent home or asked to watch the games in their classrooms. The country of 20 million people would stop working, shutdown in the middle of a workweek. Ken Dryden would later write in his book *Home Game*:

> *A game is a game. But a symbol is not. We had to win this series.*

The final game was emotional for both teams, and in the fifth minute Jean-Paul Parise would be penalized two minutes for interference. He would react to the call by banging his stick on the ice followed by him lifting the stick up over his shoulder and threatening to hit referee Kompella with it, causing the West German to cower in fear in anticipation of Parise's attack. For his actions Parise would be given an additional 10-minute misconduct penalty and thrown out of the game.

In a hard fought game, the Soviet's would hold a 5-3 lead into the second period intermission. In the final period, Esposito would score cutting the lead to 5-4, giving the Canadians over 17 minutes to get the tying goal. With just over seven minutes left in the game, Yvan Cournoyer would score the apparent tying goal but the red light goal indicator did not turn on. Eagleson, who was sitting behind the Canadian bench, attempted to walk down towards the ice surface to complain about the red light not turning on:

> *I just wanted to go down to tell the referee. The next thing I know I was on my way to Siberia.*

The Soviet police would grab him and attempt to take him into custody. Pete Mahovlich would swing his stick at the Russian police. Other players on the bench began to do the same until Eagleson was released. He climbed into the player's bench, stopping the game and Eagleson would eventually be led by a couple of players and the team trainer towards the Canadian dressing room. As Eagleson walked across the rink he would do and "up yours" gesture to the goal judge that did not turn on the red light, while the trainer was giving the whistling Russian spectators "the finger." For this, Eagleson would receive the Russian nickname *"nekulturny,"* meaning *"cultureless."* The goal would stand and with less than two minutes left in the game, Russian hockey officials would tell Eagleson that the Soviets were going to declare themselves the series victor due to a 32 to 30 goal differential in the eight games. It had come to the wire between the two greatest teams ever assembled. Each team had skated to a level never before seen exhibiting emotions never equaled since. For all who witnessed the event, time stood still. Not since the First Battle of Moytura, 3600 years earlier, had so much rested on the outcome of a hockey showdown. With 40 seconds left in the series, Paul Henderson, while sitting on the bench, stood up and yelled to Pete Mahovlich to come off the ice. *"I let him on,"* Pete Mahovlich later said, *"he told me to get off because; he was going to score a bleeping goal."*

Paul Henderson jumped on the ice and skated towards the Soviet goal. The puck was centered toward the Soviet net; Henderson would take an off-balance swing at the puck sending himself crashing into the boards behind the goal. Henderson got up, skated around the net, as Phil Esposito shot - the puck came to Henderson in front of the net, stopped by Vladislav Tretiak. The rebound would come back to Henderson who flipped the puck over a fallen Tretiak. Goal!!! The Canadians would take their first lead of the game and win the series. In the end a series five thousand years in the making had come down to thirty-four seconds. Thirty-four seconds that would last eternity.

Special Thanks

We would like to thank the following people for their assistance and support during the course of this project: Fred & Ann Buscaglia, Ken Greenwood, Joe Francis, Bret Talbot, Dennis Sita, Mary Margaret McDonough, Scott Wolter, Richard Nielsen, Dylan Jones, Harvey Rubin, Francine Goodman, Esq., Arleen Tortorelli, Torkia Nzidee, Jeff Eigen, David Crow, Pratibha Patel, Doug Robertson, Esq., Leslie Bauchelle, Paul Patskou, Dan Ammann, Basil M. Tomlinson, Michael Kessel, Esq., Jim & Shirl Talbot, Michael Talbot, Michael Schorr, Frits Locher, and Larry Reisenouer, Laurence Weeks, Barbra & Ted Terrone, Jo-Anne & Adrian Taylor, Evin Dobson, Bruce Wohl, Moneer Cherie, Kevin Thompkins, Noemi Fasullo, Susan Ginch, and Rachael Dean.

SELECTED BIBLIOGRAPHY

Adams, Henry H. *1942: The Year That Doomed The Axis*. New York: David Mckay Co., 1967.

After The Battle. *"Dieppe 1942."* No. 5, 1974.

Allen, Camelli. *Great Moments In Pro Hockey*. New York: Bantam Books, 1971.

Allen, D. *Totem Poles of the Northwest*. Saanichton: Hancock Publishers, 1977.

Allen, Kevin. *USA HOCKEY: A Celebration Of A Great Tradition*. Chicago:Triumph Books, 1997.

Allen, Ralph. *Ordeal By Fire*. Toronto: Popular Library, 1961.

Altieri, James J. *"Doomed Strike Force."* World War Two Magazine, May 1986.

Anderson, Rasmus B. *America Not Discovered By Columbus: An Historical Sketch Of The Discovery Of America By The Norsemen In The Tenth Century*. Chicago: S.C. Griggs and Company, 1891.

Andrews, Ron et al. *The Leafs: The First 50 Years.* McClelland & Stewart, Toronto, 1976.

Arlott, John. *The Oxford Companion To Sports and Games*. London: Oxford University Press, 1976.

Aristotle. *Minor Works*. Boston: Trans. By W.S. Lett, Loeb Classic Library, Harvard University, 1955.

Atkin, Ronald. *Dieppe 1942, The Jubilee Disaster*. London: Macmillan Co. Ltd., 1980.

Ayteo, Don. *Blood & Guts: Violence In Sports.* New York: Paddington Press Ltd., 1979.

Bartlett, Lt. Col. Merrill L. *Assault From The Sea*. Annapolis: Naval Institute Press, 1983.

Batten, Jack. *Quest for the Cup*. Key Porter Books, Toronto, 2001.

Baxter, Collins F. *"Winston Churchill: Military Strategist?"* Military Affairs February 1983.

Beardsley, Doug. *Country On Ice*. Polestar Press, 1987.

Beatty, Jerome. *"Canada Rolls Up Her Sleeves"* Current History and Forum, Nov. 7,1940.

Beddoes, Dick and Roberts, John. *Summit 74: The Canada/Russia Hockey Series -Larceny In Luzhniki, The Inside Story*. Toronto: Methuen, 1974.

Beddoes, Dick. *Hockey! The Story Of The World's Fastest Sport*. New York: Macmillan, 1973.

Beddoes, Dick. *Greatest Hockey Stories*. Toronto: Macmillan, 1990.

Benedict, Michael. *Canada On Ice: 50 Years Of Great Hockey*. Toronto: Viking Press, 1998.

Benoist-Melchin, Jacques. *Sixty Days That Shook The West*. New York: G.P. Putnam's Sons, 1963.

Bentley, Mary and Bentley, Ted. *Gabriola: Petroglyph Island*. Victoria: Sono Nis Press, 1981.

Berton, Pierre. *Vimy*. Toronto: Simon and Schuster, 1985.

Boas, Dr. Franz. *The Central Eskimo*. Washington: Government Printing Office, 1888.

Bocca, Geoffrey. *The Adventurous Life of Winston Churchill*. New York: Avon Books, 1958.

Boelcke, Willi A. *The Secret Conferences of Dr. Goebbels 1939-43*. New York: E.P. Dutton & Co., 1970.

Boyce, Trevor. *British Ice Hockey Players From The Golden Days*.

Harefield: Yore Publishers, 1997.

Brasch, R. *How Did Sports Begin? A Look At The Origins Of Man At Play*. New York: David McKay Company, Inc., 1970.

British Broadcasting Corporation. *The World At War Documentary Series: "The Soviet Union 1941-43"* London: Thames Productions, 1971.

British Columbia Government Tourist Bureau. *Thunderbird Park Victoria, British Columbia, Canada*. Victoria: Queen's Printer, n.d.

Broadfoot, Barry. *Six War Years*. Don Mills: Paper Jacks, 1979.

Broderick, Doc. *Ice Hockey*. Nicolas Kaye Publishers, London, 1951.

Brown, Anthony Cave. *Bodyguard of Lies*. New York: Bantam, 1976.

Brown, E. K. *"Mackenzie King of Canada."* Harper's Magazine, Jan. 1943.

Bryant, Arthur. *The Turn of the Tide*. New York: Doubleday, 1957.

Buckley, Christopher. *Norway, The Commandos, Dieppe*. London: H.M. Stationery Office, 1951.

Buchanan, Lt. Col. *March of the Prairie Men*. Privately Printed, 1957.

Buffey, Vern. *Black & White & Never Right*. Toronto: Wiley, 1980.

Burns, Lt. Gen. E.L.M. *General Mud*. Toronto: Clarke, Irwin & Co., 1970.

Butcher, Harry C. *My Three Years With Eisenhower*. New York: Simon & Schuster, 1946.

Cadogan, Alexander. *The Diaries of Sir Alexander Cadogan*. New York: Putnam's Sons, 1972.

Calvocoressi, Peter. *Total War*. Middlesex: Penguin Books, 1972.

Campbell, John P. *"Deception and D-Day."* Canadian Defence Journal, Winter, 1980.

Canadian Broadcasting Corporation. *"Dieppe 1942."* Network Production/Promotion Kit, 1978.

Canadian Historical Review. *"The Suicide Battalion."* Volume LXI No.1 , March 1980.

Canada's Weekly. *"Canada In England."* No. 3603 Vol. CXVIII , December. 18, 1941.

Carling O'Keefe Breweries. *Canada Cup 1976.* Official Series Programme.

Carter, Hodding. *The Commandos of World War Two.* New York: Random House, 1966.

Cave, Joy B. *What Became of Corporal Pittman?* Portugal Cove: Breakwater Books Limited, 1976.

Cheesman, Paul R. and Cheesman, Millie F. *Ancient American Indians Their Origins, Civilizations & Old World Connections.* Bountiful: Horizon Publishers & Distributors, 1991.

Cherry, Don and Fischler, Stan. *GRAPES -A Vintage View Of Hockey.* Scarborough: Avon Books, 1983.

Churchill, Winston S. *The Hinge of Fate.* London: Cassell & Co., 1951.

Churchill, Winston S. *The War Speeches of the Rt. Hon. Winston S. Churchill Vol. II. June 25, 1941 - September 6, 1942.* ed. Charles Eade. London: Shenval Press, 1953.

Churchill, Winston S. *The Fall of France.* London: Cassell & Co., 1964.

Clagett, Marshall. *Greek Science in Antiquity.* London: Collier Books, 1976.

Coleman, Jim. *Hockey Is Our Game: Canada In The World Of International Hockey.* Toronto: Key Porter, 1987.

Collins, Frank D. *Popular Sports: Their Development.* Chicago: Rand McNally & Company, Inc., 1935.

Combined Operations. *The Official History of Combined Operations.* London: H.M. Stationery Office, 1943.

Colombo, John Robert. *Colombo's Concise Canadian Quotations.* Edmonton: Hurtig Publishers, 1976.

Conacher, Brian. *Hockey In Canada, The Way It Is!* Toronto: Pocket Books, 1971.

Conrad, Harold E. *"Canada's All-Out War Effort."* Current History Magazine, November 1941.

Cooper, Duff. *Old Men Forget: The Autobiography of Duff Cooper.* London: Rupert Hart-Davis, 1954.

Crescent Athletic Club Of Brooklyn. *Club Book 1904.* Brooklyn: City Club House, 1904.

Crogdon, Don et al. *Combat Theatre of World War Two.* New York: Dell Publishing, 1958.

Cross, Collin. *The Fall of the British Empire.* New York: Coward-McCann, Inc. 1969.

Curator Hockey Hall of Fame. *Hockey's Heritage.* Toronto: Hockey Hall of Fame, 1982.

Current History Magazine. *"Planning The Second Front."* August 1942.

Dancocks, Daniel G. *In Enemy Hands: Canadian Prisoners of War 1939-45.* Edmonton: Hurtig Publishers, 1983.

Debarats, Peter. *Rene: A Canadian In Search Of A Country.* Toronto: McClelland and Stewart, 1976.

De Breubeuf, Jean. *The Jesuit Relations and Allied Documents, Travels and Explorations of the Jesuit Missionaries in New France 1610-1791 Vol. X, Huron.* n.d.

De Breubeuf, Jean. *The Jesuit Relations and Allied Documents, Travels and Explorations of the Jesuit Missionaries In New France 1610-1791:*

The Original French, Latin and Italian texts, with English Translations and Notes. n.d.

DeGaulle, Charles. *The Speeches of Charles DeGaulle.* New York: Oxford University Press, 1944.

Diamond, Dan, Duplacey,James, Ralph Dinger, Igor Kuperman, Eric Zwieg
Total Hockey: The Official Encyclopedia of the National Hockey League. Kansas City: Andrews McMeel, 1999

D'Este, Carlo. *Decision In Normandy.* London: Collins, 1983.

Devins, Joseph H. *The Vaagso Raid.* New York: Bantam Books, 1983.

Dewar, Jane. *True Canadian War Stories.* Toronto: Legion Magazine, 1987.

Diamond, Dan, Editor. *Forever Rivals: The Montreal Canadiens - Toronto Maple Leafs.* Toronto: Random House, 1996.

Diamond, Dan et al. *Years Of Glory 1942-1967, The National Hockey League's Official Book Of The Six Team Era.* Toronto: McClelland & Stewart, 1994.

Diamond, Dan et al. *Total Hockey: The Official Encyclopedia Of The National Hockey League.* Kingston: Total Sports Publishing, 2000.

Donaghy, Greg et al. *Canada At The Early Cold War 1943-1957.* Ottawa: Department of Foreign Affairs and International Trade, 1998.

Drackett, Phil. *Flashing Blades: The Story Of British Ice Hockey.* Marlborough: The Crowood Press, 1987.

Drew, Stephen. *"Tough, Versatile, Courageous."* The New York Times Magazine Supplement, Aug. 22, 1942.

Dryden, Ken. *The Game.* Toronto: Macmillan, 1983.

Dryden, Ken and MacGregor, Roy. *Home Game: Hockey and Life in Canada.* Toronto: McClelland & Stewart, 1989.

Duff, Wilson. *The Indian History of British Columbia Volume I The*

Impact of the White Man. Anthropology in British Columbia Memoir No.5. Victoria: Provincial Museum of Natural History and Anthropology, 1964.

Duggan, John P. *Neutral Ireland and the Third Reich*. Dublin: Ginn and Macmillan, 1985.

Durnsford-Slater, Brigadier John. *Commando*. London: William Kimber, 1953.

Eden, Anthony. *The Eden Memoirs, Volume II: The Reckoning*. Boston: Houghton Mifflin Co., 1965.

Eisenhower, David. *Eisenhower At War, 1943-1945*. New York: 1986.

Encyclopedia Titanica: First Class Passenger: Quigg Edmond Baxter [www.encyclopedia-titanica.org] Accessed Fri Apr 04 08:35:32 2003.

Eskenazi, Gerald. *The Fastest Sport.* Chicago: Follett, 1974.

Esposito, Phil; Eskenazi, Gerald. *Hockey is My Life*. New York: Warner Books, 1972.

Fay, Sidney B. *"The First Second Front."* Current History Magazine. December 1942.

Ferguson, Bernard. *The Watery Maze: The Story of Combined Operations*. London, Collins, 1961.

Fischler, Stan and Shirley, Walton Fischler. *The Hockey Encyclopedia: The Complete Record of Professional Ice Hockey.* New York: Macmillan, 1983.

Fischler, *Stan. Hockey's 100 A Personal Ranking of the Best Players in Hockey History*. New York: Beaufort Books, 1994.

Fischler, Stan. *Fischler's Illustrated History of Hockey*. Toronto: Warwick Publishing, 1993.

Fischler, Stan. *Golden Ice - The Greatest Teams In Hockey History, A Personal Ranking By*

Stan Fischler. Toronto: McGraw Hill, 1990.

Fischler, Stan. *Slashing! A Tough Look At Hockey From A Writer Who Loves The Game*. New York: Crowell, 1974.

Fischler, Stan. *Offside. Hockey From The Inside*. New York: Methuen, 1985.

Fischler, Stan and Shirley. *Great Book Of Hockey: More Than 100 Years Of Fire On Ice*. Lincolnwood: Publications International, 1996.

Fischler, Stan and Shirley. *20th Century Hockey Chronicle*. Lincolnwood: Publications International Ltd., 1994.

Fleming, Fergus. *Barrow's Boys: A Stirring Story of Daring, Fortitude, and Outright Lunacy*. New York: Grove Press, 1998.

Fleming, Peter. *Operation Sea Lion*. New York: Simon and Schuster, 1957.

Fosty, George Robert. *The Desperate Glory: The Battle of Dieppe, France August 19, 1942*. Wichita Falls: Midwestern State University, Unpublished Master's Thesis, 1991.

Fotheringham, Alan. *"Behind The Myths."* Maclean's Magazine, August 11. 1981.

Franks, Norman L.R. *The Greatest Air Battle*. London; William Kimber, 1978.

Frayne, Trent and Gzowski, Peter. *Great Canadian Sports Stories: A Century Of Competition*. Toronto: McClelland & Stewart, 1965.

Frayne, Trent. *The Mad Men of Hockey*. Toronto: McClelland & Stewart, 1974.

Gaffen, Fred. *Unknown Warriors: Canadians In The Vietnam War*. Toronto: Dundern Press, 1990.

Ganier-Raymond, Phillippe. *The Tangled Web*. New York: Pantheon Books, 1968.

Gershoy, Leo. *"A Second Front - When?."* Current History Magazine, November 1942.

Gilbert, Martin. *Winston Churchill: Road To Victory 1941-1945*. Boston: Houghton Mifflin Co., 1986.

Gilchrist, Donald. *Castle Commando*. Edinburgh: Oliver and Boyd, 1960.

Goodhart, Philip and Chataway, Christopher. War Without Weapons. London: W.H. Allen, 1968.

Goodspeed, D.J. *The Road Past Vimy*. Toronto: MacMillan , 1969.

Goodspeed, D. J. *Battle Royal: A History of the Royal Regiment of Canada 1862-1962*. Toronto: Royal Regiment of Canada, 1962.

Granatstein, J.L. and Morton, Desmond. *A Nation Forged In Fire: Canadians And The Second World War 1939-1945.* Toronto: Lester & Orpen Dennys, 1989.

Griesler, Patricia. *Valour Remembered: Canada and the First World War*. Ottawa: Department of Veteran's Affairs, 1995.

Grigg, John. *1943*. London: Methuen, 1985.

Greig, Murray. *Trail on Ice: A Century of Hockey in the Home of Champions.* Trail, Canada: Trail City Archives, 1999.

Grogan. John Patrick. *Dieppe and Beyond*. Renfrew: Juniper Books, 1982.

Grun, Bernard. *The Timelines Of History. 3rd Edition.* New York: Simon & Schuster, 1991.

Haliburton, Thomas Chandler. *The Attache or Sam Slick in England (2 Volumes)*. London: Richard Bentley, 1843.

Halifax Herald Newspaper: *Letter to the Editor*, December 27, 1940.

Hamilton, Nigel. *Monty: The Making of a General 1887-1942*. New York: McGraw-Hill, 1981.

Hamilton, Robert M. *Canadian Quotations & Phrases Literary and Historical.* Toronto: McClelland & Stewart, 1965.

Harman, Nicholas. *Dunkirk: The Patriotic Myth*. New York: Simon and Schuster, 1980.

Harris, Billy. *The Glory Years -Memories Of A Decade, 1955 -1965*. Toronto: Prentice-Hall, 1969

Hastings, Max. *Overlord: D-Day and the Battle of Normandy 1944*. London: M. Joseph, 1984.

Hatch, Alden. *The Mountbatten's: The Last Royal Success Story*. New York: Random House, 1965.

Henry, Alexander. *Travels and Adventures in Canada and the Indian Territories between the Years 1760 and 1776*. Parts I and II. New York: Burt Franklin, 1969.

Henry, Alexander. *"Journal"* (Edited by Elliott Coues). New York: Frances P. Harper Company, 1897

Henry, Bill. *An Approved History Of The Olympic Games*. New York: G.P. Putnam's Sons, 1948.

Hewitt, Foster. *Hello, Canada And Hockey Fans In The United States*. Toronto: Thomas Allen, 1950.

Hewitt, Foster. *Hockey Night In Canada, The Maple Leaf's Story*. Toronto: Ryerson, 1953.

Higgins, Trumbull. *Winston Churchill and the Second Front*. New York: Oxford University Press, 1957.

Hill, Beth. *Guide to Indian Rock Carvings of the Pacific Northwest Coast*. North Vancouver: Hancock Publishers, 1980.

Hinsley, F. H. *British Intelligence in the Second World War, Volume Two*. New York: Cambridge University Press, 1981.

Hockey Hall of Fame. *Legends Of Hockey: The Official Book Of The Hockey Hall Of Fame*. Toronto: Penguin Canada, 1996.

Hollander, Zander and Bock, Hal. *The Complete Encyclopedia of Hockey*. Englewood Cliffs: Prentice-Hall, 1974.

Holmes, Richard. *Acts of War*. New York: The Free Press, 1985.

Hopkins, J. Castell. *Canada At War*. Toronto: The Canadian Annual Review, 1919.

Homer. *The Iliad: translated by W.H.D. Rouse*. New York: Mentor Book, 1938.

Homer. *The Odyssey: The story of Odysseus translated by W. H. D. Rouse*. New York: Mentor Book, 1938.

Honolulu Star Bulletin: *"U.S. Fight 6-Hour Battle" (August 20, 1942)*.

Hopkins, J. Castell. *Canada At War*. Toronto: The Canadian Annual Review, 1919.

Howe, Gordie et al. *After The Applause*. Toronto: McClelland & Stewart, 1989.

Hovgaard, William. *The Voyages of the Norsemen to America*. New York: The American-Scandinavian Foundation, 1914.

Hull, Cordell. *The Memoirs of Cordell Hull*. London: Stroughton and Hodder, 1948.

Hunter, Douglas. *War Games: Conn Smythe and Hockey's Fighting Men*. Toronto: Viking-Penguin Books Canada Ltd., 1996.

Hunter, Murray T. *Canada At Dieppe*. Ottawa: Canadian War Museum, 1982.

Hutchison, Bruce. *The Incredible Canadian*. Toronto: Longmans, Green and Co., 1952.

Imlach, Punch and Young, Scott. *Hockey Is A Battle*. Toronto: Macmillan, 1969

Inglis, Joy. *Spirit In The Stone*. Victoria: Horsdal & Schubart, 1998.

Isaacs, Neil D. *Checking Back: A History Of The National Hockey League*. New York: W.W. Norton, 1977.

Ismay, General Lord. *The Memoirs of General Lord Ismay*. New York:

Viking Press, 1960.

Jackdaw. *"Dieppe 1942."* No. C8. London: Clarke Irwin, 1967.

James, Admiral Sir William. *The Portsmouth Letters*. London: Macmillan, 1946.

Jenish, Darcy. *The Stanley Cup: One Hundred Years Of Hockey At Its Best*. Toronto: McClelland & Stewart, 1992.

Keegan, John. *Six Armies In Normandy*. New York: The Viking Press, 1982.

Keller, W. *The Bible As History*. London: Hodder & Stoughton, 1963.

Kennan, George F. *Russia and the West*. New York: Mentor Books, 1962.

Kennedy, Sir John. *The Business of War: The War Narratives of Major-General Sir John Kennedy*. New York: William Morrow and Company, 1958.

Kidd, Bruce and MacFarlane, John. *The Death of Hockey*. Toronto: New Press, 1972.

King James Version. *The Holy Bible*. New York: Three Lions, Inc. 1964.

Kruger, Arnd and Riordan, James. *The Story Of Worker Sport*. Champaign: Human Kinetics, 1996.

Ladd, James. *The Commandos and Rangers of World War Two*. New York: St. Martin's Press, 1978.

Lapp, Richard M. *The Memorial Cup*. Madeira Park: Harbour Publishing Company, Ltd., 1997.

Leasor, James. *War At The Top*. London: Cape, 1958.

Leasor, James. *Green Beach*. London: Heinemann, 1975.

Leonetti, Mike. *The Game We Knew: Hockey In The Fifties*. Vancouver: Raincoast Book Distribution, 1997.

Lenoir, Maurice. *"Province of Quebec."* New Republic, September 16, 1940.

Lepotier, Contre-Amiral. *Raiders From The Sea*. London: Weidenfeld and Nicholson, 1954.

Leverkuehn, Paul. *German Military Intelligence*. London: Weidenfeld and Nicholson, 1954.

Lewin, Ronald. *Ultra Goes To War*. New York: McGraw Hill, 1978.

Liddell Hart, Sir Basil. *History of the Second World War*. New York: G.P. Putnam's Sons, 1971.

Life Magazine: *"Commander Of The Canadians" (December 18, 1939)*.

Life Magazine. *"Canada At War: U.S. Neighbor Grids For Actions."*, December 18, 1939.

Liss, Howard. *Strange But True Hockey Stories*. New York: Random House, 1972.

Ludwig, Jack. *Hockey Night In Moscow*. Toronto: McClelland Stewart, 1972.

MacCormac, John. *Canada: America's Problem*. New York: Viking Press, 1940.

MacDonald, Robert. *The Owners Of Eden: The Life And Past Of The Native People*. Vancouver: Evergreen Press, Ltd., 1974.

MacFarlane, John. *Twenty-Seven Days In September*. Toronto: Hockey Canada & Prospect Publications, 1973.

Macksey, Kenneth. *Vimy Ridge 1914-18*. New York: Ballantine, 1972.

Maclean's Magazine: *"Quebec's Angry Young Men." (February 24, 1962)*.

Macpherson, Stewart. *Mike And I*. London: Home & Van Thal, 1948

Macskimming, Roy. *Cold War: The Amazing Canada-Soviet Hockey Series Of 1972*. Vancouver: Greystone Books Ltd., 1996.

Maguire, Eric. *Dieppe, August 19th, 1942.* London: Cape, 1963.

Majdalany, Fred. *The Crossroads of World History.* Garden City: Doubleday and Co., Ltd., 1968.

Margolin, Malcolm. *The Ohlone Way: Indian Life in the San Francisco-Monterey Bay Area.* Berkeley: Heyday Books, 1975.

Mason, David. *Churchill.* New York: Ballantine Books, 1972.

Massey, Raymond. *When I Was Young.* Toronto: Little, Brown and Company, 1976.

Maund, Rear-Admiral L.E.H. *Assault From The Sea.* London: Methuen and Co., 1949.

Meade, Edward. *Indian Rock Carvings of the Pacific Northwest.* Sidney: Gray's Publishing Ltd., 1971.

McAuley, Jim. *The Ottawa Sports Book: Vignettes From Ottawa's Sport History.* Burnstown: General Store Publishing House, 1987.

McFarlane, Brian. *50 Years of Hockey 1917-1967.* Toronto: Pagurian Press, 1967.

McFarlane, Brian. *60 Years of Hockey.* Toronto: McGraw-Hill Ryerson, 1976.

McFarlane, Brian. *The Story of the National Hockey League An Intimate History Of Hockey's Most Dramatic Century.* New York: Charles Scribner's Sons, 1973.

McFarlane, Brian. *History Of Hockey.* Champaign: Sports Publishing Inc. 1997.

McFarlane, Brian. *Stanley Cup Fever 100 Years of Hockey Greatness.* Toronto: Stoddart, 1992.

McFarlane, Brian. *Everything You Always Wanted To Know About Hockey.* New York: Scribner's, 1971.

McFarlane, Brian. *One Hundred Years Of Hockey.* Toronto: Deneau Publishers, 1989.

McLean, John. *The Indians Their Manners and Customs*. Halifax: William Buggs, 1889.

McLennan, W. *"Hockey In Canada."* Harper's Weekly, January 12, 1895.

Mellor, John. *Dieppe –Canada's Forgotten Heroes*. Toronto: Methuen, 1975.

Millar, George. *The Bruneval Raid*. London: Pan Books, 1976.

Montgomery, Field-Marshal Bernard. *Normandy to the Baltic*. London: Hutchinson, 1947.

Montgomery, Field-Marshal Bernard. *Memoirs of Field-Marshal Montgomery of Alamein*. London: Collins, 1958.

Moogk, Capt. Peter. *"Hell Was Hottest On Blue Beach."* Sentinel Magazine, March 1987.

Moore, Robert W. *"Rehearsal At Dieppe."* National Geographic Magazine, October 1942.

Mordal, Jacques. *Dieppe: The Dawn of Decision*. Toronto: Ryerson, 1963.

Morgan, Sir. F. *Overture to Overlord*. Toronto: Macmillan, 1946.

Morison, Rear-Admiral Samuel E. *Strategy and Compromises*. Boston; Little, Brown, 1957.

Morton, Desmond. *When Your Number's Up: The Canadian Soldier In The First World War*. Toronto: Random House, 1993.

Morton, Desmond and Granatstein, J.L. *Marching To Armageddon: Canadians And The Great War 1914-19*. Toronto: Lester & Orpen Dennys, 1989.

Morton, Desmond. *When Your Number's Up: The Canadian Soldier In The First World War*. Toronto: Random House, 1993.

Mouton, Claude. *The Montreal Canadiens; a Hockey Dynasty*. Toronto: Van Nostrand Reinhold Company, 1980.

Mullen, Willard and Kamm, Hubert. *The Junior Illustrated Encyclopedia of Sports*. New York: The Bobbs-Merrill Company, Inc., 1966.

Mulvoy, Mark et al. *Ice Hockey: Sports Illustrated*. Philadelphia: J.B. Lippincott, 1971.

Munro, John A. and Ingles, Alex I. *Mike: The Memoirs Of The Right Honourable Lester B. Pearson. Volume I: 1897-1948*. Toronto: University Of Toronto Press, 1972.

Munro, John A. and Ingles, Alex I. *Mike: The Memoirs Of The Right Honourable Lester B. Pearson. Volume II: 1948 -1957*. Scarborough: New American Library of Canada, Ltd., 1975.

Munro, Ross. *Gauntlet to Overlord*. Toronto: Macmillan, 1946.

Murphy, Tony and Kenney, Paul. *The Trail Of The Caribou: Newfoundland In The First World War, 1914-18*. St. John's: Harry Cuff Publications Ltd., 1991.

New Republic Magazine. July 7, 1941 to August 31, 1942: *"Create A Second Front!"* (July 7, 1941); *"America and the Second Front."* (November 24, 1941); *"Is Churchill's Star Setting?"* (May 18, 1942); *"The Politics of the Second Front."* (July 27, 1942); *"Commandos On All Fronts."* (August 31, 1942).

Newsweek Magazine: *"Hockey On To Moscow" (March 22, 1954)*. *"Olympics: The Stuff Of Glory" (March 7, 1960)*.

Nicolson, Harold. *Diaries and Letters. Volume II: The War Years 1939-1945. New York: Atheneum*, 1967.

Nolan, Brian. *King's War: MacKenzie King and the Politics of War 1939-1945*. Toronto: Fawcett Crest, 1988.

O'Brien, Andy. *Fire-Wagon Hockey*. Toronto: Ryerson, 1967.

O'Brien, Andy. *Headline Hockey*. Toronto: The Ryerson Press, 1963

O'Brien, Andy. *Superstars: Hockey's Greatest Players*. Toronto,

Canada: McGraw-Hill Ryerson Ltd, 1973

Office of Chief of Military History, Dept. of the Army. *The European Theatre of Operations, United States Army in World War Two.* Washington: Dept. of Army, 1951.

Official Website: *International Ice Hockey Federation.*

Official Website: *Rosslyn-Chapel.com.*

Official Website: *University of Harvard Hockey.*

Official Website: *University of Notre Dame.*

Official Website: *University of Oklahoma.*

Official Website: *University of Southern California.*

Olney, Roos R. *This Game Called Hockey: Great Moments In The World's Fastest Team Sport.* Northbrook: Dodd, Mead & Co., 1978.

Orr, Frank. *The Story Of Hockey.* New York: Random House, 1971.

Orr, Frank. *Tough Guys Of Hockey.* New York: Random House, 1974.

Orr, Frank. *Great Goalies Of Pro Hockey.* New York: Random House, 1973.

Padden, Ian. *U.S. Rangers.* Toronto: Ballantine, 1967.

Paine, Lauran. *German Military Intelligence in World War Two.* New York: Stein and Day, 1984.

Peat, Harold R. *Private Peat.* Brooklyn: Bobbs-Merrill Company, Inc., 1917.

Pearson, Lester B. *The Four Faces Of Peace.* New York: Dodd, Mead & Company, 1964.

Pearson, Lester B. *Words And Occasions.* Toronto: University of Toronto Press, 1970.

Percival, Lloyd. *The Hockey Handbook.* Toronto: Copp Clark, 1957.

Perreault, Gilles. *The Secret of D-Day.* Toronto: Ballantine, 1967.

Pickersgill, J.W. *The Mackenzie King Record, Volume I: 1939-1944.* Chicago: University of Chicago Press, 1960.

Podnieks, Andrew. *Canada's Olympic Hockey Teams The Complete History 1920-1998.* Toronto: Doubleday, 1997.

Pohl, Frederick J. *Atlantic Crossings Before Columbus.* New York: WW Norton & Company, 1961.

Power, C.G. *The R.C.A.F. Overseas.* Toronto: Oxford University Press, 1944.

Powers, John, and Kaminsky, Arthur C. *One Goal: A Chronicle Of The U.S. Olympic Hockey Team. New York.* Harper Collins, 1984.

Prouse, Robert A. *A Ticket to Hell via Dieppe.* Toronto: Van Nostrand, 1982.

Qarrington, Paul. *Hometown Heroes. On The Road With Canada's National Team.* Toronto: Collins, 1988.

Raddall, Thomas H. *Halifax: Warden of the North.* New York: Doubleday & Company, 1965.

Rand, Silas Tertius. *Dictionary of the Language of the Mic Mac Indians.* Halifax: Nova Scotia Printing Company, 1888.

Rastvorov, Yuri A. *"Red Amateurs Are Pros"* (Article: No Date).

Rees, Goronwy. *A Bundle of Sensations.* Toronto: Clarke Irwin, 1960.

Reyburn, Wallace. *Some Of It Was Fun.* Toronto: T. Nelson, 1949.

Reyburn, Wallace. *"Street Fighting In Dieppe."* Life Magazine, August 31, 1942.

Reynolds, Quentin. *Dress Rehearsal.* New York: Random House, 1943.

Roberts, Leslie. *"Canada's Place in the War and After."* Free World

Magazine, May, 1942.

Robertson, Heather. *A Gentleman Adventurer: The Arctic Diaries of R.H.G. Bonnycastle*. Toronto: Lester & Orpen Dennys, 1984.

Robertson, Terence. *The Shame and the Glory: Dieppe*. Toronto: McClelland, 1967.

Ronberg, Gary. *The Ice Men*. New York: Rutledge, 1973.

Ronberg, Gary. *The Hockey Encyclopedia*. New York: MacMillan Company, 1974.

Roskill, Stephen. *"The Dieppe Raid and the Question of German Foreknowledge."* Royal United Service Institute Journal, February, 1964.

Ross, Alexander. *Adventures Of The First Settlers On The Oregon Or Columbia River, 1810-1813*. Chicago: Lakeside Press, 1923.

Roxborough, Henry. *One Hundred-Not Out: The Story Of Nineteenth-Century Canadian Sport*. Toronto: Ryerson, 1966.

Roy, R. H. *"Morale in the Canadian Army in Canada During World War Two."* Canadian Defence Quarterly. 1986.

Salmaggi, Cesare et al. *2194 Days of War*. New York: Windward Books, 1977.

Saunders, Hillary St. George. *The Green Beret*. London: Michael Joseph, 1949.

Scott, F.R. and Smith, A.J.M. *The Blasted Pine*. Toronto: Macmillan, 1957.

Scott, Peter. *Eye of the Wind*. New York: Houghton Mifflin, 1961.

Scott, Peter. *The Battle of the Narrow Seas*. London: Country Life, 1946.

Scott, Walter. *2nd Front Now 1943*. Montgomery: University of Alabama, 1985.

Sherwood, Robert E. *The White House Papers of Harry L Hopkins, Volume I, II*. London: Eyre and Spottiswoode, 1948.

Senn, Alfred E. *Power Politics And The Olympic Games: A History Of The Power Brokers, Events, And Controversies That Shaped The Games*. Champaign: Human Kinetics, 1999.

Simonds, Peter. *Maple Leaf Up, Maple Leaf Down*. New York: Island Press, 1946.

Sinden, Harry. *Hockey Showdown: The Canada-Russia Hockey Series*: Toronto: Doubleday, 1973.

Skelton, John, Trans. *Bibliotheca Historica of Diodorus Sculus II, Vol.I, II*. London: Oxford University Press, 1955, 1963.

Smith, Don and Mueser, Dr. Anne Marie. *How Sports Began*. Danbury: Starting Point Library, 1972.

Smith, Waldo. *What Time The Tempest*. Toronto: Ryerson, 1953.

Smythe, Thomas Stafford and Shea, Kevin. *Centre Ice: The Smythe Family, The Gardens And The Toronto Maple Leafs Hockey Club*. Bolton: H.B. Fenn Publishing, 2000.

Snyder, Louis L. *Masterpieces of War Reporting*. New York: Julian Messner, Inc., 1962.

Soames, Mary. *Clementine Churchill: The Biography of a Marriage*. Boston: Houghton Mifflin, 1979.

Soward, F.W. et al. *Canada In World Affairs, Volume I*. London: Oxford University Press, 1941.

Spicer, Stanley T. *Glooscap Legends*. Hansport: Lancelot Press, 1991.

Sports Illustrated Magazine:*"Red Faces in Canada: Russia-Team Canada Match."* (September 11, 1972);*"Still Blushing at the Face Off: Russia-Team Canada Match."* (September 18, 1972); *"So the Canadians Go to Hockeyland: Russia-Team Canada Match in Soviet Union."* (October 2, 1972);*"Waking Up From A Nightmare: Team Canada's Victory Over Russia."* (October 9, 1972).

Spokane -Review Newspaper: *"Begun In 1916 By Les Patrick Spokane Has Glorious, Erratic Hockey History -Not Over Yet."* (March 16, 1975 by Howie Stalwick).

Stacey, Colonel C.P. *Official History of the Canadian Army at War.* Ottawa: King's Printer, 1948.

Stacey, Colonel C.P. *Six Years of War, Volume I.* Ottawa: Queen's Printer, 1955.

Stacey, Colonel C.P. *A Very Double Life: The Private World of Mackenzie King.* Toronto: Macmillan, 1976.

Strange, Joseph L. *"The British Rejection of Operation Sledgehammer."* Military Affairs, October 1981.

Strange, William. *Canada the Pacific and War.* Toronto: Thomas Nelson and Sons, Ltd., 1937.

Strong, emory. *Stone Age On The Columbia River.* Portland: Binford & Mort, 1959.

Stafford, David. *Camp X.* Toronto: Lester and Orpen Dennys, 1987.

Stanley, F.G. *Canada's Soldiers: The Military History of an Unmilitary People.* Toronto: Macmillan Co., 1960.

Steele, Richard W. *The First Offensive 1942.* Bloomington: Indiana University Press, 1973.

Stevenson, William. *A Man Called Intrepid.* London; Heinemann, 1976.

Stokes, William. *"A War Election In Canada."* New Republic, October 25, 1939.

Stokesbury, James L. *A Short History of World War Two.* New York: William Morrow, 1980.

Strange, Joseph L. *"The British Rejection of Operation Sledgehammer."* Military Affairs, October 1981.

Strange, William. *Canada the Pacific and War.* Toronto: Thomas Nelson and Sons, Ltd., 1937.

Strong, Emory. *Stone Age on the Columbia River.* Portland: Binfords & Mort Publishers, 1960.

Sweet, Waldo E. *Sport And Recreation In Ancient Greece.* New York: Oxford University Press, 1987.

Swinson, Arthur. *Defeat in Malaya: The Fall of Singapore.* New York: Ballantine, 1970.

Tait, Major Robert H. *The Trail Of The Caribou: The Newfoundland Regiment 1914-1918.* Boston: Newfoundland Publishing Co., 1933.

Tarasov, Anatoly. *Road to Olympus.* Montreal: Griffin House, 1969.

Tarasov, Anatoly and McFarlane, Brian. *Tarasov's Hockey Techniques.* Toronto: Holt, Rinehart, 1973.

Taylor, A.J.P. *Beaverbrook.* New York: Simon and Schuster, 1972.

Taylor, Leonard W. The Sourdough and the Queen: *The Many Lives of Klondike Joe Boyle.* Toronto: Methuen Publishers, 1983.

Teatero, William. *Mackenzie King: Man of Mission.* Toronto: Personal Library Publishers, 1979.

Teit, James. Traditions of the Thompson Indians of British Columbia. Boston:
Houghton Mifflin Company, 1898.

Terroux, Gilles and Brodeur, Denis. *Face-Off Of The Century.* New York: The Macmillan Company, 1972.

The Hockey News: *"Century Of Hockey"* (2000).
The Holy Bible Revised Standard Version. New York: Thomas Nelson & Sons, 1952.

The London Times: *"Rapid Demobilization" (December 19, 1918).*

The New York Times: *"Canadian Troops Arrive In Britain" (December 19, 1939 by Jack Brayley); "Decision By Allies To Aid Russia Seen" (August 1, 1942); "Russian Recall 1914 'Second Front'" (August 2, 1942); "Warning By Laval On Aiding Invasion" (August 2, 1942);*

"Invasion Choices Studied By Allies" (August 6, 1942); "2nd Front Nearing" (August 9, 1942); "British Premier In Moscow" (August 17, 1942); "New Strategy Set" (August 17, 1942); "U.S.- Alliesd Troops, Tanks Raid Dieppe 9 Hours" (August 20, 1942); "Raid Heroes Sing" (August 20, 1942); "Nazi's Dieppe Loss Put At 4,000 Men" (August 25, 1942); "Russia Upsets Canada In World Hockey Final" (March 8, 1954 by United Press); "Willing To Tour Russia" (March 9, 1954 by United Press); "Russian Hockey Team Is Praised For Its Victory In World Tourney" (March 9, 1954 by United Press); "Penticton V's Dominate Test So Thoroughly Russia Gets Only Two Shots On Goal" (March 7, 1955 by United Press) "11-Mile Parade Marks Victory" (March 7, 1955 by Canadian Press); "Donerty's Tally Brings 1-1 Draw" (March 6, 1956 by United Press);" Czechs Tie Russians 2-2, In Tourney" (March 4, 1957 by Associated Press); "Soviets Six Routes N.H.L. Stars, 6-0" (February 12, 1979 by Gerald Eskenazi); "A Legacy Of Slapstick And Slap Shots" (November 30, 1997 by Ed Willes).

The Toronto Globe and Mail: *"Czechs Tie V's, Hinting Hard Tests Coming In Series" (February 21, 1955 by Reuters); "Doug Kilburn Nets Two To Lead Penticton V's Past Czech B's, 6-0" (February 22, 1955 by Reuters); "Sports Digest" (February 24, 1955 by Jim Vipord); "V's Assert Czechs Rate Toughest" (February 24, 1955 by Canadian Press); "Sports Digest" (February 25, 1955 by Rex MacLeod); "Penticton V's Crush Americs In Opener" (February 27, 1955 by Canadian Press); Sports Digest" (February 28, 1955 by Al Nickelson); "Rally To Beat Czechs, 5-3, In Rugged Tilt Saturday; Blank Polish Aces, Sunday" (February 28, 1955 by Canadian Press); "Sports Reel" (February 29, 1955 by Bobbie Rosenfeld); "V's Win Fourth Game By Defeating Finns, 12-0" (February 29, 1955 by Canadian Press); "World Hockey Matches Are ALL Who-Dunnits To Canadian Reporters" (March 2, 1955 by Canadian Press); "V's Blank Stubborn Swedes, 3-0 (March 3, 1955 by Canadian Press); "V's Win From Swiss For Fifty In Row, 11-1" (March 3, 1955 by Canadian Press); "Leafs and Habs May Join Forces For Europe Tour" (March 3, 1955 by Canadian Press);"Sports Digest" (March 4, 1955 by Rex MacLeod); "Canada Defeats Russia" (March 7, 1955 by Arch Mackenzie); "V's Make Maple Leaf World's Top Hockey Emblem" (March 7, 1955 by Canadian Press); "Sports Digest" (March 7, 1955 by Al Nickleson); "Sports Digest" (March 8, 1955 by Bobbie Rosenfeld); "Swedes, Russian Meet Today For Puck Title" (March 5, 1957 by Canadian Press); "Sweden Captures World Hockey Crown" (March 6, 1957 by Canadian Press); "Dunlops Wallop Poland, 14-1; Norway, 12-0" (March 3, 1958 by Ed Simon); "Canada Crushes Finland, 24-0" (March 4, 1958 by Ed Simon);"Canucks Expect Swedes To Give Tough Test*

Today" (March 6, 1958 by Ed Simon); "Early Tension Slows Whitby Hockey Team" (March 10, 1958 by Bruce West);"Canada Defeats Russia To Win World Hockey" (March 10, 1958 by Bruce West); "Team Canada Players Say Ballard's Worries Are Groundless"(August 14, 1972 by Dan Proudfoot); "WHA Given Less Than A Year" (August 15, 1972 by Dan Proudfoot); "Clubs Spending Money But New Pro League Facing Identity Crisis" (August 15, 1972 United Press International Article) ; "WHA Competition Raises NHL Salaries" (August 17,1972 by Dick Beddoes); "Russian Scouts Disappointed By Lack Of Hitting" (August 18, 1972 by Dan Proudfoot); "By Dick Beddoes" (August 18, 1972 by Dick Beddoes); "Jean Ratelle's Hook-Check Breaks Bill Goldworthy's Nose In Practice" (August 23, 1972 by Dan Proudfoot); "Team Canada Display Draws Meagre Crowd" (August 23, 1972 by Dick Beddoes); "Puck Sweep Possible Scout Says" (August 24, 1972 by Dan Proudfoot); "Sinden, Ferguson Have Six Days To Correct Weaknesses" (August 28, 1972 by Dan Proudfoot); "Mental Attitude, Physical Condition Equal To Sinden" (August 29, 1972 by Dick Beddoes); "Scowling Scout Kulagin Chortles Happily"(August 29, 1972 by Dan Proudfoot); "By Dick Beddoes" (August 29, 1972 by Dick Beddoes); "Russian Hockey Team Has An Aggregate Sameness" (September 1, 1972 by Dick Beddoes); "Team Canada Players Confident, Glad Training Over" (September 1, 1972 by Dan Proudfoot); "Only A Game, But 15 Million Fans Want Fame, Not Shame" (September 1, 1972 by Dick Beddoes); "Air Canada Goof Almost Condemns Team To Go Stickless Against Russians" (September 2, 1972 by Staff); "Canada Mourns Hockey Myth" (September 4, 1972 by Louis Cauz); "Sinden Goes For Checking In Shaking Up Roster" (September 4, 1972 by Dan Proudfoot); "Canadian Team Outplayed In Every Area, Stunned Coach Admits" (September 4, 1972 by Dan Proudfoot); "By Dick Beddoes" (September 4, 1972 by Dick Beddoes); "CAHA President Ignored. Labels Series 'Political'" (September 4, 1972 by Staff); "Failure To Shake Hands Annoys PM; A Misunderstanding, Players Say" (September 4, 1972 by Staff); "Bergman Denies Team Underestimates Russians" (September 4, 1972 by Dan Proudfoot); "It's Even: Canada Beats Russia 4-1" (September 5, 1972 by Dan Proudfoot); "Tony Esposito Spikes Red Guns" (September 5, 1972 by Dick Beddoes); "Backyard Hockey Way Of Life For Russian Youngsters, Too" (September 5, 1972 by Scott Young); "Ferguson Points To Russians' Harsh Sticks" (September 6, 1972 by Jack Marks); "Canadians Can Expect Stricter Officiating In Russia, Bobrov Says" (September 6, 1972 by Dan Proudfoot); "Referees Target of Tass" (Septenber 6, 1972 by Associated Press); "By Dick Beddoes" (September 6, 1972 by Dick Beddoes); "Leafs Buy Tretiak To Replace Parent" (September 6, 1972 by Staff); "Russians Play In 4-4 Game Shows Hockey Belongs To Both

Countries" (September 7, 1972 by Dan Proudfoot); "Discontent Grows, Two Team Members Threaten To Quit." (September 7, 1972 by Dan Proudfoot); "Leafs Still Woo Parent, Open Camp" September 14" (September 7, 1972 by Rex Macleod); "Russia's Tretiak Earned Ultimate - Praise From NHL Goalies" (September 8, 1972 by Dan Proudfoot); "Parent Turns Down $750,000 To Remain With Philadelphia" (September 8, 1972 by Dan Proudfoot); "Booing Bewilders Esposito, 'Fans Ridicule Below My Dignity'" (September 9, 1972 by Dick Beddoes); "By Dick Beddoes" (September 11, 1972 by Dick Beddoes); "Canada Russian Telecast. Now Bobby Hull's Commercial Banned" (September 11, 1972 by Staff); "Tarasov's Hockey Book Helps To Make Masters Of Pupils" (September 11, 1972 by Dan Proudfoot); "$1 Million Bush Bid" (September 12, 1972 by Associated Press); "Mission To Moscow. Team Canada To Work Out On Sweden's Wide Ice" (September 12, 1972 by Dick Beddoes); "Orr May Play In Sweden. Regaining Prestige Sinden's Goal" (September 14, 1972 by Canadian Press); "Soviet Coach wary, NHLers First Class But Not Quite Gods" (September 15, 1972 by Vsevolod Bobrov); "'Guys were Completely Lost.' Dimensions Of European Rinks Frighten Canadian Coaches" (September 15, 1972 by Dan Proudfoot); "WHA Dates Czechs" (September 15, 1972 by United Press International); "Norris Signs Up 5 Countries For European Pro Puck Loop" (September 15, 1972 by Canadian Press); "WHA, NHL Pushing For Pro Hockey In Europe" (September 17, 1972 by Staff); "NHL Owners Complain About Hockey Series" (September 17, 1972 by Staff); "Crude Team Canada Ties Sneaky Sweden 4-4" (September 18, 1972 by Dan Proudfoot); "Criminal Assault. Swedish Writers Hurl Harpoons" (September 18, 1972 by Associated Press); "CAHA Could Use Veto On WHA European Tour" (September 18, 1972 by Canadian Press);"Hockey Opener Letdown For Swedes, Sinden" (September 18, 1972 by Dan Proudfoot); "Tarnished Play Disturbs Team Canada Players" (September 19, 1972 by Dan Proudfoot); "Parise Makes Reputation With Team Canada" (September 20, 1972 by Dan Proudfoot); "Angry Canadian Blame Selves For 5-4 Moscow Loser" (September 23, 1972 by Dan Proudfoot); "Mention Moscow Kelly Sees Red" (September 23, 1972 by Rex MacLeod); "Team Canada Leaders Have Flaws: Smythe" (September 24, 1972 by Canadian Press); "Mighty Mite Spearheads Russian Comeback. Anisin Creates Headache For Canadians" (September 24, 1972 by Staff-Canadian Press); "Bunny At His Needling Best After Canadian Team Collapse" (September 24, 1972 by Staff); "Habs Adopting Russian Ideas For Training" (September 24, 1972 by Canadian Press); "Team Canada Is Confident It Can Win Series. Russians Defeated 3-2" (September 25, 1972 by Dan Proudfoot); "'Ahearne-Style Refereeing' Worst sinden Has Ever Seen" (September

252

25, 1972 by Colin McCullough); "*Team Canada Defectors Annoyed At Coach*" (September 25, 1972 by New York Times Service); "*250,000 Czechs Want To See Team Canada Game*" (September 26, 1972 by Colin McCullough); "*Finns Perform Well In First Workout With Leafs*" (September 26, 1972 by Staff); "*Canada Ties Series With 4-3 Triumph*" (September 27, 1972 by Dan Proudfoot); "*Kompalla's Performance Disappoints Morrison*" (September 27, 1972 by Dan Proudfoot); "*Leaf's Ballard Foresees Russ, Czechs In NHL*" (September 27, 1972 by Colin McCullough); "*Soviet Series Crowns Esposito A Superstar*" (September 28,1972 by Dan Proudfoot); "*Canadian Threaten Withdrawal*" (September 28, 1972 by Dan Proudfoot); "*From Russia With Glory*" (September 29, 1972 by Dan Proudfoot); "*Horns Blow Fans Howl As Canada Wildly Celebrates Hockey Triumph*" (September 29, 1972 by Staff); "*Esposito Remembers Every Dramatic Minute (Almost)*" (September 29, 1972 by Dan Proudfoot); "*Czech Club Short On Practice. Sinden Ponders Lineup Change*" (September 30, 1972 by Dan Proudfoot); "*Refs Resign After Fun Flight*" (September 30, 1972 by Staff); "*Series Points Gaps In Cultures*" (September 30, 1972 by Hedrick Smith); "*Wings Didn't Need Russian Spur To Break Tradition*" (September 30, 1972 by Gord Walker);"*Challenge Cup Ready To Meet Russian Might*" (February 3, 1979 by Donald Ramsay); "*Soviet Road To Olympus*" (February 9, 1979 by Scott Young); "*NHL Stars Solve Soviet Mystique*" (February 10, 1979 by Donald Ramsay); "*Russian Tie Series*" (February 12, 1979 by Donald Ramsay); "*NHL Appears Second Rate*" (February 12, 1979 by Donald Ramsay); "*NHL Requires All-Star Salesman To Kill Hockey's U.S. Test Pattern*" (February 12, 1979 by Dave Anderson).

The Toronto Star: "*Face It, NHL-You're No longer World's Best*" (February 12, 1979 by Milt Dunnell).

The Vancouver Province: "*In This Corner*" (February 28, 1939 by Bill Forst);"*Smoke Eaters Retain World Crown With Win Over U.S.*" (February 28, 1939). "*Canada Starts Fast In World Hockey*" (1954 by the Canadian Press); "*Swedes Startle Russians Get Tie As Canada Wins*" (March 6, 1954 by Canadian Press); "*Soft Ice Hampers Players*" (March 6, 1954 by Canadian Press); "*Germans Top Fins, Advance*" (March 6, 1954 by Canadian Press); "*Anti-Canada. C.A.H.A. Studies Charges*" (March 6, 1954 by Reuters); "*Russia Wins World Hockey, Trounces East York, 7-2*" (March 8, 1954 by Canadian Press); "*Russ Win Will Get Pondering*" (March 8, 1954 by Canadian Press);"*Toronto Starts Campaign. Send Leafs To Russia? Local Experts Laugh!*" (March 9, 1954 by Canadian Press); "*A Tragedy At Stockholm*"(March 9, 1954 by

Alf Cottrell); "*Russians Win 28-0*" *(December 17, 1966 by Canadian Press);* "*Canada Dumps Russia -All Over Ice*" *(December 19, 1966);* "*Brewer Basks In New Light*" *(December 19, 1966);* "*Poles Post Win No. 5*" *(December 19, 1966 by Canadian Press);* "*Nats' Tie Is Really A Victory*" *(December 21, 1966 by Canadian Press);* "*Iron Curtain Men Work Well On Ice*" *(December 30, 1966 by Provincial Wire Service);*

The Vancouver Sun: *"Ottawa Rushes Preparations" (September 3, 1939); "Fighting For A Just Cause" (September 3, 1939): "Canadian Dagger Pointed At Berlin" (June 6, 1944).*

The Washington Post: *"Soviet Skill Prevailed" (February 12, 1979 by Robert Fachet).*

The Winnipeg Free Press: *"Stars Shoulder Blame As Soviets Humble NHL" (February 12, 1979 by Claude Adams).*
Thom, Douglas J. *The Hockey Bibliography: Ice Hockey Worldwide.* Toronto: Ontario Institute for Studies In Education, 1978.

Thomas, Bruce. *"The Commando."* Harper's Magazine, March 1942.

Thompson, R.W. *D-Day.* New York: Ballantine, 1968.

Thompson, R.W. *Churchill and the Montgomery Myth.* New York: M. Evans and Co., Inc., 1967.

Thordarson, Bruce. *Lester Pearson Diplomat And Politican.* Toronto: Oxford University Press, 1974.

Time Magazine: *"Canadians Abroad Upsets on Ice" (March 15, 1954); "Home Town Hockey" (March 7, 1955); "There Goes The 8 Game Sweep" (September 11, 1972); "Team Canada To Russia With Misgivings" (September 18, 1972); "What A Difference A Goal Makes" (October 9, 1972); "The Unpretentious Ambassadors" (October 14, 1974); " Canada A House Divided" (February 13, 1978).*

Touny, A.D. and Wenig, Dr. Steffen. *Sport In Ancient Egypt.* Leipzig: Edition Leipzig, 1969.

Traill, Henry Duff. *The Life of Sir John Franklin, R.N.* London: John Muray, 1896.

Trevor-Roper, H.R. *Blitzkreig to Defeat: Hitler's War Directives 1939-*

1945. New York: Holt, Rinehart and Winston, 1965.

Truscott, Lt. Gen. L.K. *Command Decisions.* New York: Dutton, 1954.

Tunis, John R. *"Everybody's On A Skate."* American Legion Magazine, February 1939.

University of Chile, official website "History" by Sylvia Ríos Montero [http://www.uchile.cl/cultura/mapa/artesamapuche/ingles/histor.htm]

USA Today: *"1960 U.S. Hockey Team Crafted First Miracle On Ice"* (January 16, 2002 by Kevin Allen).

Vagts, Alfred. *A History of Militarism.* New York: Free Press, 1959.

Vallieres, Pierre. *White Niggers Of America: The Precocious Autobiography Of A Quebec Terrorist.* New York: Motnhly Review Press, 1971.

Villa, Brian Loring. *Unauthorized Action: Mountbatten and the Dieppe Raid.* New York: Oxford University Press, 1989.

Villiers, Captain Alan. Men, Ships, and The Sea. Washington: National Geographic, 1962.

Von Daniken, Erich. *Chariots Of The Gods: Unsolved Mysteries Of The Past.* New York: G.P. Putnam's Sons, 1969.

Von der Porten, Edward. *The German Navy In World War Two.* New York: Ballantine, 1969.

Voltaire. *Candide.* New York: Bantam Books, 1984.

Webb, Marshall. *"An Intimate Record of Defeat."* Maclean's Magazine, August 15, 1982.

Weekes, Don. *The Original Six: Old Time Hockey Trivia.* Vancouver: Douglas & McIntyre, Ltd., 1995.

Werth, Alexander. *Russia At War 1941-1945.* New York: Avon Books, 1964.

White, Wilbur W. *"Russia's Fight For Time."* Current History Magazine, October 1942.

Whitehead, Eric. *Cyclone Taylor A Hockey Legend.* Toronto: Doubleday, 1977.

Wighton, Charles et al. *They Spied on England.* London: Odhams Press, 1958.

Wilmot, Chester. *The Struggle for Europe.* London: Collins, 1952.

Wintringham, Tom. *"The Second Front -Someday."* Free World Magazine, October 1942.

Wrinch, P.N. *The Military Strategy of Winston Churchill.* Boston: Boston University Press, 1961.

Wyatt, Woodrow. *Distinguished for Talent.* London: Cape, 1957.

Wynecoop, David. *Children of the Sun: A History of the Spokane Indians.* Spokane: Wellpinit, 1969.

Young, Kenneth. *Churchill and Beaverbrook.* London: Eyres and Spottiswoode, 1946

Young, Peter. *Commando.* New York: Ballantine, 1969.

Young, Scott. *The Boys of Saturday Night: Inside Hockey Night In Canada.* Toronto: McClelland & Stewart, 1991.

Young, Scott. *War On Ice: Canada In International Hockey.* Toronto: McClelland & Stewart, 1976.

Young, Scott. *Canada Cup Of Hockey '76.* Worldsport Properties, 1976.

Ziegler, Philip. *Mountbatten: The Official Biography.* London: Collins, 1985.

Zuckerman, Prof. Lord. *From Apes to Warlords.* London: Cape, 1978.

About the Authors

☼ **George Robert Fosty**

George Robert Fosty is a Canadian historian and documentary filmmaker currently living in New York City. He was born in 1960 in Prince Rupert, British Columbia, Canada. In 1980, he received a Diploma in International Law from The London City Polytechnic, London, England. In 1983 he was awarded an Associate of Arts in History from Western Wyoming Community College in Rock Springs, Wyoming. He obtained his Bachelor of Arts in History from the University of Hawaii at Hilo in 1985. From 1986 to 1988, he traveled throughout Western Canada working odd jobs all the while researching and interviewing Canadian military veterans of the disastrous August 19, 1942 Commando Raid on Dieppe, France. From 1988 to 1990 he was employed as a Teaching Assistant within the History Department of Midwestern State University, Wichita Falls, Texas. In 1991 he received his Master of Arts in History from Midwestern State University. Six-years of research and over one-hundred interviews with Canadian military veterans culminated in his 192-page master's thesis entitled: *"The Desperate Glory: The Battle of Dieppe 1942."* From September 1990 to November 1991 he was employed as a military historian (GS-7) with the United States Office of Personal Management under special contract to the United States Department of Defense and the United States Air Force, Sheppard AFB, Texas.

While at Sheppard he authored and edited numerous articles on USAF history, created two temporary military museums (in conjunction with Sheppard 50th Anniversary celebrations), identified, dated, and catalogued 12,000 photos on USAF history, served as a military advisor on three locally produced television documentaries, and co-authored the award winning book *Sustaining The Wings: A Fifty Year History of Sheppard AFB* the 1991 United States Air Training Command History Book-of-the-Year. In 1994 he moved his family to New York City. He is married to his wife of 14-years and is the father of two young boys.

257

☼ **Darril Fosty**

Darril Fosty is a Canadian historian and documentary filmmaker currently living in Seattle, Washington. Though he was born in Terrace, British Columbia, Canada in 1968, he spent much of his youth in Kamloops, British Columbia. He studied History and Journalism at Western Washington University in Bellingham, Washington completing his Bachelor of Arts degree in 1992 with a concentration in North American, Native North American, and post-French Revolutionary European history.

Upon leaving university, he worked in sports journalism writing game summaries for the Seattle Sounders Professional Soccer Team for distribution over the Associated Press wire service, during the 1994 season. For the past eight years he has worked in the technology field while extensively traveling to England, France, and Spain researching early forms of European hockey. He is a specialist in Canadian and West Coast Native Indian history.

☼ John Jelley

John Jelley is an international sports writer living in Nanaimo, British Columbia, Canada. He has written for publications as diverse as the *London Daily Telegraph, the Melbourne Age* and *Penthouse Magazine*. A self-confessed "information pack-rat" he collects books on most major sports played around the world and is quite open in admitting the reason he moved from his home in the United Kingdom to Canada was that he could not afford a house in England that was big enough to house his library.

Born in 1956 in Broxbourne, Hertfordshire, John Jelley was educated at the Richard Hale School in Hertford, and at the Hertfordshire College of Higher Education where he received a Bachelor of Arts degree in history. He has been a working journalist since 1985, but in between his writing assignments he founded the British Australian Rules Football League in 1989 and served that body in various capacities.

His interests in ice hockey dates from his childhood in the 1960's when he bought a second hand British Ice Hockey book. From that he acquired an interest in the "golden years" of British Ice Hockey from the 1930's through to 1960. As a spectator he ranks Borje Salming as the finest player he ever saw, and admits to a longtime passion for the Toronto Maple Leafs.

About The Editors

☼Dawn Jelley

Dawn Jelley was born in Hoddesdon Hertfordshire, and with a father and brother who were both sports fans probably was always destined to become one herself. She was educated at Sheredes School and participated in many different sports. Her greatest sports achievement came in the sport of Judo where she became a member of the Great Britain national team. With a degree in history from the Hertfordshire College of Higher Education she has been a writer and editor for many years. She now makes her home in Nanaimo, British Columbia, Canada.

☼Susan M. Schulz – Jelley

Susan M. Schulz-Jelley hails from the West Texas oil town of Andrews, where she was educated in the local school district. She holds bachelor degrees in Speech and Drama Education from Texas Tech University, and another degree in English Literature from the University of Texas of the Permian Basin. She has been a teacher, news writer and editor, and is currently a sports photographer. She is the co-author of *Lincoln School: 1950-1961, An Historical Retrospective of the School for Black Students in Andrews, Texas.* She now resides in Nanaimo, British Columbia, Canada.